Rick Steves

SNAPSHOT

Naples & the Amalfi Coast

CONTENTS

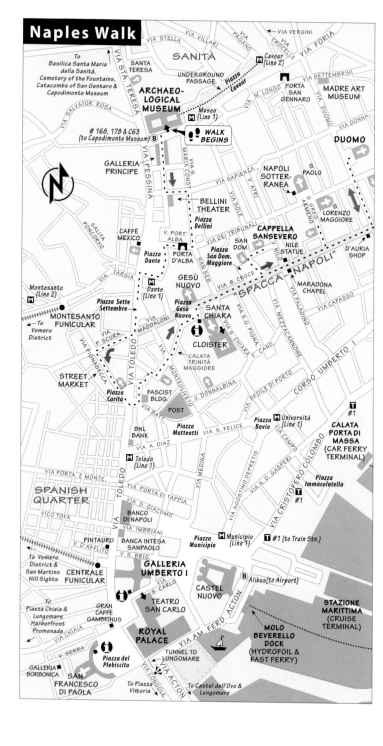

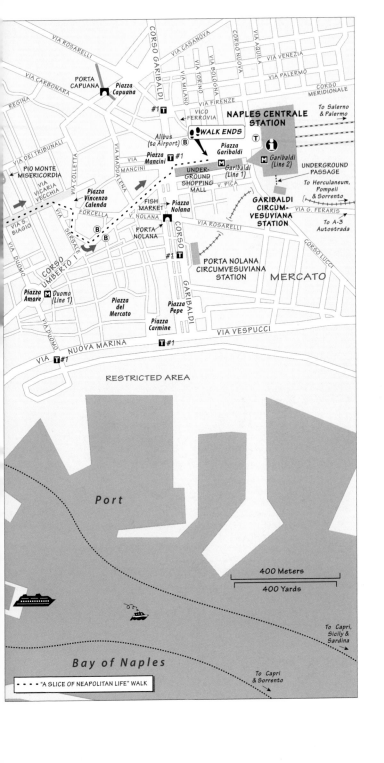

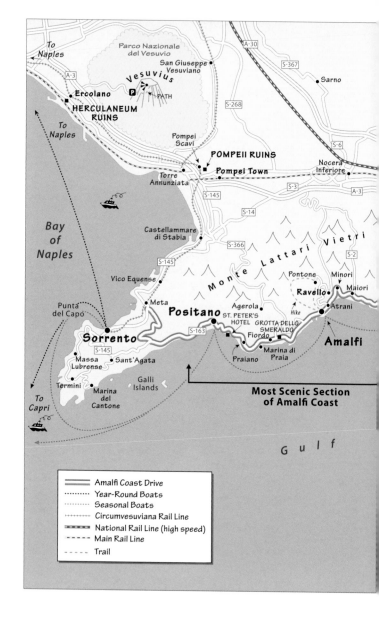

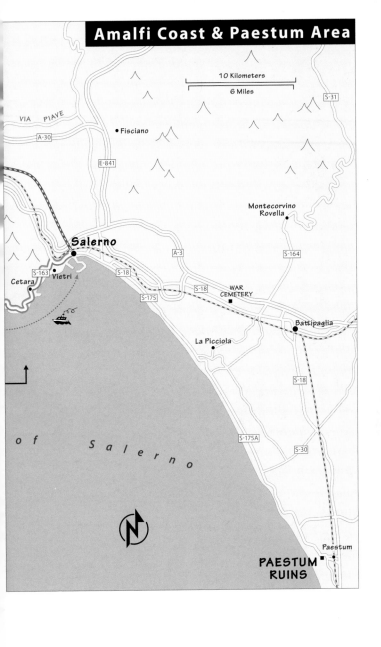

Amalfi Coast & Paestum Area

10 Kilometers

6 Miles

S-31

VIA PIAVE

A-30

• Fisciano

E-841

Montecorvino
Rovella

Salerno

A-3

S-164

S-163 Vietri

S-18

Cetara

S-18

WAR
CEMETERY

S-175

Battipaglia

La Picciola

S-18

of   Salerno

S-175A

S-30

N

Paestum

**PAESTUM
RUINS**

INTRODUCTION

This Snapshot guide, excerpted from my guidebook *Rick Steves Italy*, introduces you to Naples, Pompeii, and the Amalfi Coast. The gritty, historic port city of Naples is arguably Italy's wildest urban jungle, with a uniquely vibrant street life. Enjoy a pizza in its birthplace, and explore the city's excellent Archaeological Museum. Then head into the countryside to unearth ancient history at Pompeii and Herculaneum, well-preserved Roman towns in the shadow of the steaming Mt. Vesuvius.

An hour to the south, Sorrento kicks off the gloriously scenic Amalfi Coast, where buses filled with white-knuckle tourists take turns squeezing along an impossibly narrow sea-view road. Relax in stylish Sorrento or hilly Positano, and side-trip to the glitzy Amalfi Town and Ravello, the ancient Greek temples at Paestum, or the jet-set isle of Capri, with its otherworldly Blue Grotto.

To help you have the best trip possible, I've included the following topics in this book:

• **Planning Your Time,** with advice on how to make the most of your limited time

• **Orientation,** including tourist information (abbreviated as TI), tips on public transportation, local tour options, and helpful hints

• **Sights** with ratings:

▲▲▲—Don't miss

▲▲—Try hard to see

▲—Worthwhile if you can make it

No rating—Worth knowing about

• **Sleeping** and **Eating,** with good-value recommendations in every price range

• **Connections,** with tips on trains, buses, and driving

Practicalities, near the end of this book, has information on money, staying connected, hotel reservations, transportation, and more, plus Italian survival phrases.

To travel smartly, read this little book in its entirety before you go. It's my hope that this guide will make your trip more meaningful and rewarding. Traveling like a temporary local, you'll get the absolute most out of every mile, minute, and dollar.

Buon viaggio!

NAPLES

Napoli

If you like Italy as far south as Rome, go farther south—it gets better. If Italy is getting on your nerves, stop at Rome. Italy intensifies as you plunge deeper. Naples is Italy in the extreme—its best (birthplace of pizza and Sophia Loren) and its worst (home of the Camorra, Naples' "family" of organized crime).

Before Italy unified in the late 1800s, Naples was the country's richest city. But Naples' fortunes nosedived when the capital of modern Italy was established in Rome. Things got so bad that many of its residents emigrated. The Italy America knows—pizza, spaghetti, and "O Sole Mio"/"Santa Lucia"—came from 19th-century Naples, as brought to the US by all those immigrants.

Today, Naples impresses visitors with one of Europe's top archaeological museums (showcasing the artistic treasures of Pompeii), fascinating churches that convey the city's unique personality and powerful devotion, an underground warren of Greek and Roman ruins, fine works of art (including pieces by Caravaggio, who lived here for a time), and evocative Nativity scenes (called *presepi*). Of course, Neapolitans make great pizza and tasty pastries (try the crispy, ricotta-stuffed *sfogliatella*). But more than anything, Naples has a brash and vibrant street life—"Italy in your face" in ways both good and bad. Walking through its colorful old town is one of my favorite experiences anywhere in Europe. For a grand overlook, head to the hilltop viewpoint (San Martino) for sweeping views of the city and its bay.

Naples is southern Italy's leading city, the third-largest city in Italy, and Europe's most densely populated city, with more than one million people and few open spaces or parks. While in many ways it feels like an urban jungle, Naples surprises the observant traveler with its impressive knack for living, eating, and raising children with good humor and decency. Overcome your fear of being run down or ripped off long enough to talk with people. Enjoy a few smiles and jokes with the man running the neighborhood tripe shop, or the woman taking her daycare class on a walk through the traffic.

The pulse of Italy throbs in Naples. Like Cairo or Mumbai, it's appalling and captivating at the same time, the closest thing

to "reality travel" that you'll find in Western Europe. But this tangled mess still somehow manages to breathe, laugh, and sing—with a joyful Italian accent. Thanks to its reputation as a dangerous place, Naples doesn't get nearly as many tourists as it deserves. While the city has its problems, it has improved

a lot in recent years. And even though it remains a bit edgy, I feel comfortable here. Naples richly rewards those who venture in.

Naples is also the springboard to an array of nearby sightseeing treats: Just beyond Naples are the remarkable ruins of Pompeii and Herculaneum, and the brooding volcano that did them both in, Mount Vesuvius. A few more miles down the road is the pleasant resort town of Sorrento and the offshore escape isle of Capri. Next comes the dramatic scenery of the Amalfi Coast. Plunging even farther south, you'll reach the Greek temples of Paestum.

PLANNING YOUR TIME

Naples is an ideal day trip either from Rome or from the comfortable home base of Sorrento, each just over an hour away. Or you can stow your bag at the station and see Naples in a few hours while you change trains here on the way between Rome and Sorrento. For some, a little Naples goes a long way. If you're not comfortable in chaotic and congested cities, think twice before spending the night here. But those who are intrigued by the city's sights and street life enjoy overnighting in Naples.

On a quick visit, start with the Archaeological Museum (closed Tue), follow my self-guided Naples Walk, and celebrate your survival with pizza. With more time, dip into more churches, go underground to see Greek and Roman ruins, trek to Capodimonte to see art treasures, or consider ascending San Martino for the view. Spend an early evening strolling Naples' romantic Lungomare harborside promenade.

For a blitz tour from Rome, you could have breakfast on an

Still Naples After All These Years

For three centuries (1500-1800), Naples was one of the world's richest and most sophisticated cities. The remnants we see today are an elegant reminder of that golden age, and a fascinating case study in what went wrong.

500 B.C.-A.D. 500—Greek-Speaking Romans: Naples got its start as Neapolis ("new city"), a thriving Greek colony. Even when conquered by the Romans, the city never fully adopted the Latin language and Roman ways. Actually, those sophisticated Hellenist traditions were exactly what the Romans admired about Naples and made them want to vacation there. For the next 2,000 years, this pattern would repeat itself: The city, living under foreign rule, would evolve independently from the rest of the Italian peninsula.

500-1500—Independence Despite Foreign Rule: The city powered on relatively unchanged after the fall of Rome, ruled as the independent Duchy of Naples under Ostrogoths, Byzantines, and Lombards. Next, in late-medieval times, it was the Germans and French (or "Angevins") who possessed it as the Kingdom of Naples. As sea trade became more important to the European economy, Naples was suddenly smack-dab in the geographical heart of commerce—the Mediterranean.

1500-1800—Golden Age: In 1502, Spain conquered Naples, and their combined wealth made Naples one of the great cities on Earth. With a population of 300,000, only Paris was larger. Deputies of the Spanish king called viceroys presided over the city, and proceeded to use Spain's New World wealth to beautify Naples.

When Spain's monarchy passed to the Viennese Habsburgs and French Bourbons, the cosmopolitan nature of Naples was only enhanced. Naples was home to nobles and royalty from across Europe. Baroque culture thrived, with artists like Caravaggio and Bernini, thinkers like Giordano Bruno, composers like Scarlatti, and a new art form called opera. Naples took on the

early Rome-Naples express train (usually daily 7:35-8:45), do Naples and Pompeii in a day, and be back in Rome before you turn into a zucchini. That's exhausting, but more memorable than a fourth day in Rome.

Yes, Naples is huge. But if you stick to my suggestions and grab a cab when you're lost or tired, it's fun. Treat yourself well in Naples; the city is cheap by Italian standards. Splurging on a sane and comfortable hotel is a worthwhile investment.

On summer afternoons, Naples' street life slows and many churches, museums, and shops close as the temperature soars. The city comes back to life in the early evening.

"look" it retains today, with palatial Neoclassical buildings in pastel colors and lavishly ornamented churches.

Despite its veneer of sophistication, trouble was brewing. In 1656, a vicious bubonic plague (Europe's last) killed off half the population. Trade routes shifted west as Europe industrialized, but Naples languished, remaining feudal and agricultural, with the church owning much of the land. The gap between rich foreign elites and homegrown poor grew.

1800-2000: Napoleon conquered the city. Then the monarchy was restored under a medieval-era political arrangement called the Kingdom of the Two Sicilies (uniting Naples and Sicily). The city was still rich, thanks to its French Bourbon rulers, but it was increasingly backward, left behind by a more industrialized and democratic Europe.

Meanwhile, sweeping down from the north, there was a movement for Italian nationhood. Naples—with its legacy of independence from the rest of the peninsula—resisted. But in 1860, Naples was forcefully united with the new nation-state of Italy. Its vast wealth was confiscated and taken to the capital in Rome.

This began a century-plus of decline. There was no foreign wealth and no local economy. An estimated four million southern Italians fled, emigrating to northern Italy and the US. During World War II, Naples suffered Italy's worst bombings. The postwar economic recovery in northern Italy never trickled south, which remained backward, under the thumb of the feudal-style Camorra (the Naples-based Mafia).

Today: The lack of a postwar economic recovery actually is a boon to tourists. It preserved an independent way of life that dates back centuries. Visitors today enjoy a rare sight—a city that has been continuously inhabited and self-sustaining for 2,500 years.

Orientation to Naples

Naples is set deep inside the large, curving Bay of Naples, with Mount Vesuvius looming just five miles away. Although Naples is a sprawling city, its fairly compact core contains the most interesting sights. The tourist's Naples is a triangle, with its points at the Centrale train station in the east, the Archaeological Museum to the west, and Piazza del Plebiscito (with the Royal Palace) and the port to the south. Steep hills rise above this historic core, including San Martino, capped with a mighty fortress.

TOURIST INFORMATION

Central Naples has multiple small TIs, none of them particularly helpful—just grab a map and browse the brochures. The handiest one is in **Centrale train station** (daily 9:00-18:00, near track 23, tel. 081-268-779). Two others are by the entrance to the **Galleria Umberto I** shopping mall, across from Teatro di San Carlo (Mon-Sat 9:00-17:00, Sun until 13:00, tel. 081-402-394), and on Spaccanapoli, across from the **Church of Gesù Nuovo** (same hours as Galleria Umberto I TI, tel. 081-551-2701). For information online, the best overall website is www.inaples.it.

ARRIVAL IN NAPLES
By Train

Naples has several train stations, but all trains coming into town stop at either Napoli Centrale or Garibaldi—which are essentially the same place, with Centrale on top of Garibaldi. Stretching in front of this station complex is the vast Piazza Garibaldi, with an underground shopping mall and Metro entrance.

Centrale Station, on the ground floor, is the slick, modern main station. It has a small TI (near track 23), an ATM (at Banco di Napoli near track 24), a bookstore (La Feltrinelli, near track 24—beyond the pharmacy), and baggage check (*deposito bagagli,* near track 5). Pay WCs are down the stairs across from track 13. Shops and eateries are concentrated in the underground level. A good supermarket (Sapori & Dintorni) is out the front door and to the left.

Garibaldi Station, on the lower level of the complex, is used exclusively by the narrow-gauge Circumvesuviana commuter train (which you'll most likely use to connect to Sorrento or Pompeii). Note that this is not the terminus for the Circumvesuviana; that's one stop farther downtown, at the station called Porta Nolana.

Getting Downtown from the Station: Arriving at either station, the best bet for reaching most sights and hotels is either the Metro or a taxi. In the lower-level corridor (below the main Centrale hall), look for signs to **Metro** lines 1 and 2. Line 1 is handy for city-center stops, including the cruise port (Municipio), the main shopping drag (Toledo and Dante), and the Archaeological Museum (Museo). Line 2 is slightly quicker for reaching the Archaeological Museum (ride it to the Cavour stop and walk 5 minutes). For tips on navigating the Metro, see "Getting Around Naples," later.

A long row of white **taxis** line up out front. Ask the driver to charge you the fixed rate *(tariffa predeterminata),* which varies from €7 for the old center to €13 for the most distant hotel I list. The TI in the station can tell you the going rate.

NAPLES

Planning Your Time in the Region

On a quick trip, give the entire area—including Sorrento and Naples—a minimum of three days. If you use Sorrento as your sunny springboard, you can spend a day in Naples, a day exploring the Amalfi Coast, and a day split between Pompeii and the town of Sorrento. While Paestum (Greek temples), Mount Vesuvius, Herculaneum (an ancient Roman site like Pompeii), and the island of Capri are fine destinations, they are worthwhile only if you have more time. For a map, see page 59.

The **Campania ArteCard** regional pass may save you a few euros if you're here for two or three days, use public transportation, and visit multiple major sights (such as Pompeii, Herculaneum, Paestum, Naples' Archaeological Museum, and several other museums in Naples). There are three versions of the card: The **three-day,** €32 Tutta la Regione version is good if you'll be visiting both Naples and Sorrento; it includes free entry to two sights (plus a 50 percent discount off others) and transportation within Naples, on the Circumvesuviana train, and on Amalfi Coast buses. A **seven-day,** €34 Tutta la Regione option covers five sights (and discounts on the others) but no transportation. If you're focusing on Naples, the **three-day,** €21 **Napoli-only** version covers transportation within Naples and three city sights, plus discounts on the others (but it doesn't cover the outlying ancient sites). You can buy the card at some Naples TIs and at participating sights (cards activate on first use, expire 3 days later at midnight, www.campaniartecard.it).

By Ferry or Cruise Ship

Ferries and cruise ships dock next to each other in the shadow of the old fortress (Castel Nuovo), a short walk from all the old town sightseeing action. Naples has great ferry connections to Sorrento, Capri, and other nearby destinations. Cruise ships use the giant Stazione Marittima cruise terminal, hydrofoils and faster ferries use the Molo Beverello dock (to the west of the terminal), and slower car ferries leave from Calata Porta di Massa, east of the terminal.

Whether arriving by ferry or cruise ship, you can get to the city center by taxi, tram, Metro, or on foot; the Alibus shuttle bus runs to the airport (see "By Plane," later).

The **taxi** stand is in front of the port area. There's a fixed €11 rate to the train station or to the Archaeological Museum.

If you're taking public transportation, a €1 single ticket covers either the tram or the Metro. You can buy tickets at any tobacco shop: Caffè Moreno is under the canopy between the two buildings of the cruise terminal, and Caffè Beverello is along the busy street. Remember to validate your ticket as you board the tram or enter the Metro station.

Tram #1 (6/hour, 15 minutes) stops at the busy road directly in front of the cruise terminal, at the corner of the big, orange brick building, and heads to Piazza Garibaldi and the train station, where you can connect to trains to sights outside of town. If you're taking the Circumvesuviana commuter line to Pompeii or Sorrento, hop off this tram a bit earlier, at Porta Nolana, where you can catch the train at its starting point.

Straight ahead across the road from the cruise terminal (on the right side of the big fortress) is Piazza Municipio, with the handy Municipio **Metro** stop. From here, line 1 zips you right to the Archaeological Museum (Museo stop) or, in the opposite direction, to the train station (Garibaldi stop).

On foot, it's a seven-minute **walk**—past the gigantic Castel Nuovo—to Piazza del Plebiscito and the old city center.

By Plane

Naples International Airport (a.k.a. Capodichino, code: NAP) is close to town (tel. 081-789-6767, handy info desk just outside baggage claim, www.gesac.it). Alibus shuttle buses zip you in 20 minutes from the airport to Piazza Garibaldi, by Naples' Centrale train station, and then head to the port/Piazza Municipio for boats to Capri and Sorrento (buses run daily 6:00-23:00, 4/hour, 30 minutes to the port, €4 on board, stops at train station and port only). The shuttle bus leaves and departs from the bus platforms at the northwest corner of Piazza Garibaldi—the far-right corner when exiting the train station. If you take a taxi to or from the airport, ask the driver for the fixed price (€16 to the train station, €19 to the port, €23 to the Chiaia district near the waterfront).

To reach **Sorrento** from Naples Airport, take the direct Curreri bus. A taxi to Sorrento costs about €100.

HELPFUL HINTS

Tours: ∩ Download my free Rick Steves audio tours of the Naples Archaeological Museum and my Naples Walk.

Theft Alert: While most travelers visit Naples safely, err on the side of caution. Don't venture into neighborhoods that make you uncomfortable. While the train station has been nicely spruced up, its glow only extends for a block or so. The areas a little farther away are seedy and frequented by some of Italy's most downtrodden people. Walk with confidence, as if you know where you're going and what you're doing. Touristy Spaccanapoli and the posh Via Toledo shopping boulevard are more upscale, but you'll still see rowdy kids and panhandlers. Assume able-bodied beggars are thieves.

Stick to busy streets and beware of gangs of hoodlums.

A third of the city is unemployed, and past local governments have set an example that the Mafia would be proud of. Assume con artists are more clever than you. Any jostle or commotion is probably a thief-team smokescreen. To keep bags safe, it's probably best to leave them at your hotel or at the left-luggage office in Centrale Station.

Always walk on the sidewalk (even if the locals don't) and carry your bag on the side away from the street—thieves on scooters have been known to snatch bags as they swoop by. The less you have dangling from you (including cameras and necklaces), the better. Keep valuables buttoned up.

Thieves and con-artists hang out close to where cruise travelers tumble into Naples. But perhaps your biggest risk of theft is while catching or riding the Circumvesuviana commuter train. At the train station, carry your own bags—there are no official porters. If you're connecting from a long-distance express, you'll be going from a relatively secure compartment into an often-crowded and dingy train, where disoriented tourists with luggage delicately mix with the residents of Naples' most down-and-out districts. It's prime hunting ground for thieves. While I ride the Circumvesuviana comfortably and safely, each year I hear of many travelers who get ripped off on this ride. You won't be mugged—but you may be conned or pickpocketed. Be ready for this very common trick: A team of thieves blocks the door at a stop, pretending it's stuck. While everyone rushes to try to open it, an accomplice picks their pockets. Wear your money belt, and avoid the Circumvesuviana train late at night when it's plagued by intimidating ruffians. For maximum safety and peace of mind, sit in the front car, where the driver will double as your protector.

Traffic Safety: In Naples, red lights are discretionary, and pedestrians need to be wary, particularly of motor scooters. Even on "pedestrian" streets, stay alert to avoid being sideswiped by scooters that nudge their way through the crowds. Keep children close. Smart tourists jaywalk in the shadow of bold locals, who generally ignore crosswalks. Wait for a break in traffic, cross with confidence, and make eye contact with approaching drivers. The traffic will stop.

Bookstore: La Feltrinelli, conveniently located in Centrale Station, carries a small selection of English-language books (daily 7:00-21:00, near track 24).

Laundry: Lavasciuga, a block from the Università Metro stop, is convenient but has just three washers (Mon-Sat 9:00-19:00, closed Sun, Via Sedile di Porto 54, mobile 327-754-6639).

NAPLES

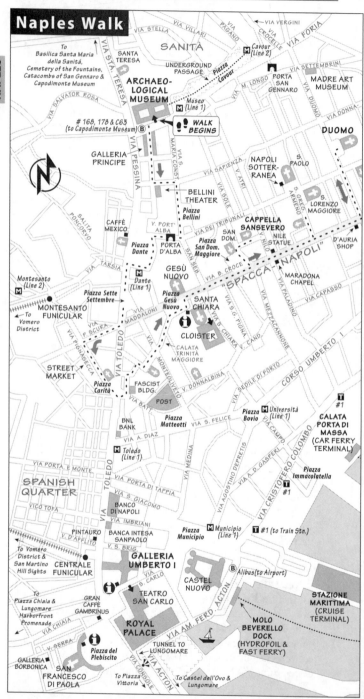

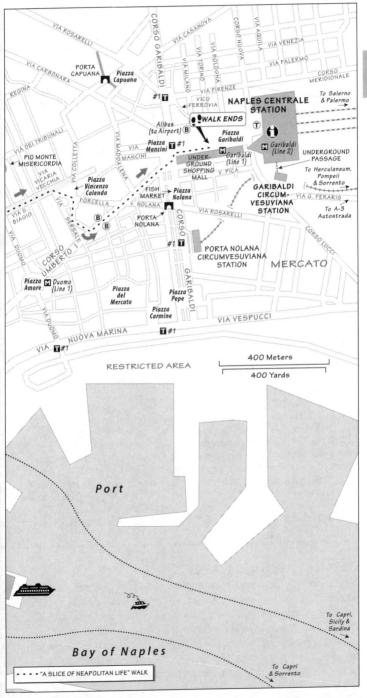

NAPLES

Mondo Guide Tours of Pompeii, Naples, the Amalfi Coast, and Capri for My Readers

Mondo Guide, a big Naples-based company, offers "shared tours" for Rick Steves readers. These allow you the luxury of a private, professional guide at a fraction of the usual cost, because you'll be sharing the expense with other travelers using this book. Their tours, which run from April through October, include **Pompeii,** a walking tour of **Naples,** and two longer-distance trips from Sorrento: an **Amalfi Coast** van tour and a private boat to the **isle of Capri.** The Pompeii and Naples tours are designed to work together—they are timed so you can do both on the same day. Mondo also offers shore excursions for cruise passengers arriving in Naples or Salerno. I don't receive a cut from the tours; I set this up with Mondo Guide to help my readers have the most economical experience in this region.

Reservations are required. For specifics and to sign up, go to www.sharedtours.com (Mondo tel. 081-751-3290, mobile 340-460-5254, www.mondoguide.com, info@mondoguide.com). On the website, use your credit-card number to reserve a spot. You'll then pay cash for the tour. If you must cancel, email more than three days in advance or you'll be billed.

Each tour requires a minimum of six participants. You'll be sent an email confirmation as soon as they're sure your tour will run. If there's not enough demand to justify the trip, they'll notify you three days before the departure date (giving you time to come up with an alternative plan). Confirmed departures are continually updated on the website.

Pompeii Tour: This two-hour guided walk brings to life the ruins of the excavated city (€15, Pompeii entry extra—your guide will collect money and buy tickets, daily at 11:00; meet at Hotel/Ristorante Suisse, a 5-minute walk from the train station—exiting the station, turn right, pass the Porta Marina entrance, and continue down the hill to the restaurant, on the right).

Historic Naples Walk: Naples is a challenge to enjoy and understand; on this three-hour walk, a local Neapolitan guide helps you uncover the true character of the city (€25; daily at 15:00; meet at the steps of the Archaeological Museum—you

GETTING AROUND NAPLES

Naples' entire public transportation system—Metro, buses, funicular railways, and the single tram line—uses the same tickets, which must be stamped as you enter (in yellow or blue machines). A €1 single ticket *(corsa singola)* covers any ride on most modes of transportation (bus, tram, funicular, or Metro line 1), with no transfers; for Metro line 2 you need the €1.20 version (it's considered a "suburban" line). If you need to transfer, buy the €1.50 *90 minuti* ticket.

can do the museum on your own before joining your guide).

Full-Day Amalfi Coast Minibus Tour from Sorrento: The Amalfi Coast can be complicated and time-consuming to visit on your own, making a shared minibus the simplest and most affordable way to enjoy the sights. (Small groups use an eight-seat minibus with only a driver; larger groups use a 19-seat minibus that comes with a driver and a guide.) This nine-hour trip will save time and money and maximize your experience. It begins in Sorrento and heads south for the breathtaking (and lightly narrated) drive, several photo stops, and an hour or two on your own in each of the three main towns—Positano, Amalfi, and Ravello—before returning to Sorrento. Lunch isn't included; to save time for exploring, just grab a quick lunch in one of the towns (€50, daily at 9:00; meet in front of Hotel Antiche Mura, at Via Fuorimura 7, a block inland from Piazza Tasso).

Full-Day Capri Boat Trip from Sorrento: To sidestep the hassles of taking public boats from Sorrento for a Capri side-trip, Mondo offers a trip to the island on a small private boat (12 people maximum), which includes an early visit to the Blue Grotto sea cave when conditions allow (€13, optional) and about four hours of free time to explore the island on your own. After your time on land, the boat takes you on a lightly narrated trip around the island with drinks, snacks, and a chance to swim if the weather cooperates (€90, daily at 8:00, pickup at hotel, may be cancelled in bad weather).

Shore Excursions from Naples or Salerno: If you're arriving on a cruise ship at the port of Naples or the port of Salerno, Mondo Guide offers an all-day itinerary that combines three big sights in the region and the scenic Amalfi Coast. From Naples, a guided visit to Pompeii with an hour of free time each in Sorrento and Positano; from Salerno, a guided visit to Pompeii with an hour of free time each in Sorrento and Amalfi town (€65/person, departing daily at 8:00-8:30 from the main exit of the Naples cruise terminal building or from your ship in Salerno).

Tickets are sold at *tabacchi* stores, some newsstands, clunky machines at Metro stations (coins and small bills only), and occasionally at station windows. A *giornaliero* day pass costs €3.50 (or €4.50 including Metro line 2), and pays for itself quickly, but can be hard to find; many *tabacchi* stores don't sell them. A weekly ticket (Monday to Sunday) costs €12, or €15.80 including Metro line 2. Several versions of the Campania ArteCard include free public transport in Naples. For general information, maps, and fares in English,

visit www.unicocampania.it. The TI hands out a good free map showing bus, Metro, and funicular routes. For schedules, your only option is the Italian-only site www.anm.it. For journey planning, use maps.google.com.

By Metro: Naples' subway, the *Metropolitana*, has three main lines *(linea)*. Station entrances and signs to the Metro are marked by a red square with a white *M*.

Line 1 is very useful for tourists. Starting from the train station (stop name: Garibaldi), it heads to Università (the university), Municipio (at Piazza Municipio, just above the harbor and cruise terminal), Toledo (south end of Via Toledo, near Piazza del Plebiscito), Dante (Piazza Dante), and Museo (Archaeological Museum). Four stops beyond Museo is the Vanvitelli stop, near the hilltop San Martino sights. Many of line 1's new stations are huge and elaborate, designed by prominent artists and architects; Naples is proud of them, and locals are excited to tell you about their favorite.

NAPLES

Line 2 (part of the Italian national rail system) is most useful for getting quickly from the train station to Piazza Cavour (a 5-minute walk from the Archaeological Museum) or Montesanto (the top of the Spanish Quarter and Spaccanapoli street, and base of one funicular up to San Martino).

The new, under-construction **line 6** will begin at Municipio and head west to Mergellina and beyond—but it's unlikely to be of much use to tourists.

By Funicular: Central Naples' three funiculars *(funicolare)* carry commuters and sightseers into the hilly San Martino neighborhood just west of downtown. All three converge near Piazza Fuga, a short walk from the hilltop fortress and monastery/museum. The Centrale line runs from the Spanish Quarter, just near Piazza del Plebiscito and the Toledo Metro stop; the Montesanto line from the Montesanto Metro stop and Via Pignasecca market zone; and the Chiaia line from near the Piazza Amadeo Metro stop.

By Bus: Buses can be handy for certain trips, such as getting to Capodimonte. But buses are crowded and poorly signed, and aren't a user-friendly option for uninitiated newcomers.

By Tram: Tram line #1 runs along Corso Garibaldi (at the other end of the big square from Centrale Station) and down to the waterfront, terminating by the ferry and cruise terminals (direction: Stazione Marittima). It's useful if you're connecting from boat to train, or returning to the port after finishing my self-guided walk.

By Taxi: A short ride in town should cost €10-12. Ask for the *tariffa predeterminata* (a fixed rate). Your hotel or a TI can tell you the going rate for a given ride. You can also ask the driver to use the meter—for metered rides there are some legitimate extra charges (baggage fees, €2.50 supplement after 22:00 or all day Sun and holidays). Radio Taxi 8888 is one reputable company (tel. 081-8888).

Tours in Naples

Local Guides

Pina Esposito has a Ph.D. in ancient archaeology and art and does fine private walking and driving tours of Naples and the region (Pompeii, Capri, the Amalfi Coast, etc.), including Naples' Archaeological Museum (€60/hour, 2-hour minimum, 10 percent off with this book, mobile 338-763-4224, annamariaesposito1@ virgilio.it).

The team at **Mondo Guide** offers private tours of the Archaeological Museum (€120/2 hours) and city (€240/4 hours), and can provide guides or drivers throughout the region (tel. 081-751-3290, www.mondoguide.com, info@mondoguide.com).

Walking Tours

Mondo Guide offers my readers special shared tours of Naples and of Pompeii, as well as other trips in the region. For details, see the sidebar.

Hop-On, Hop-Off Bus Tours

CitySightseeing Napoli tour buses make three different hop-on, hop-off loops through the city. Only one of these—the red line, which loops around the historical center and stops at the Archaeological Museum and Capodimonte—is particularly helpful. The bus route will give you a sense of greater Naples that this chapter largely ignores (€22, ticket valid 24 hours, infrequent departures, buy from driver or from kiosk at Piazza Municipio in front of Castel Nuovo near the port, scant recorded narration; for details, see the brochure at hotels and TI, tel. 081-551-7279, www.napoli.citysightseeing.it). The same company offers a shorter, more frequent route around the old center in an open-top minibus (€7, €25 combo-ticket with the main route, 40-minute loop, departs in front of the Church of Gesù Nuovo).

Cruise-Ship Excursions

Mondo Guide offers shared shore excursions for my readers (see sidebar).

Convenient for cruise-ship passengers, the **Can't Be Missed** tour company takes you from the port of Naples on an all-day, big-bus trip along the Amalfi Coast that also includes a stop in Sorrento and a guided tour of Pompeii (€65, meet at 8:00 in front of port, bus leaves at 8:30, returns at 17:15, Pompeii ticket extra, mobile 329-129-8182, www.cantbemissedtours.com, 10 percent discount with this book—use promo code "RICKSTEVES" on their website).

Archaeological Museum Tour

Naples' Archaeological Museum (Museo Archeologico), worth

▲▲▲, is one of the world's great museums of ancient art. It boasts supersized statues as well as art and decorations of Pompeii and Herculaneum, the two ancient burgs that were buried in ash by the eruption of Mount Vesuvius in A.D. 79. For lovers of antiquity, this museum alone makes Naples a worthwhile stop. When Pompeii was excavated in the late 1700s, Naples' Bourbon king bellowed, "Bring me the best of what you find!" The finest art and artifacts ended up here, leaving the ancient sites themselves barren (though still impressive). It's here at the Archaeological Museum that you can get up close and personal with the ancient world.

ORIENTATION

Cost and Hours: €8, sometimes more for temporary exhibits, free first Sun of the month, Wed-Mon 9:00-19:30, closed Tue. Early and temporary closures are noted on a board near the ticket office: Expect some rooms to be closed in July and August.

Getting There: To take the **Metro** *(Metropolitana)* from Centrale Station, first buy a single €1.20 transit ticket at a newsstand or tobacco shop. Then follow the signs for *Metro Linea 2* (down the stairs in front of track 13). Validate your ticket in the small yellow or blue boxes near the escalator going down to the tracks. You're looking for line 2 trains heading in the direction of Pozzuoli (they generally depart from track 4, but may depart temporarily from track 2). Ride one stop to Piazza Cavour, and follow the *Museo* signs through the underground passage. Or exit and walk five minutes uphill through the park along the busy street. Look for a grand old red building located up a flight of stairs at the top of the block.

You can also take the Metro's cheaper line 1 five stops from Centrale Station to Museo—it's only a little slower. Figure on €11 for a **taxi** from the train station to the museum.

Information: The shop sells a worthwhile *National Archaeological Museum of Naples* guidebook for €12. Tel. 081-442-2149, www.museoarcheologiconapoli.it.

Tours: My self-guided tour (below) covers all the basics. For more detail, the decent audioguide (€5, leave ID at ticket desk) focuses largely on the provenance of the artifacts and how they ended up here. For a guided tour, book Pina Esposito (see "Tours in Naples," earlier).

☊ Download my free Archaeological Museum **audio tour** (available in 2018).

Baggage Check: Bag check is obligatory and free.

Eating: The museum has no café, but vending machines sell drinks and snacks. There are several good places to grab a meal within a few blocks.

◗ SELF-GUIDED TOUR

Entering the museum, stand at the base of the grand staircase. To your right, on the ground floor, are the larger-than-life statues of the Farnese Collection, starring the *Toro Farnese* and the *Farnese Hercules.* Up the stairs on the mezzanine level are mosaics and fres-

NAPLES

Naples Archaeological Museum

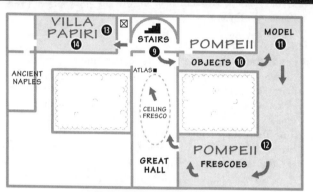

Second Floor (2)

Mezzanine (1)

Not to Scale

⊠ Elevator

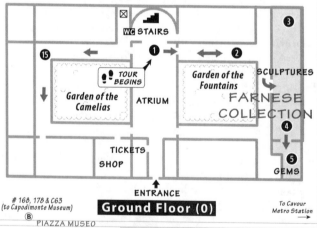

Ground Floor (0)

① Grand Staircase
② Hall of the Busts
③ Toro Farnese
④ Farnese Hercules
⑤ Farnese Cup
⑥ Various Mosaics
⑦ Dancing Faun & Battle of Alexander
⑧ Secret Room
⑨ Great Hall
⑩ Metal, Ivory & Glass Objects
⑪ Model of Pompeii
⑫ Frescoes
⑬ Papyrus Scrolls
⑭ Bronze Statues
⑮ Doriforo

coes from Pompeii, including the Secret Room of erotic art. On the top floor are more artifacts from Pompeii, a scale model of the city, and bronze statues from Herculaneum. WCs are behind the staircase.

• *From the base of the* ❶ *grand staircase, turn right through the door marked* Collezione Farnese *and head for the far end, walking through a rich collection of ancient portrait* ❷ *busts.*

   Pause at the busts of **Caracalla** *(a third of the way down, on the left), and marvel at how he evolved from idealistic youth to cruel tyrant (and nemesis of Russell Crowe in the movie* Gladiator*). Admire the* **Seated Agrippina** *(two-thirds of the way down) with her typical hairstyle, realistic face, and pensive look. Nearby, look in* **Vespasian**'s *right ear and see how the huge head was hollowed out in medieval times. Now, continue to the end, jog right, then left, entering Room 13.*

Ground Floor: The Farnese Collection

The Farnese Collection statues are not from Pompeii, but from Rome. Today they're displayed in this grand hall of huge, bright, and wonderfully restored statues excavated from Rome's Baths of Caracalla. Peruse the larger-than-life statues filling the hall. They were dug up in the 1540s at the behest of Alessandro Farnese (by then Pope Paul III) while he was building the family palace on the Campo de' Fiori in Rome. His main purpose in excavating the baths was to scavenge quality building stone. The sculptures were a nice extra and helped the palace come in under budget on decorations. In the 1700s, the collection ended up in the hands of Charles, the Bourbon king of Naples (whose mother was a Farnese). His son, the next king, had it brought to Naples.

• *Quick—look down to the left end of the hall. There's a woman being tied to a snorting bull.*

   The tangled ❸ *Toro Farnese* tells a thrilling Greek myth. At 13 feet, it's the tallest ancient marble group ever found, and the largest intact statue from antiquity.

A third-century A.D. copy of a lost bronze Hellenistic original, it was carved out of one piece of marble. Michelangelo and others "restored" it at the pope's request—meaning that they integrated surviving bits into a new work. Panels on the wall show which pieces were actually carved by Michelangelo (in blue on the chart): the head of the woman in back, the torso of the aunt under the bull, and the dog. (Imagine how the statue would stand out if it were thoughtfully lit and not surrounded by white walls.)

Here's the tragic story behind the statue: Once upon an ancient Greek time, King Lycus was bewitched by Dirce. He abandoned his pregnant wife, Antiope (standing regally in the background). The single mom gave birth to twin boys. When they grew up, they killed their deadbeat dad and tied Dirce to the horns of a bull to be bashed against a mountain. Captured in marble, the action is thrilling: cape flailing, dog snarling, hooves in the air. You can almost hear the bull snorting. And in the back, Antiope oversees this harsh ancient justice with satisfaction.

At the opposite end of the hall stands the ❹ *Farnese Hercules.* The great Greek hero is exhausted. He leans wearily on his club (draped with his lion skin) and bows his head. He's just finished the daunting Eleventh Labor, having traveled the world, fought men and gods, freed Prometheus from his rock, and carried Atlas' weight of the world on his shoulders. Now he's returned with the prize: the golden apples of the gods, which he cups behind his back. But, after all that, he's just been told he has to return the apples and do one final labor: descend into hell itself. Oh, man.

The 10-foot colossus is a third-century A.D. Roman marble copy (signed by "Glykon") of a fourth-century B.C. Greek bronze original (probably by Lysippos). The statue was enormously famous in its day. Dozens of copies— some marble, some bronze—have been found in Roman villas and baths. This version was unearthed in Rome's Baths of Caracalla in 1546, along with the *Toro Farnese.*

The *Farnese Hercules* was equally famous in the 16th-18th centuries. Tourists flocked to Rome to admire it, art students studied it from afar in prints, Louis XIV made a copy for Versailles, and petty nobles everywhere put small-scale knock-offs in their gardens. This curly-haired version of Hercules became the modern world's image of the Greek hero.

• *Behind Hercules is a doorway into the impressive Farnese gem collection (Rooms 9 and 10). You'll see cameos and the ancient cereal bowl-shaped* ❺ **Farnese Cup,** *which features a portrait thought to be of Cleopatra. When you're ready to move on, backtrack to the main entry hall with its grand staircase, then head up to the mezzanine level (turn left at the lion and go under the* Mosaici *sign), and enter Room 57.*

Mezzanine: Pompeiian Mosaics and the Secret Room

These ❻ **mosaics**—mostly of animals, battle scenes, and geometric designs—were excavated from the walls and floors of Pompeii's ritzy villas. The *Chained Dog* once graced a home's entryway. The

colorful mosaic columns (to your right in adjoining Room 58) shaded a courtyard, part of an ensemble of wall mosaics and bubbling fountains. In Room 59, admire the realism of the tambourine-playing musicians, the drinking doves, and the skull—a reminder of impending death.

Continue a few steps into Room 60, with objects taken from one of Pompeii's greatest villas, the House of the Faun. The 20-inch-high statue was the house's delightful centerpiece, the ❼ *Dancing Faun*. This rare surviving Greek bronze statue (from the fourth century B.C.) is surrounded by some of the best mosaics of that age. (Find the little cat, who's caught a bird.)

A museum highlight, just beyond the statue, is the grand *Battle of Alexander*, a second-century B.C. copy of the now-lost original

Greek fresco, done a century earlier. It decorated a floor in the House of the Faun and was found intact. (The damage you see occurred as this treasure was moved from Pompeii to the king's collection here.) Alexander (left side of the scene, with curly hair and sideburns) is about to defeat the Persians under Darius (central figure, in chariot with turban and beard). This pivotal victory allowed Alexander to quickly overrun much of Asia (331 B.C.). Alexander is the only one without a helmet...a confident master of the battlefield while everyone else is fighting for their lives, eyes bulging with fear. Notice how the horses, already in retreat, add to the scene's propaganda value. Notice also the shading and perspective, which Renaissance artists would later work so hard to accomplish. (A modern reproduction of the mosaic is now back in Pompeii, at the House of the Faun.)

Farther on, the ❽ **Secret Room** (Gabinetto Segreto, Room 65) contains a sizable assortment of erotic frescoes, well-hung pottery, and perky statues that once decorated bedrooms, meeting rooms, brothels, and even shops at Pompeii and Herculaneum.

These bawdy statues and frescoes—many of them once displayed in Pompeii's grandest houses—were entertainment for guests. (By the time they made it to this museum, in 1819, the frescoes could be viewed only with permission from the king—see the letters in the glass case just outside the door.) The Roman nobles commissioned the wildest scenes imaginable. Think of them as ancient dirty jokes.

At the entrance, you're enthusiastically greeted by big stone penises that once projected over Pompeii's doorways. A massive phallus was not necessarily a sexual symbol, but a magical amulet used against the "evil eye." It symbolized fertility, happiness, good luck, riches, straight A's, and general wellbeing.

Circulating counterclockwise through this section, look for the following: the fresco—high up—of a faun playfully pulling the sheet off a beautiful woman (#12), only to be grossed out by a hermaphrodite's plumbing (perhaps the original *"Mamma mia!"*). A few steps farther, see horny pygmies from Africa in action *(#27)*. There's a toga with an embarrassing bulge (#34). A particularly high-quality statue depicts a goat and a satyr engaging in a lewd act (#36). And, watching over it all with remarkable aplomb, Venus, the patron goddess of Pompeii (#39).

The back room is furnished and decorated the way an ancient brothel might have been. The 10 frescoes on the wall functioned as both a menu of services offered and as a kind of *Kama Sutra* of sex positions. The glass cases contain more phallic art, including dangling mobiles used as party favors at rowdy banquets.

• *So, now that your travel buddy is finally showing a little interest in art...finish up your visit by climbing the stairs to the top floor.*

At the top of the stairs, pause and get oriented to our final sights. Directly ahead is a doorway (marked Salone Meridiana*) that leads into a big, empty hall. To the left of this grand hall is a series of rooms with more artifacts from Pompeii. To the right are rooms of statues from Herculaneum. Keep this general layout in mind, because occasionally doorways and routes are altered, and you may have to improvise a bit to find your way.*

Top Floor: Frescoes, Statues, Artifacts, and a Model of Pompeii

First, step into the Salone Meridiana. This was the ❾ **great hall** of the university (17th and 18th centuries) until the building became the royal museum, in 1777. Walk to the center. The sundial (from 1791) still works. Look up to the far-right corner of the hall and find the tiny pinhole. At noon (13:00 in summer), a ray of sun enters the hall and strikes the sundial, showing the time of the year... if you know your zodiac.

Now enter the series of rooms to the left of the grand hall, with ❿ **Metal, Ivory, and Glass Objects** found in Pompeii. You enter through a doorway marked *Vetri e Avori*, which leads into Room 89. Browse your way to the far end, with the stunning *Blue Vase* (Room 85), decorated with cameo Bacchuses harvesting grapes. Turn left, then right, to find the huge, room-filling ⓫ **model of Pompeii**, a 1:100 scale model of the ruins (Room 96). Face the model from the side labeled *plastico di Pompeii*. This is how tourists enter today, up the street, and spilling into the large rectangular forum with the Temple of Jupiter at one end. Farther up in the model are the city's two amphitheater-shaped theaters. This was all that had been excavated when the model was made in 1879. Another model (displayed on the wall) shows the site in 2004, after more excavations, when they'd dug up as far as the huge oval-shaped arena.

Continue on (through Rooms 83-80) and enter Room 75 (marked *affreschi)* to see the museum's impressive collection of (nonerotic) ⓬ **frescoes** taken from the walls of Pompeii villas. Pompeiians loved to decorate their homes with scenes from mythology (Hercules' labors, Venus and Mars in love), landscapes, everyday market scenes, and faux architecture. Look for the scene featuring Bacchus dressed in a robe of grapes standing alongside Mt. Vesuvius—a rare portrait of the volcano before it blew its top. To the left (in Room 78), find the famous dual portrait of baker Terentius Neo and his wife—possibly two of the 2,000 victims when Vesuvius erupted.

• *Browse through more frescoes and objects from Pompeii in this labyrinth of rooms until, eventually, you end up back near the great hall. From here (facing the hall entrance), turn right and find the entrance*

to the wing labeled La Villa dei Papiri.

These artifacts came from the Herculaneum holiday home of Julius Caesar's father-in-law. To the right of the entrance, in Room 114, find two of the 2,000 ⓭ **papyrus scrolls** that gave the villa its name. Displays explain how the half-burned scrolls were unrolled and (with luck) read after excavation in the 1750s. Apparently Caesar's father-in-law was an educated man who appreciated everything from Greek philosophy to Latin history.

Continuing into Room 116, enjoy some of the villa's ⓮ **bronze statues.** Look into the lifelike blue eyes of the intense *Corridore* (runners), bent on doing their best. The *Five Dancers*, with their inlaid-ivory eyes and graceful poses, decorated a portico. The next room (CXVII) has more fine works: *Resting Hermes* (with his tired little heel wings) is taking a break. Nearby, the *Drunken Faun* (singing and snapping his fingers to the beat, a wineskin at his side) is clearly living for today. This statue epitomizes the *carpe diem* life-style of the Epicurean philosophy followed by Caesar's father-in-law and so many other Romans living in Herculaneum and Pompeii on that fateful morning of August 24, A.D. 79, when Vesuvius changed everything.

• *Ka-pow. The artistic explosion you've just experienced in this mighty museum is now over. To exit, return to the ground floor. To reach the exit, circle around the museum courtyard to the gift shop. But for extra credit, stop at one more sight on your way out.*

Doriforo

As you circle the courtyard toward the exit, find ⓭ **Doriforo**. (If he's been moved, ask a guard, *"Dov'è il* Doriforo?") This seven-foot-tall "spear-carrier" (the literal translation of *doriforo*) just stands there, as if holding a spear. What's the big deal about this statue, which looks like so many others? It's a marble rep-lica made by the Romans of one of the most-copied statues of antiquity, a fifth-century B.C. bronze Greek original by Polyclitus. This copy once stood in a Pompeii gym, where it inspired ancient athletes by showing the ideal propor-tions of Greek beauty. So full of motion, and so realistic in its *contrapposto* pose (weight on one foot), the *Doriforo* would later inspire Do-natello and Michelangelo, helping to trigger the Renaissance. And so the glories of ancient Pompeii, once buried and forgotten, live on today.

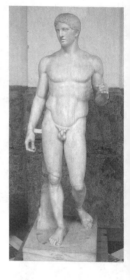

Naples Walk

A SLICE OF NEAPOLITAN LIFE

This self-guided walk, worth ▲▲▲, takes you from the Archaeo-logical Museum through the heart of town and back to Centrale Station. Allow at least two hours, plus time for pizza and sight-seeing stops. (If you have the time and interest, you can make a side-trip to the Royal Palace/Piazza del Plebiscito area—covered in "Sights in Naples," later—halfway through this walk.) You can also ∩ download my free Naples City Walk audio tour (available in 2018).

Naples, a living medieval city, is its own best sight. Couples artfully make love on Vespas surrounded by more fights and smiles per cobblestone than anywhere else in Italy. Sure, Naples has its important sights. But to capture its essence, take this walk through the core of the city.

Part 1: From the Archaeological Museum to Piazza Gesù Nuovo

Start at the Archaeological Museum, at the top of Piazza Cavour (Metro: Cavour or Museo). From here, we'll ramble down a fine boulevard before cutting into the medieval heart of the city.

Archaeological Museum: The palatial building, built in the mid-1700s, captures the glory of Naples at its peak, and is a great introduction to the Naples we'll see. Back then, the city was rich from sea trade and home to erudite nobles from abroad. They built a magnificent capital of buildings like this one. On this walk we'll see that grand city they built...and its remnants following centuries of decline.

• *From the door of the Archaeological Museum, cross the street, veer right, and enter the arched doorway of the beige-colored Galleria Principe di Napoli mall. (If the entrance is blocked, simply loop around the block to another entrance or pick up our walk behind the Galleria.)*

Galleria Principe di Napoli: There's no better example of Naples' grandeur—and decline—than this elegant 19th-century shopping mall. You'll enjoy a soaring skylight, carved woodwork,

ironwork lanterns, playful cupids, an elegant atmosphere...and empty shops. Built with great expectations, the galleria was named for the first male child of the royal Savoy family, the Prince of Naples. Malls like these were popular in Paris and London. In the US, we call this decorative style Art Nouveau; in Italy it's "Liberty Style," named for a British department store that was in vogue at a time when Naples was nicknamed the "Paris of the South." (Parisian artist Edgar Degas even left Paris to adopt Naples—which he actually considered more cosmopolitan and sophisticated—as his hometown.) But despite its grandeur, the mall has suffered from the economic stagnation that began in the late-1800s. Even ambitious renovations in recent years have failed to attract much business.

• *Leaving the gallery through the opposite end, walk one block downhill. You'll pass alongside the palatial golden facade of the Academy of Fine Arts, fronted by tropical plants and (usually) busy with students at its outdoor cafés. At Via Conte di Ruvo, turn left, passing the fine*

Bellini Theater (also in the Liberty Style). All along our walk, be sure to enjoy the architecture of the late 19th century, when Naples was the last stop on Romantic Age travelers' Grand Tour of Europe. After one block, turn right on Via Santa Maria di Costantinopoli. Walking between two grand churches, continue directly downhill to a small park with a statue in the center called...

Piazza Bellini: Suddenly you're in neighborhood Napoli. The statue honors the opera composer Vincenzo Bellini, whose career was launched in Naples in the early 1800s, when opera itself was being born. Just past the statue, peer down into the sunken area to see Naples' ancient origins as a fifth-century B.C. Greek colony called Neapolis—literally, "the new city." These tuff blocks without mortar were part of a tower in the city wall. (And you're standing on land that, back then, was outside of the town.) You can see how the street level has risen from the rubble of centuries.

Now look around at the city of today. Survey the many balconies—and the people who use them as a "backyard" in this densely packed city. The apartment blocks were originally the palaces of noble families, as indicated by the stately family crests above grand doorways. For 2,500 years, laundry has blown in the breeze right here.

• *Walk 30 yards downhill. Stop at the horseshoe-shaped **Port'Alba gate** (on the right). Spin slowly 360 degrees and take in the scene. The proud tile across the street (upstairs, between the two balconies) shows Piazza Bellini circa 1890. Learn to ignore graffiti (as the locals do). Pass through the gate, down Via Port'Alba, and stroll through this pleasant passage lined with book stalls. You emerge into a big square called...*

Piazza Dante: This square is marked by a statue of Dante, the medieval poet. Fittingly, half the square is devoted to bookstores. Old Dante looks out over an urban area that was once grand, then chaotic, and is now slowly becoming grand again.

Along one side is a grandiose, orange-and-gray **pseudo-facade** of columns and statues designed by Luigi Vanvitelli, the architect who remade the city in the late 1700s. Vanvitelli remade an existing monastery into this new structure, representing the power of the Bourbon monarchy when Naples was at its peak. Originally, a statue of the king stood in the square. But in 1799, the Bourbon monarchy was toppled when Napoleon invaded. The king's statue was removed and replaced with the generic figure of Dante. And note the name that was later added to the big facade—Victor Emmanuel. These suggest the next phase of Naples' history—its decline—which we'll see in just a bit.

The Neapolitan people are survivors. A long history of corrupt and greedy colonial overlords (German, Norman, French, Austrian, Spanish, Napoleon, etc.) has taught Neapolitans to deal creatively with authority. Many credit this aspect of Naples' past for the strength of organized crime here.

• Before moving on, note the red "M" that Dante seems to be gesturing to. This marks the **Dante Metro station,** *the best of Napoli's art-splashed Metro stations. (To take a look, go down three flights of escalators and then back up; you'll need a ticket, unless you can sweet-talk a guard.) Then, exit Piazza Dante at the far end, walking downhill on...*

Via Toledo: The long, straight street heading downhill from Piazza Dante is Naples' principal shopping drag. It originated as a military road built by the Spanish viceroys (hence the name) who made Naples great in the 16th century. Back then, Via Toledo skirted the old town wall to connect the Spanish military headquarters (now the museum where you started this walk) with the Royal Palace (down by the bay). As you stroll, peek into the many lovely atriums, which provide a break from the big street.

After a couple hundred yards, you'll reach **Piazza Sette Settembre.** This square represents the event that precipitated Naples' swift decline. On September 7, 1860, from the white marble balcony of the Neoclassical building overlooking the square, the famous revolutionary Giuseppe Garibaldi celebrated his conquest of Naples. He declared Italy united and Victor Emmanuel II its first king. And a decade later, that declaration became reality when Rome also fell to unification forces. It was the start of a glorious new era for Italy, Rome, and the Italian people. But not for Naples.

Naples' treasury was confiscated to subsidize the industrial expansion of the north, and its bureaucrats were transferred to the new capital in Rome. Within a few decades, Naples went from being a thriving cultural and political capital to a provincial town, with its economy in shambles and its dialect considered backward.

• Continue straight on Via Toledo. A block past Piazza Sette Settembre,

you'll come to Via Maddaloni, which marks the start of the long, straight, narrow street nicknamed...

Spaccanapoli: Via Maddaloni is the modern name for this thin street that, since ancient times, has bisected the city. The name Spaccanapoli translates as "split Naples." Look left down the street (toward the train station), and right (toward San Martino hill), and you get a sense of how Spaccanapoli divides this urban jungle of buildings.

• *At this point in our walk, take a moment to plan your next move. From here, our walk loops to the right, through the edge of the intense residential Spanish Quarter neighborhood to Piazza Carità before cutting over to the Spaccanapoli district. (If you were to side-trip to the Royal Palace and Piazza del Plebiscito-area sights—described later in "Sights in Naples"—you'd do that from here...but that makes this walk pretty long.)*

At the Spaccanapoli intersection, go right (toward the church facade on the hill), heading up Via Pasquale Scura. After about 100 yards, you hit a busy intersection. Stop. You're on one of Naples' most colorful open-air market streets...

Via Pignasecca Market: Take in the colorful scene at the intersection. Then, turn left down Via Pignasecca and stroll this colorful strip. You'll pass fish stalls, tripe vendors, butchers, produce stands, cheap clothes stores, street-food vendors, and much more.

This is a taste of Naples' famous **Spanish Quarter** (its center is farther down Via Toledo—see map—but this area provides a good sampling).

The Spanish Quarter is a classic world of *basso* (low) living. The streets—which were laid out in the 16th century for the Spanish

military barracks outside the city walls—are unbelievably narrow (and cool in summer), and the buildings rise five stories high. In such tight quarters, life—flirting, fighting, playing, and loving—happens in the road. This is *the* cliché of life in Naples, as shown in so many movies. The Spanish Quarter is Naples at its most characteristic. The shopkeepers are friendly, and the mopeds are bold (watch out). Concerned locals will tug on their lower eyelids, warning you to be wary. Hungry? Pop into a grocery shop and ask the clerk to make you his best prosciutto-and-mozzarella sandwich (it should cost you about €4).

• *Turn left and follow Via Pignasecca as it leads back to Via Toledo at the square called...*

Piazza Carità: This square, built for an official visit by Hitler to Mussolini in 1938, is full of stern, straight, obedient lines. The big building belonged to an insurance company. (For the best example of fascist architecture in town, take a slight detour from here: With your back to Via Toledo, leave Piazza Carità downhill on the right-hand corner and walk a block to the Poste e Telegrafi building. There you'll see several government buildings with stirring reliefs singing the praises of lobotomized workers and a totalitarian society.)

In Naples—long a poor and rough city—rather than being heroic, people learn from the cradle the art of survival. The modern memorial statue in the center of this square celebrates Salvo d'Acquisto, a rare hometown hero. In 1943, he was executed after falsely confessing to sabotage...saving 22 fellow Italian soldiers from a Nazi revenge massacre.

• *Need a WC? Pop into the Burger King. From Piazza Carità, veer northwest (past more fascist-style architecture) on Via Morgantini through Piazza Monteoliveto. Cross the busy street, then angle up Calata Trinità Maggiore to the fancy column in the piazza at the top of the hill.*

Part 2: From Piazza Gesù Nuovo to Centrale Station

• *You're in Piazza Gesù Nuovo, and you're back on the straight-as-a-Greek-arrow Spaccanapoli, formerly the main thoroughfare of the Greek city of Neapolis. (Spaccanapoli changes names several times: Via Maddaloni, Via B. Croce, Via S. Biagio dei Librai, and Via Vicaria Vecchia.) Stop for a while at...*

Piazza Gesù Nuovo: This square is marked by a towering 18th-century Baroque monument to the Counter-Reformation.

Although the Jesuit order was powerful in Naples because of its Spanish heritage, locals never attacked Protestants here with the full fury of the Spanish Inquisition.

If you'd like, you can visit two bulky old churches, starting with the dark, fortress-like, 17th-century **Church of Gesù Nuovo,** followed by the simpler **Church of Santa Chiara** (in the courtyard across the street; both described under "Sights in Naples"). There's also a **TI** on this square.

• *Continue along the main drag for another 200 yards. Since this is a university district, you may see students and bookstores. As this neighborhood is also famously superstitious, look for incense-burning women with carts full of good-luck charms for sale.*

Passing Palazzo Venezia—the embassy of Venice to Naples when both were independent powers—you'll emerge into the next square...

Piazza San Domenico Maggiore: This square is marked by another ornate 17th-century monument built to thank God for ending the plague. From this square, detour left along the right side of the castle-like church, then follow yellow signs, taking the first right and walking one short block to the remarkable Baroque **Cappella Sansevero** (described later, under "Sights in Naples").

• *After touring the chapel, return to Via B. Croce (a.k.a. Spaccanapoli), turn left, and continue your cultural scavenger hunt. At the intersection of Via Nilo, find the...*

Statue of the Nile (on the left): A reminder of the multiethnic makeup of Greek Neapolis, this statue is in what was the Egyptian quarter. Locals like to call this statue *The Body of Naples*, with the overflowing cornucopia symbolizing the abundance of their fine city. (I once asked a Neapolitan man to describe the local women, who are famous for their beauty, in one word. He replied, simply, "Abundant.") This intersection is considered the center of old Naples.

• *Directly opposite the statue, inside of Bar Nilo, is the...*

"Chapel of Maradona": The small "chapel" on the right wall is dedicated to Diego Maradona, a soccer star who played for Naples in the 1980s. Locals consider soccer almost a religion, and this guy was practically a deity. You can even see a "hair of Diego" and a teardrop from the city when he went to another team for more money. Unfortunately, his reputation has since been sullied by problems he's had with organized crime, drugs, and police. Perhaps inspired by Maradona's example, the coffee bar has posted a quadrilingual sign (though, strangely, not in English) threatening that those who take a picture without buying a cup of coffee may find their camera damaged... *Capisce?*

• *Continue on another 100 yards. You may pass gold and silver shops. Some say stolen jewelry ends up here, is melted down immediately, and gets resold in some other form as soon as it cools. Look for* compro oro *("I buy gold") signs—an enduring sign of Naples' tough economic times. Continue to a tiny square at the intersection with Via San Gregorio Armeno.*

Via San Gregorio Armeno: Stroll up this tiny lane toward the fanciful tower that arches over the street. The street is lined with stalls selling lots of souvenir kitsch, as well as some of Naples' most distinctive local crafts. Among the many figurines on sale, find items relating to *presepi* (Nativity scenes). Just as many Americans keep an eye out year-round for Christmas-tree orna-

ments, Italians regularly add pieces to the family *presepe,* the centerpiece of their holiday decorations. You'll see elaborate manger scenes made of bark and moss, with niches to hold baby Jesus or mother Mary. You'll also see lots of jokey figurines caricaturing local politicians, soccer stars, and other celebrities. (Some of the highest-quality *presepi* pieces are sold at the D'Auria shop, a little farther down Spaccanapoli, on the right at #87. They even sell the classy *campane* version, under a glass bell.)

Another popular Naples souvenir sold here—and all over—is the *corno,* a skinny, twisted, red horn that resembles a chili pepper. The *corno* comes with a double symbolism for fertility: It's a horn of plenty, and it's also a phallic symbol turned upside-down. Neapolitans explain that fertility isn't sexual; it provides the greatest gift a person can give—life—and it ensures that one's soul will live on through the next generation. Interestingly, in today's Naples, just as in yesterday's Pompeii (where bulging erections greeted visitors at the entrance to a home), fertility is equated with good luck.

(By the way, a bit farther up Via San Gregorio Armeno, you'll find the underground **Napoli Sotterranea archaeological site,** along Via dei Tribunali, which also has some of the city's best **pizzerias**—both are described later.)

• *Continue down Spaccanapoli another 100 yards until you hit busy Via Duomo. Consider detouring five minutes north (left) up Via Duomo to visit Naples'* **Duomo;** *just around the corner from that is the* **Pio Monte della Misericordia Church,** *with a fine Caravaggio painting (both described later, under "Sights in Naples"). But for now, continue straight, crossing Via Duomo. Here, Spaccanapoli is named...*

Via Vicaria Vecchia: Here along Via Vicaria Vecchia, the main "sight" is the vibrant street life. It's grittier, less touristy, and less atmospheric than what we've been seeing. The street and side-street scenes intensify. The area is said to be a center of the Camorra (the Naples-based version of the Sicilian Mafia), but as a tourist, you won't notice. Paint a picture with these thoughts: Naples has the most intact street plan of any surviving ancient Greek or Roman city. Imagine this city during those times (and retain these images as you visit Pompeii), with streetside shop fronts that close up after dark, and private homes on upper floors. What you see today is just one more page in a 2,000-year-old story of a city: all kinds of meetings, beatings, and cheatings; kisses, near misses, and little-boy pisses.

You name it, it occurs right on the streets today, as it has since ancient times. People ooze from crusty corners. Black-and-white death announcements add to the clutter on the walls. Widows sell ciga-rettes from buckets. For a peek behind the scenes in the shade of wet laundry, venture down a few side streets. Buy two carrots as a gift for the woman on the fifth floor, if she'll lower her bucket to pick them up. The neighborhood action seems best at about 18:00.

At the tiny fenced-in triangle of greenery, hang out for a few minutes to just observe the crazy motorbike action and teen scene.

• *From here, veer right onto Via Forcella. You emerge into Piazza Vin-cenzo Calenda, where there's a round fence protecting another chunk of that ancient **Greek wall** of Neapolis. Hungry? Turn right here, on Via Pietro Colletta, and close out the walk with three typical Neapolitan...*

Eateries: Step into the North Pole at the recommended **Polo Nord Gelateria** (at #41). The oldest *gelateria* in Naples has had four generations of family working here since 1931. Before you order, sample a few flavors, including their *bacio,* or "kiss," flavor (choco-late and hazelnut)—all are made fresh daily.

Two of Napoli's most competitive **pizzerias** are nearby. **Tri-anon da Ciro** (across the street from Polo Nord) has been serving them up hot and fast for almost a century. A half-block farther, on the right, is the place where some say pizza was born—at **Antica Pizzeria da Michele.** (For more on both, see "Eating in Naples," later).

• *Our walk is over. It's easy to return to Centrale Station. Continue straight ahead, downhill, until you hit the grand boulevard, Corso Um-berto I. Turn left here, and it's a straight 15-minute walk to Centrale Station. (Or cross the street and hop on a bus; they all go to the station.) You'll pass a gauntlet of purse/CD/sunglasses salesmen and shady char-acters hawking stolen mobile phones. You'll soon reach the vast Piazza Garibaldi, with a shiny new modern canopy in the middle. On the far side is the station. You made it.*

Sights in Naples

Naples' best sights are the Archaeological Museum and my self-guided Naples Walk, both covered earlier. For extra credit, con-sider these sights.

CHURCHES ON OR NEAR SPACCANAPOLI

These churches are linked—in this order—on my self-guided walk.

▲Church of Gesù Nuovo

This church's unique pyramid-grill facade survives from a fortified 15th-century noble palace. Step inside for a brilliant Neapolitan Baroque interior. The second chapel on the right features a much-adored **statue of St. Giuseppe Moscati** (1880-1927), a Christian doctor famous for helping the poor. In 1987, Moscati became the first modern doctor to be canonized. Sit and watch a steady stream of Neapolitans taking turns to kiss and touch the altar, then hold the good doctor's highly polished hand.

Continue on to the third chapel and enter the **Sale Moscati.** Look high on the walls of this long room to see hundreds of ex-votos—tiny red-and-silver plaques of thanksgiving for prayers answered with the help of St. Moscati (each has a symbol of the ailment cured). Naples' practice of using ex-votos, while incorporated into its Catholic rituals, goes back to its pagan Greek roots. Rooms from Moscati's nearby apartment are on display, and a glass case shows possessions and photos of the great doctor. As you leave the Sale Moscati, notice the big bomb casing that hangs high in the left corner. It fell through the church's dome in 1943, but caused almost no damage...yet another miracle.

Cost and Hours: Free, daily 6:45-13:00 & 16:00-19:30, Piazza del Gesù Nuovo, www.gesunuovo.it.

Church of Santa Chiara

Dating from the 14th century, this church is from a period of French royal rule under the Angevin dynasty. Consider the stark contrast between this church (Gothic) and the Gesù Nuovo (Baroque), across the street. Inside, look for the faded Trinity on the back wall (on the right as you face the door, under the stone canopy), which shows a dove representing the Holy Spirit between the heads of God the Father and Christ (c. 1414). This is an example of the fine frescoes that once covered the walls. Most were stuccoed over during Baroque times or destroyed in 1943 by Allied bombs. Continuing down the main aisle, you'll step over a huge inlaid-marble Angevin coat of arms on the floor. The altar is adorned with four finely carved Gothic tombs of Angevin kings. A chapel stacked with Bourbon royalty is just to the right.

Cost and Hours: Free, daily 7:30-13:00 & 16:30-20:00, Piazza del Gesù Nuovo, www.monasterodisantachiara.com. Its tranquil cloistered courtyard, around back, is not worth its €6 entry fee.

▲▲Cappella Sansevero

This small chapel is a Baroque explosion mourning the body of Christ, who lies on a soft pillow under an incredibly realistic veil. It's also the personal chapel of Raimondo de Sangro, an eccentric Freemason, containing his tomb and the tombs of his family. Like other 18th-century Enlightenment figures, Raimondo was a wealthy man of letters, scientist and inventor, and patron of the arts—and he was also a grand master of the Freemasons of the Kingdom of Naples. His chapel—filled with Masonic symbolism—is a complex ensemble, with statues representing virtues such as self-control, religious zeal, and the Masonic philosophy of freedom through enlightenment. Though it's a pricey private enterprise, the chapel is worth a visit.

Cost and Hours: €7, buy tickets at office at the corner—or skip the long ticket-buying line by reserving ahead online (€2 fee) and printing out a voucher; open Wed-Mon 9:30-18:30, closed Tue; Via de Sanctis 19, tel. 081-551-8470, www.museosansevero. it. The least crowded time to visit is after 16:00—the later the better. Pick up the free floor plan, which identifies each of the statues lining the nave.

Visiting the Chapel: Study the incredible *Veiled Christ* in the center. Carved out of marble, it's like no other statue I've seen (by

Giuseppe "Howdeedoodat" Sammartino, 1753). The Christian message (Jesus died for our salvation) is accompanied by a Masonic message (the veil represents how the body and ego are obstacles to real spiritual freedom). As you walk from Christ's feet to his head, notice how the expression on Jesus' face goes from suffering to peace.

Raimondo's mom and dad are buried on either side of the **main altar.** To the right of the altar, marking his father's tomb, a statue representing *Despair* or *Disillusion* struggles with a marble rope net (carved out of a single piece of stone), symbolic of a troubled mind. The flames on the head of the winged boy represent human intellect—more Masonic symbolism, showing how knowledge frees the human mind. To the left of the main altar is a statue of *Modesty,* marking the tomb of Raimondo's mother (who died after his birth, and was only 20). The veiled woman fingers a broken tablet, symbolizing an interrupted life.

Raimondo de Sangro himself lies buried in a side altar (on the right). Among his inventions was the deep-green pigment used on the ceiling fresco. The inlaid M. C. Escher-esque maze on the floor around de Sangro's tomb is another Masonic reminder of how the quest for knowledge gets you out of the maze of life. This tilework once covered the floor of the entire chapel.

Your Sansevero finale is downstairs: two mysterious...**skeletons.** Perhaps another of the mad inventor's fancies: Inject a corpse with a fluid to fossilize the veins so that they'll survive the body's decomposition. While that's the legend, investigations have shown that the veins were artificial, and the models were created to illustrate how the circulatory system works.

▲Duomo

Naples' historic cathedral, built by imported French Anjou kings in the 14th century, boasts a breathtaking Neo-Gothic facade. Step

into the vast interior to see the mix of styles along the side chapels—from pointy Gothic arches to rounded Renaissance ones to gilded Baroque decor.

Cost and Hours: Free, Mon-Sat 8:30-13:30 & 14:30-20:00, Sun 8:30-13:30 & 16:30-19:30, Via Duomo.

Visiting the Church: Explore the two largest side-chapels (flanking the nave, about halfway to the transept). Each is practically a church in its own right. On the left, the **Chapel of St. Restituta** stands on the site of the original, early-Christian church that predated the cathedral (at the far end, you can pay a small fee to see its sixth-century baptismal font under mosaics and go downstairs to see its even earlier foundations; shorter hours than cathedral). On the right is the **Chapel of San Gennaro**—dedicated to the beloved patron saint of Naples—decorated with silver busts of centuries of bishops, and seven paintings done on bronze.

The cathedral's **main altar** at the front is ringed by carved wooden seats, filled three times a year by clergy to witness the Miracle of the Blood. Thousands of Neapolitans cram into this church for a peek at two tiny vials with the dried blood of St. Gennaro. As the clergy roots—or even jeers—for the miracle to occur, the blood temporarily liquefies. Neapolitans take this ritual with deadly seriousness, and believe that if the blood remains solid, it's terrible luck for the city. Sure enough, on the rare occasion that the miracle fails, locals can point to a terrible event soon after—such as an earthquake, an eruption of Mount Vesuvius, or an especially disappointing soccer loss.

The stairs beneath the altar take you to a **crypt** with the relics of St. Gennaro and (across the room) a statue of the bishop who rescued the relics from a rival town and returned them to Naples.

Pio Monte della Misericordia

This small church (near the Duomo, and run by a charitable foundation) displays one of the best works by Caravaggio, *The Seven*

Works of Mercy. Upstairs is a ho-hum art gallery. The price is steep, but it may be worth it for Caravaggio fans.

Cost and Hours: €7, includes audioguide, Thu-Tue 9:00-14:30, closed Wed, Via dei Tribunali 253, tel. 081-446-944, www.piomontedellamisericordia.it.

Visiting the Church: Caravaggio's *The Seven Works of Mercy* hangs over the main altar in a humble gray chapel. It's well lit, allowing Caravaggio's characteristically dark canvas to really pop. In one crowded canvas, the great early-Baroque artist illustrates seven virtues: burying the dead (the man carrying a corpse by the ankles); visiting the imprisoned and feeding the hungry (Pero breastfeeding her starving father—a scene from a famous Roman story); sheltering the homeless (a pilgrim on the Camino de Santiago, with his floppy hat, negotiates with an innkeeper); caring for the sick and clothing the naked (St. Martin offers part of his cloak to the injured man in the foreground); and giving drink to the thirsty (Samson chugs from a jawbone in the background)—all of them set in a dark Neapolitan alley and watched over by Mary, Jesus, and a pair of angels. Caravaggio painted this work in Naples in 1607, while in exile from Rome, where he had been sentenced to death for killing a man in a duel.

IN THE CITY CENTER

This cluster of important sights can be found between the big ceremonial square, Piazza del Plebiscito, and the cruise ship terminal. If touring the entire neighborhood, I'd see it in the order described here.

▲Piazza del Plebiscito

This square celebrates the 1861 vote (*plebiscito,* plebiscite) in which Naples chose to join Italy. Dominating the top of the square is the Church of San Francesco di Paola, with its Pantheon-inspired dome and broad, arcing colonnades. If it's open, step inside to ogle the vast interior—a Neoclassical re-creation of one of ancient Rome's finest buildings.

• *Opposite is the...*

Royal Palace (Palazzo Reale)

Having housed Spanish, French, and even Italian royalty, this building displays statues of all those who stayed here. From the square in front of the palace, look for eight kings in the niches, each from a different dynasty (left to right): Norman, German, French, Spanish, Spanish, Spanish, French (Napoleon's brother-in-law), and, finally, Italian—Victor Emmanuel II, King of Savoy. The statues were done at the request of V. E. II's son, so his dad is the most dashing of the group. As far as palaces go, the interior is relatively unimpressive.

Cost and Hours: €4, includes painfully dry audioguide, Thu-Tue 9:00-20:00, closed Wed, last entry one hour before closing, tel. 848-082-408, www.palazzorealenapoli.it.

Visiting the Palace: The palace's grand Neoclassical staircase leads up to a floor with 30 plush rooms. You'll follow a one-way route (with some English descriptions) featuring the palace theater, paintings by "the Caravaggio Imitators," Neapolitan tapestries, fine inlaid-stone tabletops, chandeliers, gilded woodwork, and more. The rooms do feel quite grand, but they lack the personality and sense of importance of Europe's better palaces. Don't miss the huge, tapestry-laden Hercules Hall. On the way out, step into the chapel, with a fantastic Nativity scene—a commotion of 18th-century ceramic figurines.

• *Continue 50 yards past the Royal Palace (toward the trees) to enjoy a...*

Fine Harbor View

While boats busily serve Capri and Sorrento, Mount Vesuvius smolders ominously in the distance. Look back to see the vast "Bourbon red" palace—its color inspired by Pompeii. The hilltop

above Piazza del Plebiscito is San Martino, with its Carthusian monastery-turned-museum and Castle of St. Elmo (remember, the Centrale funicular to the top is just across the square and up Via Toledo). The promenade you're on continues to Naples' romantic harborfront—the fishermen's quarter (Borgo Marinaro)—a fortified island connected to the mainland by a stout causeway, with its fanciful, ancient Castel dell'Ovo (Egg Castle) and trendy harborside restaurants. From there, the Lungomare harborside promenade—described later—continues past the Santa Lucia district, stretching out along the Bay of Naples. This long promenade, running along Via Francesco Caracciolo to the Mergellina district and beyond, is a delightful people-watching scene on balmy nights.

• *Head back through the piazza and pop into...*

Gran Caffè Gambrinus

This coffeehouse, facing the piazza, takes you back to the elegance of 1860. It's a classic place to sample a crispy *sfogliatella* pastry, or perhaps the mushroom-shaped, rum-soaked bread-like cakes called *babà*, which come in a huge variety. Stand at the bar *(banco)*, pay double to sit *(tavola)*, or just wander around as you imagine the café buzzing with the ritzy intellectuals, journalists, and artsy bohemian types who munched on *babà* here during Naples' 19th-century heyday (daily 7:00-24:00, Piazza del Plebiscito 1, tel. 081-417-582).

• *A block away, tucked behind the palace, you can peek inside the Neoclassical...*

Teatro di San Carlo

Built in 1737, 41 years before Milan's La Scala, this is Europe's oldest opera house and Italy's second-most-respected (after La Scala). The theater burned down in 1816, and was rebuilt within the year. Guided 35-minute visits in English basically just show you the fine auditorium with its 184 boxes—each with a big mirror to reflect the candlelight (€6; tours Mon-Sat at 10:30, 11:30, 12:30, 14:30, 15:30, and 16:30; Sun at 10:30, 11:30, and 12:30; tel. 081-797-2468, www.teatrosancarlo.it).

• *Beyond Teatro di San Carlo and the Royal Palace is the huge, harborfront...*

Castel Nuovo

This imposing castle now houses government bureaucrats and the **Civic Museum.** It feels like a mostly empty shell, with a couple of dusty halls of Neapolitan art, but the views over the bay from the upper terraces are impressive (€6, Mon-Sat 8:30-19:00, closed Sun, last entry one hour before closing, tel. 081-795-7722, www.comune.napoli.it).

• *Head back to Teatro di San Carlo, cross the street, and go through the tall yellow arch into...*

▲Galleria Umberto I

This Victorian iron-and-glass shopping mall was built in 1892 to reinvigorate the district after a devastating cholera epidemic occurred here. Gawk up, then walk left to bring you back out on Via Toledo.

• *Just up the street and behind Piazza del Plebiscito is an interesting subterranean experience.*

▲Galleria Borbonica

Beneath Naples' Royal Palace was a vast underground network of caves, aqueducts, and cisterns that originated as a quarry in the 15th century. In the mid-1800s, when popular revolutions were threatening royalty across Europe, the understandably nervous king of Naples, Ferdinand II, had this underground world expanded to create an escape tunnel from the palace to his military barracks nearby. In World War II, it was used as an air-raid shelter; after the war, the police used it to store impounded cars and motorcycles. Today, enthusiastic guides take the curious on a fascinating 70-minute, 500-yard-long guided walk through this many-layered world littered with disintegrating 60-year-old vehicles upon which Naples sits.

Cost and Hours: €10 English-language tours leave Fri-Sun at 10:00, 12:00, 15:30, and 17:30, tel. 081-764-5808. The most convenient entry is just behind Piazza del Plebiscito—up Via Gennaro Serra and down Vico del Grottone to #4 (to avoid that entrance's 90 steep steps, enter at Via Morelli 61).

NORTH OF SPACCANAPOLI
▲Napoli Sotterranea

This archaeological site, a manmade underground maze of passageways and ruins from Greek and Roman times, can only be toured with a guide. You'll descend 121 steps under the modern city to explore two underground areas. One is the old Greek tuff quarry used to build the city of Neapolis, which was later converted into an immense cistern by the Romans. The other is an excavated portion of the Greco-Roman theater that once seated 6,000 people. It's clear that this space has been encroached upon by modern development—some current residents' windows literally look down into the theater ruins. The tour involves a lot of stairs, as well as a long, narrow 20-inch-wide walkway—lit only by candlelight—that uses an ancient water channel (a heavyset person could not comfortably fit through this, and claustrophobes will be miserable). Although there's not much to actually see, the experience is fascinating and includes a little history from World War II—when the quarry/cistern was turned into a shelter to protect locals from American bombs.

Cost and Hours: €10; includes 1.5-hour tour. Tours in English are offered daily every two hours from 10:00 to 18:00. Bring a light sweater. Tel. 081-296-944, www.napolisotterranea.org.

Getting There: The site is at Piazza San Gaetano 68, along Via dei Tribunali. It's a 15-minute walk from the Archaeological Museum, and just a couple of blocks uphill from Spaccanapoli's statue of the Nile. The entrance is immediately to the left of the Church of San Paolo Maggiore (look for the *Sotterranea* signs).

MADRE

MADRE, a museum of contemporary art, displays works by Jeff Koons, Anish Kapoor, Francesco Clemente, and other big names in the art world. Aficionados of modern art consider it one of the better collections in the country. Some descriptions are in English—you'll need them.

Cost and Hours: €7, free on Mon; Wed-Mon 10:00-19:30, closed Tue, last entry one hour before closing; Via Settembrini 79, tel. 081-1931-3016, www.madrenapoli.it.

▲▲Sanità District

While the characteristic Spaccanapoli and Spanish Quarter are being tamed, today's clear winner for wild-and-crazy Neapolitan life in the streets is the gritty Sanità District, north of the Archaeological Museum.

A big part of the attraction of Naples is its *basso* living (life in the streets). Many locals with enough money to move to the sanity of the suburbs choose instead to keep living where the action is—in a cauldron of flapping laundry, police sirens, broken cobblestone lanes, singing merchants, sidewalks clogged with makeshift markets, and walls crusted with ancient posters and graffiti.

One of Naples' most historic and colorful zones, Sanità is sometimes called "the living *presepe*" for the way people live stacked on top of each other in rustic conditions, as if in an elaborate manger scene. (Because organized crime is still strong in this quarter, development is slow.) Literally "the healthy place" (named for the freshness of the air, originally so high above the dense city), this is *the* place for a photo safari.

While the reason to visit Sanità is simply to swim through its amazing river of life, there are two remarkable burial sites in the district: the Catacombs of San Gaudioso, at the Basilica Santa Maria della Sanità, and the Cemetery of the Fountains (described later, under "On Capodimonte").

Visiting the Sanità District: Check to be sure your valuables are zipped or buttoned safely away. From near the Porta San Gennaro gate (just west of Via Duomo, two blocks east of Metro: Cavour, six blocks east of Archaeological Museum), leave Via Foria and head up Via Crocelle. Venture a block up Via Crocelle and then three blocks up Via dei Vergini through a thriving daily market scene. Pop into the courtyard of the Palazzo dello Spagnuolo (#19 on the left) to peek at an extravagant 18th-century staircase.

Then dog-leg left on Via Arena della Sanità and continue uphill (past another massive staircase in the courtyard at #6) to Piazza Sanità, at the base of Capodimonte, where you'll stand before the Basilica Santa Maria della Sanità, which sits atop the Catacombs of San Gaudioso (entrance inside the church, €9 combo-ticket covers

Catacombs of San Gennaro, hourly English tours run daily 10:00-13:00). Because this area was just outside the old city walls, the dead were buried here—for details, see www.catacombedinapoli.it.

From here you have three options: Browse your way back down the way you just came; continue 10 minutes up Via Sanità and Via Fontanelle to the Cemetery of the Fountains; or ride a free elevator (just past the church, under the high viaduct) up to the modern world.

ON CAPODIMONTE
▲▲Capodimonte Museum (Museo di Capodimonte)
This hilltop, about a mile due north from the Archaeological Museum, is home to Naples' top art museum. This pleasantly uncrowded collection has lesser-known (but still masterful) works by Michelangelo, Raphael, Titian, Caravaggio, and other huge names. It fills the Bourbons' cavernous summer palace, set in the midst of a sprawling hilltop park overlooking Naples, and part of the museum showcases the palace's history and furnishings. While most visitors to Naples prefer to focus on the city's vibrant street life, characteristic churches, and ancient artifacts, art lovers and royalty buffs enjoy a visit to Capodimonte.

Cost and Hours: €8, free first Sun of the month, Thu-Tue 8:30-19:30, closed Wed, last entry one hour before closing, fine audioguide-€5 (bring earbuds for better sound), café, Via Miano 2, tel. 081-749-9111, www.museocapodimonte.beniculturali.it.

Getting There: It's easiest by taxi (figure €10-12 from the town center). You can also catch the bus from Piazza Dante or from the stop directly in front of the Archaeological Museum (#168 or #178 to the Miano stop, or #C63 to the Capodimonte stop; buy €1 ticket at a newsstand or tobacco shop before you board).

Visiting the Museum: After buying your ticket, pick up the free map and head up several flights of stairs (or ride the elevator) to the "first" floor and the Galleria Farnese.

Room 2: At the far end of the first big hall is Titian's *Portrait of John Paul III*. It depicts Alessandro Farnese, the local bigwig whose family married into Bourbon royalty; later, as Pope Paul III, he was responsible for bringing great art to Naples. Four paintings to the right, you'll see a Raphael: a portrait of the same red-attired pope as a much younger cardinal.

Room 3: In the next, smaller room, the section of an altarpiece (1426) by the early Renaissance pioneer Masaccio shows a primitive attempt at 3-D: Masaccio has left out Jesus' neck to create the illusion that he's looking down on us.

Room 4: Don't miss the adjoining room (on the left, lights go on as you enter), with large charcoal drawings by Raphael (Moses shields his eyes from the burning bush, 1514) and Michelangelo (a group of soldiers, 1546; and *Venus and Love*, 1534).

Room 8: Continuing into the Borgia Collection, look for works by Mantegna (including the medallion-like *Portrait of Francesco Gonzaga*, c. 1461, a very small but finely executed profile portrait) and Giovanni Bellini's *Transfiguration*. (Bellini was Titian's master.) Rooms 9 and 10 feature Mannerism paintings.

Room 11: Here you see one of many versions of Titian's *Danaë*, where—as told in the Greek myth—the sensuous central character looks up at a cloud containing the essence of Zeus (a shower of coins), about to impregnate her. Enjoy the cupid's surprised look at the action as the courtesan awaits her union. Nearby, Titian's poignant portrait of a penitent Mary Magdalene has finely detailed tears running down her cheeks (1565).

Room 12: Parmigianino's *Antea* (1531-35), another of the collection's highlights, addresses us with an unblinking, dilated gaze. She wears a mink stole (astonishingly lifelike, with disgusting little teeth), gold chain, and head brooch—items commonly presented by a lover. By wearing the gifts, Antea signals her acceptance of her suitor's advances.

Room 14: The small, dim, adjoining room shows off the kings' "collection of wonders." Don't miss the *Farnese Box* (*Cassetta Farnese*, 1563), a masterwork of gold decoration with engraved rock crystal, which held a prayer book.

Room 17: Down the main hall are two side-by-side works by Pieter Bruegel the Elder. *The Parable of the Blind* (*Parabola dei Ciechi*, 1568) is a literal and moralistic illustration of "the blind leading the blind." *The Misanthrope* (1568) suggests the pointlessness of giving up on life and becoming a hermit; cut off from the world and lost in thought, the title figure doesn't even notice that he's about to step on a trail of thorns. Behind him, a wild-eyed young man is stealing the misanthrope's money pouch (Hey! I saw that guy on the Circumvesuviana!).

Room 20: Looking at you from the end of the corridor, Annibale Carracci's *Hercules at the Crossroads* (1596) presents the hero with a choice: virtue (on the left, nature and letters, but a steep uphill climb) or vice (on the right, scantily clad women, music, theater masks, and an easy, flat path). While his foot points one way, he looks the other...his mind not made up.

Royal Apartments: It's easy to forget that this museum is set in a royal palace. Originally a simple hunting lodge, in the 18th century the king decided it could be a grand palace. Several dynasties enjoyed its regal ballrooms and imposing reception rooms while amassing their impressive collections of art. From here on out, you'll pass through some of the opulent apartments of this building, decorated with stunning period details and furniture.

The first room is slathered with frescoes, in the style of rooms excavated at Pompeii. The grand hall in the corner comes with a massive bronze chandelier hanging over an ancient Roman inlaid-marble floor, which originally decorated the palace of Roman Emperor Tiberius on Capri (installed here in 1877). The next three rooms tell stories of three Bourbon kings with portraits and objects from their reign. Just off Room 34 is a room filled with royal porcelain. Later, you come upon a living room decorated with porcelain c. 1750. This is a masterwork of *chinoiserie*—a style reflecting Europe's fascination with Chinese culture.

Room 54: You now find yourself face-to-face with Napoleon. Under Napoleon's portrait is a statue of his mother, Letizia, carved in chalk by Antonio Canova. She's posing like a famous ancient statue of the mother of Emperor Nero. From here are several rooms decorated in the Napoleon-pleasing Neoclassical style—a reminder that Napoleon's older brother once ruled the Kingdom of Napoli.

Second Floor: Circling back to where you started, head up four flights of stairs (or take the elevator) to the second floor where you'll find art from private collections and paintings mostly from local churches. You'll see a cycle of Flemish tapestries, then halls of Gothic altarpieces.

Room 65: Heading down the first corridor, enjoy the fine altarpiece from Nottingham, England. Carved out of alabaster in the 15th century, it shows expressive scenes from the Passion of Christ.

Room 66: At the end of the first corridor, you'll see Simone Martini's lavish and delicate portrait from 1317 of San Ludovico di Tolosa crowning Roberto king of Naples.

Room 67: Find Colantonio's painting *San Girolamo nello Studio* (c. 1445), in which the astonishing level of detail—from the words on the page of the open book, to the balled-up pages tucked away at the bottom of the frame—drives home the message: Only through complete devotion and meticulous dedication can you hope to accomplish great things...like pulling a thorn out of a lion's paw.

Room 78: Farther along on this floor, shining at the end of the long corridor, you'll reach another of the museum's top pieces, Caravaggio's *The Flagellation*. Typical of his *chiaroscuro* (light/dark) style, Caravaggio uses a ribbon of light to show us only what he wants us to see: A broken Christ about to be whipped, and the manic fury of the man (on his left) who will do the whipping. This scene could be set in a Naples alley. Compare this with most of the paintings we've seen so far—of popes, saints, and aristocrats. Caravaggio was given refuge in Naples while fleeing a murder trial in Rome. (They put him to work painting. Of the eight canvases he painted during this period, three remain in Naples). Caravaggio was revolutionary in showing real life rather than idealized scenes—helping common people to better relate to these stories.

Nearby: While people visiting the Capodimonte Museum are understandably focused on its paintings, don't overlook the lush **Capodimonte Park** surrounding it. No longer a hunting ground for royalty, the park is now a pleasure garden—beloved by Neapolitans—with elegant paths and lovely gardens sprouting trees and exotic plants from around the world. It was recently honored as Italy's most beautiful park.

▲▲Catacombs of San Gennaro

Behind the towering modern church of Madre del Buon Consiglio (Mother of Good Counsel) are tucked the most impressive ancient catacombs south of Rome. It started as a pagan tomb of little consequence, but then St. Agrippino, the local bishop, was buried here in the third century. Later, in the fifth century, the bones of St. Gennaro (patron of Naples) were moved here. Suddenly a site of special reverence—complete with miracles—it became a place where Neapolitans wanted to be buried as well. Today, the catacombs are run by a nonprofit organization of earnest young people who conduct walking tours. These half-mile walks survey more than a thousand burial niches on two levels that date from the second to sixth centuries (many with frescoes surviving...barely).

Cost and Hours: €9 combo-ticket with Catacombs of San Gaudioso; included English-language tours depart on the hour Mon-Sat 10:00-17:00, Sun 10:00-14:00; Via di Capodimonte 13, tel. 081-744-3714.

▲Cemetery of the Fountains (Cimitero delle Fontanelle)

A thousand years ago, cut into the hills at the high end of Napoli, was a quarry. Then, in the 16th century, churches with crowded cemeteries began moving the bones of their long dead here to make room for the newly dead. Later these caves housed the bones of plague victims and the city's paupers. In the 19th century, many churches again emptied their cemeteries and added even more skulls to this vast ossuary. Then a cult of people appeared whose members adopted the skulls. They named the skulls, put them in little houses, brought them flowers, and asked them to intervene with God for favors from the next life. Today, the quirky caves—stacked with human bones and dotted with chapels—are open to the public.

Cost and Hours: Tips accepted, daily 10:00-17:00, Via Fontanelle 77, tel. 081-795-6160.

Getting There: Located in a sketchy-feeling neighborhood at the top end of Sanità, you can get here by hopping in a taxi, riding the Metro to the Materdei stop and following the brown signs for 10 minutes, or by hiking 10 minutes from the Basilica Santa Maria della Sanità up Via Sanità and Via Fontanelle (see "Sanità District" listing, earlier).

SOUTH OF SPACCANAPOLI
Porta Nolana Open-Air Fish Market

Naples' fish market squirts and stinks as it has for centuries under the Porta Nolana (gate in the city wall), immediately in front of the

Napoli Porta Nolana Circumvesuviana station and four long blocks from Centrale Station. Of the town's many boisterous outdoor markets, this will net you the most photos and memories. From Piazza Nolana, wander under the medieval gate and take your first left down Vico Sopramuro, enjoying this wild and entirely edible cultural scavenger hunt (Tue-Sun 8:00-14:00, closed Mon).

Two other markets with more clothing and fewer fish are at Piazza Capuana (several blocks northwest of Centrale Station and tumbling down Via Sant'Antonio Abate, Mon-Sat 8:00-18:00, Sun 9:00-13:00) and a similar cobbled shopping zone along Via Pignasecca (just off Via Toledo, west of Piazza Carità).

▲▲Harborside Promenade: The Lungomare *Passeggiata*

Each evening, relaxed and romantic Neapolitans in the mood for a scenic harborside stroll do their *vasche* (laps) along the inviting Lungomare harborside promenade and beyond. To join in this elegant people-watching scene (best after 19:00), stroll down to the waterfront from Piazza del Plebiscito and then along Via Nazario Sauro to the beginning of a delightful series of harborside promenades that stretch romantically all the way out of the city. Along the way, you'll enjoy views of Mount Vesuvius and the Bay of Naples. The entire route is crowded on weekends and lively any evening of the week with families, amorous couples, friends hanging out, and lots of hustlers. Here's a brief run-down of its three sections:

Santa Lucia and Borgo Marinaro: Via Nazario Sauro passes the Santa Lucia district, so called because this is where the song "Santa Lucia" was first performed. (The song is probably so famous in America because immigrants from Naples sang it to remember the old country.) At the fortified causeway, make a short detour out to Borgo Marinaro ("Fisherman's Quarter"), and poke around this fabled island neighborhood. With its striking Castel dell'Ovo and a trendy restaurant scene, you can dine here amid yachts with a view of Vesuvius. From here, follow Via Partenope to Piazza Vittoria.

Piazza Vittoria and Via Francesco Caracciolo: From Piazza

Vittoria the strolling action stretches along the Lungomare on Via Francesco Caracciolo all the way to the Mergellina district. The convenient bus #140 starts at Piazza Vittoria, making stops all along the promenade to Posillipo (at the end of the nice strolling stretch). Walk as far as you like away from the city center and, when you're ready to return, just hop on the bus or grab a cab. (From Piazza Vittoria you can shortcut scenically directly back to Piazza del Plebiscito by heading inland through Piazza dei Martiri and down Via Chiaia.)

Mergellina and Via Posillipo: The promenade continues past yacht harbors and rocks popular for swimming and sunbathing, under lavish Liberty Style villas, to tiny coves and inviting fish restaurants. Perched on the hillside at Posillipo (the end of the nice stretch) awaits a delightful restaurant with majestic views (Ristorante Reginella, Via Posillipo 45a, tel. 081-240-3220) and the bus #140 stop for your quick return.

ON SAN MARTINO

The ultimate view overlooking Naples, its bay, and the volcano is from the hill called San Martino, just above (and west of) the city center. Up top you'll find a mighty fortress (which charges for entry but offers the best views from its ramparts) and the adjacent monastery-turned-museum. While neither of these sights is exciting in its own right, the views are. And the surrounding neighborhood (especially Piazza Fuga) has a classy "uptown" vibe compared to the gritty city-cen-

ter streets below. Cheapskates can enjoy the views for free from the benches on the square in front of the monastery.

Getting There: From Via Toledo, the Spanish Quarter gradually climbs up San Martino's lower slopes, before steep paths take you up the rest of the way. But the easiest way to ascend San Martino is by **funicular.** Three different funicular lines lead from lower Naples to the hilltop: the Centrale line from near the bottom of Via Toledo; the Montesanto line from the Metro stop of the same name (near the top end of Via Toledo); and the Chiaia line from farther out, near Piazza Amadeo (all three are covered by any regular local transit ticket). Ride any of these three up to the end of the line. All three lines converge within a few blocks at the top of the hill—Centrale and Chiaia wind up at opposite ends of the charming Piazza Fuga, while Montesanto terminates a bit closer to the fortress and museum.

Leaving any of the funiculars, head uphill, carefully tracking the brown signs for *Castel S. Elmo* and *Museo di San Martino* (strategically placed escalators make the climb easier). Regardless of where you come up, you'll pass the Montesanto funicular station—angle right (as you face the station) down Via Pirro Ligorio, and then continue following the signs. You'll reach the castle first, and then the monastery/museum (both about 10 minutes' walk from Piazza Fuga).

Another convenient—if less scenic—approach is via the Metro's line 1 to the Vanvitelli stop, which is near the upper funicular terminals.

Castel Sant'Elmo

While it's little more than an empty husk with a decent modern art museum, this 16th-century, Spanish-built, star-shaped fortress boasts commanding views over the city and the entire Bay of Naples. Buy your ticket at the booth, then ride the elevator up to the upper courtyard and climb up to the ramparts for a slow circle to enjoy the 360-degree views. In the middle of the yard is the likeable little Museo del Novecento, a gallery of works by 20th-century Neapolitan artists (covered by same ticket); the castle also hosts temporary exhibits.

Cost and Hours: €5, open Wed-Mon 9:00-19:00, closed Tue, last entry one hour before closing, Via Tito Angelini 22, tel. 081-229-4401, www.polomusealecampania.beniculturali.it.

▲San Martino Carthusian Monastery and Museum (Certosa e Museo di San Martino)

The monastery, founded in 1325 and dissolved in the early 1800s, is now a sprawling museum with several parts. The square out front

has city views nearly as good as the ones you'll pay to see from inside, and a few cafés angling for your business.

Cost and Hours: €6, Thu-Tue 8:30-19:30, closed Wed, last entry one hour before closing, audio-guide-€5, Largo San Martino 8, tel. 081-229-4502.

Visiting the Monastery and Museum: If you want to tour the place, buy your ticket and head into the complex. Step into the church, a Baroque explosion with beautifully decorated chapels. Around the humble cloister is a variety of museum exhibits. The Naval Museum has nautical paintings, model boats, and giant ceremonial gondolas. In an adjacent hall is an excellent collection of *presepi* (Nativity scenes), both life-size and miniature, including a spectacular one by Michele Cucinello—the best I've seen in this *presepi*-crazy city. Beyond that is the larger garden cloister, ringed with a painting gallery (with lots of antique maps and artifacts of old Naples), and an entrance to a pretty view terrace.

Sleeping in Naples

As an alternative to intense Naples, most travelers prefer to sleep in mellow Sorrento, just over an hour away. But, if needed, here are a few good options. High season in Naples is spring and late fall. Prices are soft during the hot, slow summer months (July-Sept) and plunge during the pleasantly cool winters.

ON AND AROUND VIA TOLEDO

To see the city's best face, stay in the area that stretches between the Archaeological Museum and the port.

$$$ Decumani Hotel de Charme is a classy oasis tucked away on a residential lane in the very heart of the city, just off Spaccanapoli. While the street is Naples-dingy, the hotel is an inviting retreat, filling an elegant 17th-century palace with 42 rooms and a gorgeous breakfast room (air-con, elevator, Via San Giovanni Maggiore Pignatelli 15, Metro: Università; if coming from Spaccanapoli, this lane is one street toward the train station from Via Santa Chiara, tel. 081-551-8188, www.decumani.com, info@decumani.com).

$$$ Hotel Piazza Bellini is an artistically decorated hotel with 48 stripped-down, minimalist but comfy rooms surrounding a peaceful and inviting courtyard. Two blocks below the Archaeological Museum and just off the lively Piazza Bellini, it offers modern sanity in the city center (air-con, elevator, Via Santa Maria di Constantinopoli 101, Metro: Dante, tel. 081-451-732, www.hotelpiazzabellini.com, info@hotelpiazzabellini.com).

$$$ Chiaja Hotel de Charme, with the same owner as the Decumani (listed earlier), rents 33 rooms on the Via Chiaia pedestrian shopping drag near Piazza del Plebiscito. The building has a fascinating history: Part of it was the residence of a marquis, and the rest was one of Naples' most famous brothels (some view rooms, air-con, elevator, Via Chiaia 216, first floor, Metro: Toledo, tel. 081-415-555, www.hotelchiaia.it, info@hotelchiaia.it, Pietro Fusella).

$$$ Art Resort Galleria Umberto has 15 rooms in two different buildings inside the Umberto I shopping gallery at the bottom of Via Toledo, just off Piazza del Plebiscito. This genteel-feeling place gilds the lily, with an aristocratic setting and decor but older bathrooms. Consider paying €20 extra for a room overlooking the gallery (air-con, elevator, Galleria Umberto 83, fourth floor—ask at booth for coin to operate elevator if needed, Metro:

Toledo, tel. 081-497-6224, www.artresortgalleriaumberto.com, booking@hotelgalleriaumberto.com).

$$$ Hotel Il Convento, with 14 small but comfortable rooms with balconies, is a good choice for those who want to sleep in the gnarly, tight tangle of lanes called the Spanish Quarter—quintessential Naples. While the neighborhood can feel off-putting after dark, it's not especially unsafe. You're only a couple of short blocks off the main Via Toledo drag, and heavy-duty windows help block out some—but not all—of the scooter noise and church bells. A rare haven in this characteristic corner of town, it's in all the guidebooks (family rooms, air-con, elevator; Via Speranzella 137A, Metro: Toledo—from just below Banco di Napoli entrance, walk two blocks up Via Tre Re a Toledo; tel. 081-403-977, www.hotelilconvento.com, info@hotelilconvento.com).

AT THE TRAIN STATION
These hotels are less convenient for sightseeing and dining, and the neighborhood gets dodgy as you move away from the station. But they're handy for train travelers, practical for a quick stay, and less expensive.

$$ Hotel Stelle has 38 sterile, identical, newly remodeled rooms with modern furnishings. It feels very secure, and a back entrance leads directly into the train station (air-con, elevator, Corso Meridionale 60, exit station near track 5, tel. 081-1889-3090, www.stellehotel.com, info@stellehotel.com).

$$ Ibis Styles Napoli Garibaldi, with 88 rooms, offers chain predictability and a bright, youthful color scheme a three-minute walk from the station (air-con, elevator, pay parking; Via Giuseppe Ricciardi 33, exit station onto Piazza Garibaldi, then take second left onto Via G. Ricciardi; tel. 081-690-8111, www.ibis.com, h3243@accor.com).

$ Grand Hotel Europa, across the seedy street right next to the station, has 89 decent rooms whimsically decorated with not-quite-right reproductions of famous paintings. Though a bit worn, the hotel is a decent value, and its 1970s-era tackiness (including the Kool-Aid and canned fruit at breakfast) is good for a laugh (RS%, family rooms, air-con, elevator, restaurant, Corso Meridionale 14, across street from station's north exit near track 5, tel. 081-267-511, www.grandhoteleuropa.com, info@grandhoteleuropa.com).

Eating in Naples

CHEAP AND FAMOUS PIZZA
Naples is the birthplace of pizza. Its pizzerias bake just the right combination of fresh dough (soft and chewy, as opposed to Roman-style, which is thin and crispy), mozzarella, and tomatoes in

NAPLES

traditional wood-burning ovens. You can head for the famous, venerable places, but these can have long lines stretching out the door, and half-hour waits for a table. If you want to skip the hassle, just ask your hotel for directions to the neighborhood pizzeria. An average one-person pie (usually the only size available) costs

€4-8; most places offer both takeout and eat-in, and pizza is often the only thing on the menu.

Near the Station

These two pizzerias—the most famous—are both a few long blocks from the train station, and at the end of my self-guided Naples Walk.

$ Antica Pizzeria da Michele is for pizza purists. Filled with locals (and tourists), it serves just two varieties: *margherita* (tomato sauce and mozzarella) and *marinara* (tomato sauce, oregano, and garlic, no cheese). Come early to sit and watch the pizza artists in action. A pizza with beer costs around €7. As this place is often jammed with a long line, arrive early or late to get a seat. If there's a mob, head inside to get a number. If it's just too crowded to wait, the less-exceptional Pizzeria Trianon (described next) generally has room (Mon-Sat 10:30-24:00, closed Sun; look for the vertical red *Antica Pizzeria* sign at the intersection of Via Pietro Colletta and Via Cesare Sersale at #1; tel. 081-553-9204).

$ Pizzeria Trianon da Ciro, across the street and left a few doors, has been da Michele's archrival since 1923. It offers more choices, higher prices, air-conditioning, and a cozier atmosphere. For less chaos, head upstairs. While waiting for your meal, you can survey the transformation of a humble wad of dough into a smoldering, bubbly feast in their entryway pizza kitchen (daily 11:00-15:30 & 19:00-23:00, Via Pietro Colletta 42, tel. 081-553-9426).

Pizza on Via dei Tribunali

This street, which runs a couple of blocks north of Spaccanapoli, is legendary for its pizzerias and fun eateries. It's packed with hungry strollers and long lines marking the most popular places.

$ Gino Sorbillo is a local favorite and is on all the "best pizza in Naples" lists...as you'll learn the hard way if you show up at peak mealtimes, when huge mobs crowd outside the front door waiting for a table (Mon-Sat 12:00-15:30 & 19:00-24:00, closed Sun, Via dei Tribunali 32, tel. 081-446-643). Relatives run similarly named places at #35 (a good option for its specialty: fried pizza) and #37 (skip it) on the same street.

$ Pizzeria di Matteo is popular for its fried takeout treats. People waiting out front line up at the little window to snack on deep-fried goodies—*arancini* (with rice, gooey cheese, peas, and sausage), *melanzane* (eggplant), *frittatine* (balls of mac and cheese plus sausage), and *crocché* (croquettes)—for €1 apiece or less (sometimes closed Sun, Via dei Tribunali 94, tel. 081-455-262).

RESTAURANTS

If you want a full meal rather than a pizza, consider these options.

Near Spaccanapoli and Via Toledo

$$$ Ecomesarà serves up quality Neapolitan and *meridionale* (southern Italian) dishes, abiding by the Slow Food ethic, in a modern setting just below the Santa Chiara cloister, a long block south of Spaccanapoli. The atmosphere is mellow, modern, and international. Cristiano and his staff are happy to explain the menu (Tue-Sun 13:00-15:00 & 20:00-23:30, closed Mon, Via Santa Chiara 49, tel. 081-1925-9353).

$$ Tandem Ragù Restaurant, tiny with a few charming tables inside and out, features a fun menu specializing in Neapolitan *ragù* (beef, pork, or vegetarian option). The *scarpetta* dishes are simply various *ragùs* with baskets of bread for dunking (daily from 12:30 and 19:00, Via Giovanni Paladino 51, 50 yards off Spaccanapoli, below the statue of the Nile, tel. 081-1900-2468).

$$ Taverna a Santa Chiara is your classic little eatery buried deep in the old center of Naples. It's convivial, warmly run, and simple. Just 100 yards from the tourist commotion of Spaccanapoli, it provides a fun and easygoing break (daily from 13:00 and 20:00, closed Sun at dinner, Via Santa Chiara 6, tel. 081-048-4908).

$$ Trattoria Campagnola is a classic family place with a daily home-cooking-style chalkboard menu on the back wall, mama busy cooking in the back, and wine on tap. Here you can venture away from pastas, be experimental with a series of local dishes, and not go wrong (daily 12:30-16:00 & 19:30-23:00, between the famous pizzerias at Via Tribunali 47, tel. 081-459-034 but no reservations).

$$ Osteria il Garum is great if you'd like to eat on a classic Neapolitan square. It's named for the ancient fish sauce that was widely used in Roman cooking. These days, mild-mannered Luigi and his staff inject their pricey local cuisine with centuries of tradition, served in a cozy split-level cellar or outside on a covered terrace facing a neighborhood church. It's just between Via Toledo and Spaccanapoli, a short walk from the Church of Gesù Nuovo (daily 12:00-15:30 & 19:00-23:30, Piazza Monteoliveto 2A, tel. 081-542-3228).

$$ Trattoria da Nennella is fun-loving chaos buried in the

NAPLES

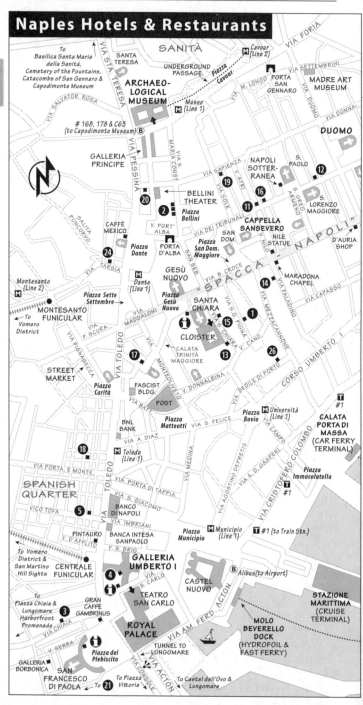

Naples Hotels & Restaurants

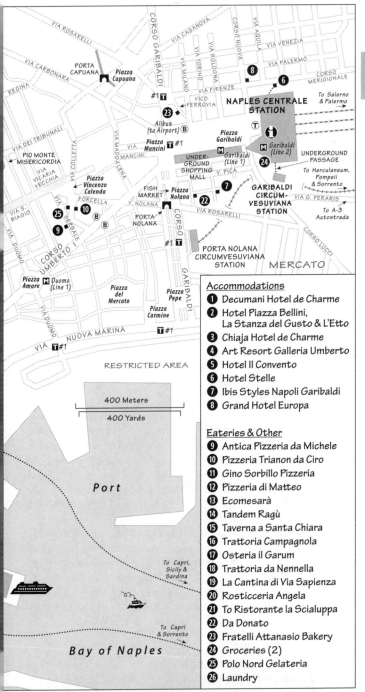

Accommodations

1 Decumani Hotel de Charme
2 Hotel Piazza Bellini,
   La Stanza del Gusto & L'Etto
3 Chiaja Hotel de Charme
4 Art Resort Galleria Umberto
5 Hotel Il Convento
6 Hotel Stelle
7 Ibis Styles Napoli Garibaldi
8 Grand Hotel Europa

Eateries & Other

9 Antica Pizzeria da Michele
10 Pizzeria Trianon da Ciro
11 Gino Sorbillo Pizzeria
12 Pizzeria di Matteo
13 Ecomesarà
14 Tandem Ragù
15 Taverna a Santa Chiara
16 Trattoria Campagnola
17 Osteria il Garum
18 Trattoria da Nennella
19 La Cantina di Via Sapienza
20 Rosticceria Angela
21 To Ristorante la Scialuppa
22 Da Donato
23 Fratelli Attanasio Bakery
24 Groceries (2)
25 Polo Nord Gelateria
26 Laundry

Spanish Quarter, with red-shirted waiters barking orders, a small festival anytime someone puts a tip in the bucket, and the fruit course served in plastic bidets. There's one price—€12 per person—and you choose three courses plus a fruit. House wine and water is served in tiny plastic cups, the crowd is ready for fun, and the food's good. You can sit indoors or on a cobbled terrace under a trellis. No reservations are taken, so put your name on the list when you arrive—the line moves pretty fast (Mon-Sat 12:00-15:00 & 19:15-23:15, closed Sun, leave Via Toledo a block down from the BNL bank and walk up Vico del Teatro Nuovo three blocks to the corner, Vico Lungo Teatro Nuovo 103, tel. 081-414-338).

$ **La Cantina di Via Sapienza** is a lunch-only hole-in-the-wall, serving up traditional Neapolitan fare in an interior that feels like a neighborhood joint (but has also been discovered by tourists). It's a block north of the congested, pizzeria-packed Via dei Tribunali, and a good alternative if those places are just too crowded and your heart isn't set on pizza (Mon-Sat for lunch only, closed Sun, Via Sapienza 40, tel. 081-459-078).

Near the Archaeological Museum

$$ **La Stanza del Gusto,** two blocks downhill from the museum, tackles food creatively and injects crusty Naples with a little modern color and irreverence. The ground floor is casual, trendy, and playful, while the upstairs is more refined yet still polka-dotted. A few tables are on the sidewalk (weekday lunch specials, Tue-Sat 12:00-15:30 & 19:30-23:30, closed Sun-Mon, Via Santa Maria di Constantinopoli 100, tel. 081-401-578).

$ **L'Etto** is fast, fun, and cheap, with tasty dishes constantly coming out of the kitchen to fill an inviting buffet line. Choose from 20 vegetable, meat, and fish options (perfect for vegetarians or vegans). It's self-serve—weigh and pay €2.50 per 100 grams (100 grams is an *etto*, hence the name). Bread and water are free at the table. It's bright, mod, and friendly with outdoor tables, too (daily from 12:30 and from 19:30, facing Piazza Bellini at Via S. Maria di Costantinopoli 102, tel. 081-1932-0967).

$ **Rosticceria Angela** is a *tavola calda* with hot ready-to-eat dishes and a coffee bar, run by a team of older gentlemen. Pricing is honest and there's simple, peaceful, air-conditioned indoor seating. Next door (same name, different management) is a tiny meat, cheese, and bread shop with all you need for a cheap meal to-go (*rosticceria* open Mon-Sat 7:30-21:30, closed Sun, 3 blocks below museum at Via Conte di Ruvo 21, between Via Pessina and Via Bellini, tel. 081-033-2928).

A Romantic Splurge on the Harbor

$$$ **Ristorante la Scialuppa** ("The Rowboat") is a great bet for a

fine local meal on the harbor. Located in the romantic Santa Lucia district, you'll walk across the causeway to the Castel dell'Ovo in the fisherman's quarter (the castle on the island) just off Via Partenope. They boast fine indoor and outdoor seating, attentive waitstaff, a wonderful assortment of *antipasti*, great seafood, and predictably high prices. Reservations are smart (Tue-Sun 12:30-15:00 & 19:30-24:00, closed Mon, Piazzetta Marinari 5, tel. 081-764-5333, www.ristorantelascialuppa.net).

Near the Station

$$ Da Donato, an excellent, traditional, family-run trattoria on a glum street near the station, serves delicious food in an unpretentious atmosphere. The best approach is for two people to share the astonishing antipasti sampler—*degustazione "fantasia" della Casa Terra e Mare*—for €25. You'll get more than a dozen small portions, each more delicious than the last. A version without seafood is €15 (Tue-Sun 12:30-14:30 & 19:30-22:00, closed Mon, two blocks from Piazza Garibaldi—turn down Via Silvio Spaventa to #39, tel. 081-287-828).

PASTRY

To get the full overview of Neapolitan pastries at good prices, visit the bakery outlet of **Fratelli Attanasio** on a small alley near the train station—with your back to the station building, it's off the far-right corner of the big square. Come early if possible (Tue-Sun 6:30-19:30, closed Mon, Vico Ferrovia 1, tel. 081-285-675).

PICNICS

A good supermarket for picnic supplies is **Sapori & Dintorni,** in the train-station complex (Mon-Sat 8:00-20:30, Sun 8:00-15:00, enter from outside, by bookstore). By Piazza Dante is a small **Superò** that's convenient to Via Toledo hotel listings (corner of Via Tarsia and Vico San Domenico Soriano, Mon-Sat 8:30-20:30, Sun 8:30-14:00).

Naples Connections

From Naples by Boat to: Sorrento (6/day, more in summer, departs roughly every 2 hours starting at 9:00, few or no boats on winter weekends, leaves from Molo Beverello, 35 minutes), **Capri** (roughly hourly, more in summer, hydrofoil: 45 minutes from Molo Beverello; ferries: 50-80 minutes from Calata Porta di Massa). Sometimes there are also seasonal boats to **Positano** and **Amalfi,** on the Amalfi Coast—ask. For timetables, visit www.capritourism. com and click "Shipping Timetable."

Getting Around the Region

To connect Naples, Sorrento, and the Amalfi Coast, you can travel on land by train, bus, and taxi. Whenever possible, consider taking a boat—it's faster, cooler, and more scenic, and you can take coastline photos that you can't get from land. For specifics, check the "Connections" sections of each chapter. Confirm times and prices locally.

By Circumvesuviana Train: This useful narrow-gauge commuter train—popular with locals, tourists, and pickpockets—links Naples, Herculaneum, Pompeii, and Sorrento. The most important Circumvesuviana station in Naples (called "Garibaldi") is underneath Naples' Centrale Station. To find it, follow the signs downstairs to *Statione Garibaldi* and then *Circumvesuviana* signs down the corridor to the Circumvesuviana ticket windows and turnstiles (no self-service ticket machines—line up). Buy your ticket, confirm time and track, insert your ticket at the turnstiles, and head down another level to the platforms.

The Circumvesuviana is covered by the Campania ArteCard (see page 9), but not by rail passes. If you're heading to **Pompeii** or **Herculaneum,** take any Circumvesuviana train marked *Sorrento*—they all stop at both places (usually depart from platform 3). Sorrento-bound trains depart twice hourly, and take about 20 minutes to reach Ercolano Scavi (for the Herculaneum ruins, €2 one-way), 40 minutes to reach Pompei Scavi-Villa dei Misteri (for the Pompeii ruins, €2.60 one-way), and 70 minutes to reach **Sorrento,** the end of the line (€3.60 one-way). Express trains to Sorrento marked *DD* (6/day) reach Sorrento 15 minutes sooner (and also stop at Herculaneum and Pompeii). For schedules, see www.eavsrl.it.

On the platform, double-check with a local that the train goes to Sorrento, as the Circumvesuviana has several lines that branch out to other destinations. When returning to Naples on the Circumvesuviana, get off at the next-to-the-last station, Garibaldi (Centrale Station is just up the escalator).

You may save a few pennies with a "TIC" ticket, which covers the Circumvesuviana plus public transport to and from the train station in Naples (for example, Pompeii to Napoli Centrale, then by Metro to your hotel).

By Regular Train: The national rail network is useful only if you need to get to Salerno (for boats and buses to Amalfi) or Paestum—direct trains run to both from Naples.

By Bus: Crowded SITA buses are most useful for traversing the popular Amalfi Coast; see "Getting Around the Amalfi Coast—By Public Bus" on page 126.

By Taxi: For €100, you can take a 30-mile taxi ride from Naples directly to your Sorrento hotel (ask the driver for the non-metered *tariffa predeterminata*). You can hire a cab on Capri for

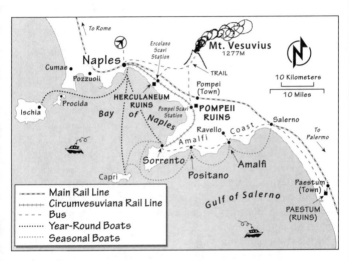

about €70/hour. Taxis on the Amalfi Coast are generally expensive, and more than willing to overcharge you, but they can be convenient, especially with a larger group. See "Getting Around the Amalfi Coast—By Taxi" on page 128.

By Boat: Major companies include Caremar (www.caremar. it), SNAV (www.snav.it), Gescab (a.k.a. NLG Jet, www.gescab. it), Navigazione Libera del Golfo (www.navlib.it), Alilauro (www. alilauro.it), Travelmar (www.travelmar.it), and Alicost (www. alicost.it). Each company has different destinations and prices; some compete for the same trips. Some lines (like Sorrento-Capri) run all year; others (on the Amalfi Coast, for example) only in summer. Trips can be cancelled in bad weather. Faster watercraft cost a little more than slow car ferries. A hydrofoil, sometimes called a "jet boat," skims between Naples and Sorrento—it's swifter, safer from pickpockets, more scenic, and more expensive than the train.

For schedules, check online (the best overview is at www. capritourism.com; click "Shipping Timetable"), or ask at any TI or at Naples' Molo Beverello boat dock. (The handy departure board on the rooftop of the Molo Beverello terminal shows all the upcoming departures.) Most boats charge €2 or so for luggage. If you plan to arrive at and leave a destination by boat, note the return times—the last boat usually leaves before 19:00.

The preset price for a taxi from Naples' Centrale train station to its port (Molo Beverello) is €11, or you can just hop on tram #1 from the far end of the big square in front of the station.

By Train to: Rome (Trenitalia: 1-4/hour, 1 hour on Frecciarossa, 2 hours on Intercity, 2.5 hours and much cheaper on regional trains; Italo: hourly, 70 minutes), **Civitavecchia** (at least hourly, 3 hours, most change in Rome), **Florence** (Trenitalia: hourly, 3 hours; Italo: hourly, 3 hours), **Salerno** (Trenitalia: at least hourly, 35-45 minutes, change in Salerno for bus or boat to Amalfi; best to take "regionale" trains—Intercity and Freccia express trains are much more expensive but no faster; also avoid slower "Metropolitana" trains that leave from the same platforms as Metro's line 2; Italo: 4/day, 45 minutes), **Paestum** (10/day, 1.5 hours, direction: Sapri), **Brindisi** (4/day, 5-6 hours, change in Caserta; from Brindisi, ferries sail to Greece), **Milan** (Trenitalia: 2/hour, 4-5 hours; Italo: 11/day, 4-5 hours), **Venice** (Trenitalia: almost hourly, 5.5 hours, some change in Bologna or Rome; Italo: 3/day, 5.5 hours, reservations required), **Palermo** (2/day direct, 9.5 hours, also an overnight train). Any train listed on the schedule as leaving Napoli PG or Napoli-Garibaldi departs not from Napoli Centrale, but from the adjacent Garibaldi Station.

By Circumvesuviana Train: See the "Getting Around the Region" sidebar for information on getting to Herculaneum, Pompeii, and Sorrento.

To Pompeii: To visit the ancient site of Pompeii, don't use national train connections to the city of Pompei (which is far from the site). Instead, ride the Circumvesuviana train, which takes you to the Pompei Scavi-Villa dei Misteri stop near the actual site.

POMPEII & NEARBY

Pompeii • Herculaneum • Vesuvius

Stopped in their tracks by the eruption of Mount Vesuvius in A.D. 79, Pompeii and Herculaneum offer the best look anywhere at what life in Rome must have been like around 2,000 years ago. These two cities of well-preserved ruins are yours to explore. Of the two sites, Pompeii is grander, while Herculaneum is smaller, more intimate, and more intact; both are easily reached from Naples on the Circumvesuviana commuter train. Vesuvius, still smoldering ominously, rises up on the horizon. It last erupted in 1944, and is still an active volcano. Buses from the train stations at Herculaneum or Pompeii drop you a half-hour hike below the crater rim.

Pompeii

A once-thriving commercial port of 20,000, Pompeii (worth ▲▲▲) grew from Greek and Etruscan roots to become an important Roman city. Then, on August 24, A.D. 79, everything changed. Vesuvius erupted and began to bury the city under 30 feet of hot volcanic ash. For the archaeologists who excavated it centuries later, this was a shake-and-bake windfall, teaching them volumes about daily

POMPEII & NEARBY

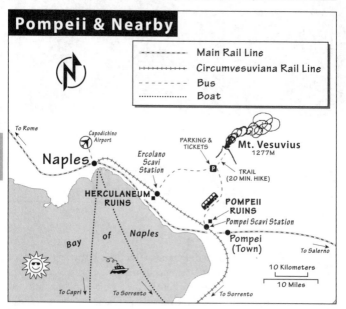

Pompeii & Nearby

Main Rail Line
Circumvesuviana Rail Line
Bus
Boat

Roman life. Pompeii was accidentally rediscovered in 1599; excavations began in 1748.

GETTING TO POMPEII

By Train: Pompeii is roughly midway between Naples and Sorrento on the Circumvesuviana train line (2/hour, 40 minutes from Naples, 30 minutes from Sorrento, either trip costs about €2.60 one-way, not covered by rail passes). Get off at the Pompei Scavi-Villa dei Misteri stop; from Naples, it's the stop after Torre Annunziata. The DD express trains (6/day) bypass several stations but do stop at Pompei Scavi, shaving 10 minutes off the trip from Naples. From the Pompei Scavi train station, it's just a two-minute walk to the Porta Marina entrance: Leaving the station, turn right and walk down the road about a block to the entrance (on your left).

Pompei vs. Pompei Scavi: Make sure you're taking the Circumvesuviana commuter train to Pompei Scavi (*scavi* means "excavations"), the station right next to the ancient site. Pompei is the name of a separate train station on the main national rail line that's a long, dull walk from the ruins. It serves the ugly modern city of Pompei (always with one "i"). Even when coming from Rome, it's better to transfer at Naples' Centrale Station to the Circumvesuviana for Pompei Scavi than to take the train straight to the Pompei city station and walk from there.

By Car: Parking is available at Camping Zeus, next to the Pompei Scavi train station (€2.50/hour, €10/12 hours, 10 percent discount with this book); several other campgrounds/parking lots are nearby.

ORIENTATION TO POMPEII

Cost: €13, includes special exhibits, free (and very crowded) the first Sun of each month, €21 combo-ticket includes Herculaneum (valid 3 consecutive days). If you plan to eat or sightsee outside of the archaeological site, ask for an entrance/exit bracelet that allows you to reenter the site up to three times on the same day. Also consider the Campania ArteCard if visiting other sights in the region.

Hours: Daily April-Oct 9:00-19:30, Nov-March 8:30-17:00, last entry 1.5 hours before closing.

Information: Tel: 081-857-5347, www.pompeiisites.org.

Closures: Some buildings and streets are bound to be closed for restoration when you visit. Make a point to use your map and numbers to find your way. Street names and building numbers are very clearly marked throughout the site.

Crowd-Beating Tip: Up to 15,000 visitors are allowed on the first Sun of the month when it's free—and packed. I'd avoid Pompeii on that day. If there's a very long ticket line at the Porta Marina entrance, continue walking three minutes to a ticket booth near Hotel Vittoria (never a line). Buy your ticket, return to Porta Marina, and walk right in. Cruise ship groups enter at the Piazza Esedra entrance.

Visitor Information: Admission to the site includes a wonderful English guide-booklet and map (be sure to get and use this). Ask for it when you buy your ticket, or check at the info window to the left of the WCs—the maps aren't available within the walls of Pompeii. The bookshop sells a couple of books with plastic overlays that allow you to re-create Pompeii from the ruins (€16; if you buy from a street vendor, pay no more than that).

Ignore the "info point" kiosk at the station, which is a private agency selling tours.

Tours: Here are several ways to enjoy an organized and educational visit to Pompeii.

Simply follow the **self-guided** tour in this chapter (or, better, enjoy the audio version with my free 🎧 Rick Steves Audio Europe app). Both cover the basics and provide a good framework for exploring the site on your own. Combined with the fine booklet and map included with your entry fee, these provide plenty of information for do-it-yourselfers.

Join a **Mondo Guide shared tour** for Rick Steves readers. This is your best budget bet for a tour with an actual guide (€15, doesn't include €13 Pompeii entry, daily at 11:00, reservations

POMPEII & NEARBY

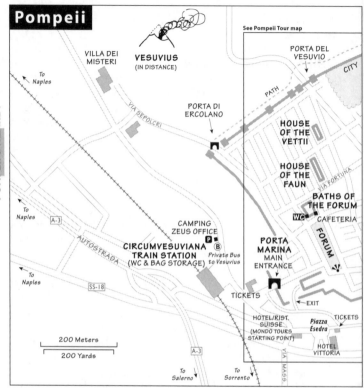

required; meet at Hotel/Ristorante Suisse, just down the hill from the Porta Marina entrance).

Hire guide **Antonio Somma** for a private or shared tour. Antonio and his team of guides offer good two-hour tours of Pompeii for €120 (mobile 393-406-3824, tel. 081-850-1992, www.tourspompeiiguide.com, info@pompeitour.com). The tour can be just for you, or, if you wish, they can try to book other travelers for the same tour to share the cost. Either way, the total price is no more than €120. For example, if six people take the tour, each pays €20. (A nice tip for the guide's extra effort is appreciated.)

Other Options: Audioguides available from a kiosk near the ticket booth at the Porta Marina entrance (€8, €13 for 2, ID required) offer basically the same info as your free booklet.

When you step off the train, you'll likely be accosted by touts for the "info point" kiosk, which sells €12 tours that depart whenever enough people sign up. Private guides (around €120/2 hours) of varying quality cluster near the ticket booth at the site and may try to herd you into a group with other travelers, which is fine if it makes the price more reasonable.

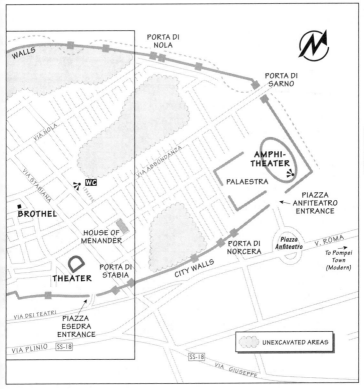

It's unethical for a guide to double charge by combining two groups into one tour. Instead, tourists should enjoy the savings and tip higher.

Rated Risqué: Parents, note that the ancient brothel and its sexually explicit frescoes are included on tours; let your guide know if you'd rather skip that stop.

Length of This Tour: Allow two hours, or three if you visit the theater and amphitheater. With less time, focus on the Forum, Baths of the Forum, House of the Vettii, House of the Faun, and brothel.

Baggage Check: Use the free baggage check near the turnstiles at the site entrance (just yards from the station). The train station also offers pay luggage storage (downstairs, by the WC).

Services: There's a pay WC at the train station. The Pompeii site has three WCs—one near the entrance, one in the cafeteria, and another near the end of this tour, uphill from the theaters.

Eating: These **$** eateries offer reasonably priced meals (though your cheapest bet may be to bring your own food for a discreet picnic). The **Ciao cafeteria,** within the site, serves good sandwiches, pizza, and pasta. You're welcome to picnic here if you buy a drink. **Bar Sgambati,** the café/restaurant at the train station, has air-conditioning, Wi-Fi, sandwiches to-go, and pastas and pizzas. **Marius Juice Shop** (run by local guide Antonio Somma's family) sells sandwiches to-go, and is located between Bar Sgambati and the Porta Marina entrance.

Starring: Roofless (collapsed) but otherwise intact Roman buildings, plaster casts of hapless victims, some erotic frescoes, and the dawning realization that these ancient people were not that different from us.

BACKGROUND

Pompeii, founded in 600 B.C., eventually became a booming Roman trading city. Not rich, not poor, it was middle class—a perfect example of typical Roman life. Most streets would have been lined with stalls and jammed with customers from sunup to sundown. Chariots vied with shoppers for street space. Two thousand years ago, Rome controlled the entire Mediterranean—making it a kind of free-trade zone—and Pompeii was a central and bustling port.

There were no posh neighborhoods in Pompeii. Rich and poor mixed it up as elegant houses existed side by side with simple homes. While nearby Herculaneum would have been a classier place to live (traffic-free streets, fancier houses, far better drainage), Pompeii was the place for action and shopping. It served an estimated 20,000 residents with more than 40 bakeries, 130 bars, restaurants, and hotels, and 30 brothels. With most of its buildings covered by brilliant white ground-marble stucco, Pompeii in A.D. 79 was an impressive town.

As you tour Pompeii, remember that its best art is in the Archaeological Museum in Naples (described in the Naples chapter).

◎ SELF-GUIDED TOUR

• Just past the ticket-taker, start your approach up to the...

❶ Porta Marina

The city of Pompeii was born on the hill ahead of you. This was the original town gate. Before Vesuvius blew and filled in the harbor, the sea came nearly to here. Notice the two openings in the gate (ahead, up the ramp).

Both were left open by day to admit major traffic. At night, the larger one was closed for better security.

• *Pass through the Porta Marina and continue up to the top of the street, pausing at the three large stepping-stones in the middle.*

❷ Pompeii's Streets

Every day, Pompeiians flooded the streets with gushing water to clean them. These stepping-stones let pedestrians cross with-

out getting their sandals wet. Chariots traveling in either direction could straddle the stones (all had standard-size axles). A single stepping-stone in a road means it was a one-way street, a pair indicates an ordinary two-way, and three (like this) signifies a major thoroughfare. The basalt stones are the original Roman pavement. The sidewalks (elevated to hide the plumbing—you'll see ancient plumbing revealed throughout the site) were paved with bits of broken pots (an ancient form of recycling) and studded with reflective bits of white marble. These "cats' eyes" helped people get around after dark, either by moonlight or with the help of lamps.

• *Continue straight ahead, don your mental toga, and enter the city as the Romans once did. The road opens up into the spacious main square: the Forum. Stand at the right end of this rectangular space and look toward Mount Vesuvius.*

❸ The Forum (Foro)

Pompeii's commercial, religious, and political center stands at the intersection of the city's two main streets. While it's the most ru-

ined part of Pompeii, it's grand nonetheless. Picture the piazza surrounded by two-story buildings on all sides. The pedestals that line the square once held statues of VIPs and various gods (now safely displayed in the museum in Naples). In Pompeii's heyday, its citizens gathered here in the main square to shop, talk politics, and socialize. Business took place in the important buildings that lined the piazza.

The Forum was dominated by the **Temple of Jupiter,** at the far end (marked by a half-dozen ruined columns atop a stair-step base). Jupiter was the supreme god of the Roman pantheon—you might

Pompeii Tour

1 Porta Marina
2 Pompeii's Streets
3 Forum
4 Basilica
5 Via Abbondanza
6 Forum Granary;
   Plaster Casts of Victims
7 Baths of the Forum
8 Fast-Food Joint
9 House of the Tragic Poet
10 Aqueduct Arch
11 House of the Faun
12 House of the Vettii
13 Bakery & Mill
14 Brothel

be able to make out his little white marble head at the center-rear of the temple. To the left of the temple is a fenced-off area, the **Forum granary,** where many artifacts from Pompeii are stored (and which we'll visit later).

At the near end of the Forum (behind where you're standing) is the **curia,** or city hall. Like many Roman buildings, it was built with brick and mortar, then covered with marble walls and floors. To your left (as you face Vesuvius and the Temple of Jupiter) is the **basilica,** or courthouse.

Since Pompeii was a pretty typical Roman town, it has the same layout and components that you'll find in any Roman city—main square, curia, basilica, temples, axis of roads, and so on. All power converged at the Forum: religious (the temple), political (the curia), judicial (the basilica), and commercial (this piazza was the main marketplace). Even the power of the people was expressed here, since this is where they gathered to vote. Imagine the hubbub of this town square in its heyday.

Look beyond the Temple of Jupiter. Five miles to the north looms the ominous backstory to this site: **Mount Vesuvius.** Mentally draw a triangle up from the two remaining peaks to reconstruct the mountain before the eruption. When it blew, Pompeiians had no idea that they were living under a volcano, as Vesuvius hadn't erupted for 1,200 years. Imagine the wonder—then the horror—as a column of pulverized rock roared upward, and then ash began to fall. The weight of the ash and small rocks collapsed Pompeii's roofs later that day, crushing people who had taken refuge inside buildings instead of fleeing the city.

• *As you face Vesuvius, the basilica is to your left, lined with stumps of columns. Step inside.*

❹ Basilica

Pompeii's basilica was a first-century palace of justice. This ancient law court has the same floor plan later adopted by many Christian churches (which are also called basilicas). The big central hall (or nave) is flanked by rows of columns marking off narrower side aisles. Along the side walls are traces of the original stucco imitating marble.

The columns—now stumps all about the same height—were not ruined by the volcano. Rather, they were left unfinished when Vesuvius blew. Pompeii had been devastated by an earthquake in A.D. 62, and was just in the process of rebuilding the basilica when

POMPEII & NEARBY

Vesuvius erupted, 17 years later. The half-built columns show off the technology of the day. Uniform bricks were stacked around a cylindrical core. Once finished, they would have been coated with marble dust stucco to simulate marble columns—an economical construction method found throughout Pompeii (and the Roman Empire).

Besides the earthquake and the eruption, Pompeii's buildings have suffered other ravages over the years, including Spanish plunderers (c. 1800), 19th-century souvenir hunters, WWII bombs, creeping and destructive vegetation, another earthquake in 1980, and modern neglect. The fact that the entire city was covered by the eruption of A.D. 79 actually helped preserve it, saving it from the sixth-century barbarians who plundered many other towns into oblivion.

• *Exit the basilica and cross the short side of the square to where the city's main street hits the Forum. Stop at the three white stones that stick up from the cobbles.*

❺ Via Abbondanza

Glance down Via Abbondanza, Pompeii's main street. Lined with shops, bars, and restaurants, it was a lively, pedestrian-only zone.

The three "beaver-teeth" stones are traffic barriers that kept chariots out. On the corner at the start of the street (just to the left), take a close look at the dark travertine column standing next to the white one. Notice that the marble drums of the white column are not chiseled entirely round—another construction project left unfinished when Vesuvius erupted.

• *Our tour will eventually end a few blocks down Via Abbondanza after making a big loop. But now, head toward Vesuvius, cutting across the Forum. To the left of the Temple of Jupiter is the...*

❻ Forum Granary

A substantial stretch of the west side of the Forum was the granary and ancient produce market. Today, it houses thousands of artifacts excavated from Pompeii. You'll see lots of crockery, pots, pans, jugs, and containers used for transporting oil and wine. You'll also see casts of a couple

of victims (and a dog) of the eruption. These casts show Pompeiians, eerily captured in their last moments, hands covering their mouths as they gasped for air. They were quickly suffocated by a

The Eruption of Vesuvius

At about 1:00 in the afternoon on August 24, A.D. 79, Mount Vesuvius erupted, sending a mushroom cloud of ash, dust, and rocks 12 miles into the air. It spewed for 18 hours straight, as winds blew the cloud southward. The white-gray ash settled like a heavy snow on Pompeii, its weight eventually collapsing roofs and floors, but leaving the walls intact. And though most of Pompeii's 20,000 residents fled that day, about 2,000 stayed behind.

Although the city of Herculaneum was closer to the volcano—about four miles away—at first it largely escaped the rain of ash, due to the direction of the wind. However, 12 hours after Vesuvius awoke, the type of eruption suddenly changed. The mountain let loose a superheated avalanche of ash, pumice, and gas. This red-hot "pyroclastic flow" sped down the side of the mountain at nearly 100 miles per hour, engulfing Herculaneum and cooking its residents alive. Several more flows over the next few hours further entombed Herculaneum, burying it in nearly 60 feet of hot material that later cooled into rock, freezing the city in time. Then, at around 7:30 in the morning, another pyroclastic flow headed south and struck Pompeii, dealing a fatal blow to those who'd remained behind.

superheated avalanche of gas and ash, and their bodies were encased in volcanic debris. While excavating, modern archaeologists detected hollow spaces underfoot, created when the victims' bodies decomposed. By gently filling the holes with plaster, the archaeologists created molds of the Pompeiians who were caught in the disaster.

A few steps to the left of the granary is a tiny alcove that contained the Mensa Ponderaria, a counter where standard units (such as today's liter or gallon) were used to measure the quantities of liquid and solid food that were sold. And just to the right of the granary is the remains of a public toilet. You can imagine the many seats, lack of privacy, and constantly flushing stream running through the room.

• *Exit the Forum by crossing it again in front of the Temple of Jupiter and turning left. Go under the arch. In the road are more "beaver-teeth" traffic blocks. On the pillar to the right, look for the pedestrian-only road sign (two guys carrying an amphora, or ancient jug; it's above the* REG VII INS IV *sign). The modern cafeteria (straight ahead) is the only eatery inside the archaeological site. Twenty yards past the cafeteria, on the left-hand side at #24, is the entrance to the...*

❼ Baths of the Forum (Terme del Foro)

Pompeii had six public baths, each with a men's and a women's section. You're in the men's zone. The leafy courtyard at the entrance was the gymnasium. After working out, clients could relax with a hot bath *(caldarium)*, warm bath *(tepidarium)*, or cold plunge *(frigidarium)*.

The first big, plain room you enter served as the **dressing room.** Holes on the walls were for pegs to hang clothing. High up, the window (with a faded Neptune underneath) was originally covered with a less-translucent Roman glass. Walk over the nonslip mosaics into the next room.

The *tepidarium* is ringed by mini statues or *telamones* (male caryatids, figures used as supporting pillars), which divided the lockers. Clients would undress and warm up here, perhaps relaxing on one of the bronze cow-footed benches near the bronze heater while waiting for a massage. Look at the ceiling—half crushed by the eruption and half intact, with its fine blue-and-white stucco work.

Next, admire the engineering in the steam-bath room, or *caldarium.* The double floor was heated from below—so it was nice for bare feet (look into the grate across from where you entered

to see the brick support towers). The double walls with brown terra-cotta tiles held the heat. Romans soaked in the big tub, which was filled with hot water. Opposite the big tub is a fountain, which spouted water onto the hot floor, creating steam. The lettering on the fountain reminded those enjoying the room which two politicians paid for it...and how much it cost them. (On the far right, the Roman numerals indicate they paid 5,250 *sestertii*). To keep condensation from dripping annoyingly from the ceiling, fluting (ribbing) was added to carry water down the walls.

• *Today's visitors exit the baths through the original entry (at the far end of the dressing room). Hungry? Immediately across the street is an ancient...*

❽ Fast-Food Joint

After a bath, it was only natural to want a little snack. So, just across the street is a fast-food joint, marked by a series of rectangular marble counters. Most ancient Romans didn't cook for themselves in their tiny apartments, so to-go places like this were commonplace. The holes in the counters held the pots for food. Each contain-

er was like a thermos, with a wooden lid to keep the soup hot, the wine cool, and so on. You could dine in the back or get your food to go. Notice the groove in the front doorstep and the holes out on the curb. The holes likely accommodated cords for stretching awnings over the sidewalk to shield the clientele from the hot sun, while the grooves were for the shop's folding accordion doors. Look at the wheel grooves in the pavement, worn down through centuries of use. Nearby are more stepping-stones for pedestrians to cross the flooded streets.

• *Just a few steps uphill from the fast-food joint, at #5 (with a locked gate), is the...*

POMPEII & NEARBY

❾ House of the Tragic Poet (Casa del Poeta Tragico)

This house is typical Roman style. The entry is flanked by two family-owned shops (each with a track for a collapsing accordion door). The home is like a train running straight away from the street: atrium (with skylight and pool to catch the rain), den (where deals were made by the shopkeeper), and garden (with rooms facing it and a shrine to remember both the gods and family ancestors). In the entryway is the famous "Beware of Dog" *(Cave Canem)* mosaic.

When it's open, today's visitors enter the home by the back door (circle around to the left). On your way there, look for the modern exposed pipe on the left side of the lane; this is the same as ones used in the ancient plumbing system, hidden beneath the raised sidewalk. Inside the house, the grooves on the marble wellhead in the entry hall (possibly closed) were formed by generations of inhabitants dragging the bucket up by rope. The richly frescoed dining room is off the garden. Diners lounged on their couches (the Roman custom) and enjoyed frescoes with fake "windows," giving the illusion of a bigger and airier room. Next to the dining room is a humble BBQ-style kitchen with a little closet for the toilet (the kitchen and bathroom shared the same plumbing).

• *Return to the fast-food place and continue about 10 yards downhill to the big intersection. From the center of the intersection, look left to see a giant arch, framing a nice view of Mount Vesuvius.*

❿ Aqueduct Arch—Running Water

Water was critical for this city of 20,000 people, and this arch was part of Pompeii's water-delivery system. A 100-mile-long aqueduct carried fresh water down from the hillsides to a big reservoir perched at the highest point of the city wall. Since overall water pressure was disappointing, Pompeiians built arches like the brick one you see here (originally covered in marble) with hidden water tanks at the top. Located just below the altitude of the main tank, these smaller tanks were filled by gravity and provided each neigh-

borhood with reliable pressure. Look closely at the arch and you'll see 2,000-year-old pipes (made of lead imported all the way from Cornwall in Britannia) embedded deep in the brick.

If there was a water shortage, democratic priorities prevailed: First the baths were cut off, then the private homes. The last to go were the public fountains, where all citizens could get drinking and cooking water.

• *If you're thirsty, fill your water bottle from the modern fountain. Then continue straight downhill one block (50 yards) to #2 on the left.*

⓫ House of the Faun (Casa del Fauno)

Stand across the street and marvel at the grand entry with *"HAVE"* (hail to you) as a welcome mat. Go in. Notice the two shrines above the entryway—one dedicated to the gods, the other to this wealthy family's ancestors. (Contemporary Neapolitans still carry on this practice; you'll notice little shrines embedded in walls all over Naples.)

You are standing in Pompeii's largest home, where you're greeted by the delightful small bronze statue of the *Dancing Faun,* famed for its realistic movement and fine proportion. (The original is in Naples' Archaeological Museum.) With 40 rooms and 27,000 square feet, the House of the Faun covers an entire city block. The next floor mosaic, with an intricate diamond-like design, decorates the homeowner's office. Beyond that, at the far end of the first garden, is the famous floor mosaic of the *Battle of Alexander.* (The original is also at the museum in Naples.) In 333 B.C., Alexander the Great beat Darius and the Persians. Romans had great respect for Alexander, the first great emperor before Rome's. While most of Pompeii's nouveau riche had notoriously bad taste and stuffed their palaces with over-the-top, mismatched decor, this guy had class. Both the faun (an ancient copy of a famous Greek statue) and the Alexander mosaic show an appreciation for history.

The house's back courtyard is lined with pillars rebuilt after the A.D. 62 earthquake. Take a close look at the brick, mortar, and fake-marble stucco veneer.

• *Leave the House of the Faun through its back door in the far-right corner, past a tiny guard's station. (If closed, exit out the front and walk around to the back.) Turn right and walk about a block until you see metal cages over the sidewalk protecting exposed stretches of ancient lead water pipes. Continue east and take your first left, walking about 20 yards to the entrance (on your left) to the...*

⑫ House of the Vettii

This is Pompeii's best-preserved home, retaining many of its mosaics and frescoes. The House of the Vettii was the bachelor pad of two wealthy merchant brothers. In the entryway, it's hard to miss the huge erection. This was not pornography. This was a symbol of success: The penis and sack of money balance each other on the goldsmith scale above a fine bowl of fruit. Translation? Only with a balance of fertility and money can you enjoy true abundance.

Step into the atrium with its replica wooden ceiling open to the sky and a lead pipe to collect water for the house cistern. The pool was flanked by two large moneyboxes (one survives, the footprint of the other shows how it was secured to the ground). The brothers wanted all who entered to know how successful they were. A variety of rooms give an intimate peek at elegant Pompeiian life. The dark room to the right of the entrance (as you face out) is filled with exquisite frescoes. Notice more white "cat's eye" stones embedded in the floor. Imagine these glinting like little eyes as the brothers and their friends wandered around by oil lamp late at night, with their sacks of gold, bowls of fruit, and enormous...egos.

• *Our next stop, the Bakery, is located about 150 yards south (downhill) from here. To get there, return to the street in front of the House of the Vettii. Walk downhill along Vicolo dei Vetti. Go one block, to where you dead-end at a T-intersection with Via della Fortuna. Go a few steps left and then right at the first corner. Continue down this gently curving road to #22.*

⑬ Bakery and Mill

The stubby stone towers are flour grinders. Grain was poured into the top and donkeys or slaves, treading in a circle, pushed wooden bars that turned the stones that ground the grain. The powdered grain dropped out the bottom as flour—flavored with tiny bits of rock. Nearby, the thing that looks like a modern-day pizza oven was...a brick oven. Each neighborhood had a bakery just like this.

• *Continue down the curvy road to the next intersection. As you walk consider the destructive power of all the plants and vines that you see around. Also, notice the chariot grooves worn into the pavement. When the curvy road reaches the intersection with Via degli Augustali, turn left. Ahead, in 50 yards, at #44, is the Taberna Hedones, an ancient tavern with an original floor mosaic still intact. A few steps past that, turn right and walk downhill to #18—one of many Pompeii brothels.*

⓮ Brothel (Lupanare)

You'll find the biggest crowds in Pompeii at a place that was likely also quite popular 2,000 years ago—the brothel. Prostitutes were nicknamed *lupe* (she-wolves), alluding to the call they made when attracting business. The brothel was a simple place, with beds and pillows made of stone and then covered with mattresses. The ancient graffiti includes tallies and exotic names of the women, indicating the prostitutes came from all corners of the Mediterranean (it also served as feedback from satisfied customers). The faded frescoes above the cells may have been a kind of menu for services offered. Note the idealized women (white, which was considered beautiful; one wears an early bra) and the rougher men (dark, considered horny). The bed legs came with little disk-like barriers to keep critters from crawling up, the tiny rooms had curtains for doors, and the prostitutes provided sheepskin condoms.

• *Leaving the brothel, go right, then take the first left, and continue going downhill two blocks to return to Via Abbondanza. This walk is over. The Forum—and exit—are to the right. If you exit now, you'll be routed through the exhibition rooms—where you'll find a scale model of the city, an interesting video, and some artifacts—and the gift shop.*

But before you leave, consider these extra stops—all worth the time and energy (if you have any left). To locate them, refer to your map.

Temple of Isis

This temple served Pompeii's Egyptian community. The little white stucco shrine with the modern plastic roof housed holy water from the Nile. Isis, from Egyptian myth, was one of many foreign gods adopted by the eclectic Romans. Pompeii must have had a synagogue, too, but it has yet to be excavated.

Theater

Originally a Greek theater (Greeks built theirs with the help of a hillside), this was the birthplace of the Greek port here in 470 b.c. During Roman times, the theater sat 5,000 people in three sets of seats, all with different prices: the five marble terraces up close (filled with romantic wooden seats for two), the main section, and the cheap

nosebleed section (surviving only on the high end, near the trees). The square stones above the cheap seats once supported a canvas rooftop. The high-profile boxes, flanking the stage, were for guests of honor. From this perch, you can see the gladiator barracks—the colonnaded courtyard beyond the theater. They lived in tiny rooms, trained in the courtyard, and fought in the nearby amphitheater. Check out the adjacent and well-preserved smaller Teatro Piccolo.

House of Menander (Casa di Menandro)

Once owned by a wealthy Pompeiian, this house takes its current name from a fresco of the Greek playwright Menander on one of the walls. Admire the grand atrium (with frescoes depicting scenes from Homer's *Iliad* and *Odyssey,* and an altar to the family gods), the wall frescoes, and the mosaics. The cloister-like back courtyard leads to a room with skeletons (not plaster casts) of eruption victims from this house. Farther back, a passage leads to the servants' quarters.

Viewpoint

You're at ground level—post-eruption. To the right (inland), the farmland shows how locals lived on top of the ruins for centuries without knowing what was underneath. To the left, you can see the entire ancient city of Pompeii spread out in front of you and appreciate the magnitude of the excavations.

Amphitheater

If you can, climb to the upper level of the amphitheater (though the stairs are often blocked). With Vesuvius looming in the back-

ground, mentally replace the tourists below with gladiators and wild animals locked in combat. Walk along the top of the amphitheater and look down into the grassy rectangular area surrounded by columns. This is the **Palaestra,** an area once used for athletic training. (If you can't get to the top of the amphitheater, you can see the Palaestra from outside—in fact, you can't miss it, as it's right next door.) Facing the other way, look for the bell tower that tops the roofline of the modern city of Pompei, where locals go about their daily lives in the shadow of the volcano, just as their ancestors did 2,000 years ago.

• *If it's too crowded to bear hiking back along uneven lanes to the entrance, you can slip out the site's "back door," which is next to the amphitheater. Exiting, turn right and follow the site's wall all the way back to the entrance.*

Herculaneum

Smaller, less crowded, and not as ruined as its famous big sister, Herculaneum (worth ▲▲, Ercolano in Italian) offers a closer, more intimate peek into ancient Roman life but lacks the grandeur of Pompeii (there's barely a colonnade).

GETTING TO HERCULANENUM

Ercolano Scavi, the nearest train station to Herculaneum, is about 20 minutes from Naples and 50 minutes from Sorrento on the same Circumvesuviana train that goes to Pompeii. Walking from the Ercolano Scavi train station to the ruins takes 10 minutes: Leave the station and turn right, then left down the main drag; continue straight, eight blocks gradually downhill, to the end of the road, where you'll run right into the grand arch that marks the entrance to the ruins. (Skip Museo MAV.) Pass through the arch and continue 200 yards down the path—taking in the bird's-eye first impression of the site to your right—to the ticket office in the modern building.

ORIENTATION TO HERCULANEUM

Cost: €11, free first Sun of each month, €22 combo-ticket includes Pompeii and three lesser sites (valid 3 consecutive days); also covered by the Campania ArteCard.

Hours: Daily April-Oct 8:30-19:30, Nov-March until 17:00, ticket office closes 1.5 hours earlier.

Information: Tel. 081-777-7008, www.pompeiisites.org.

Closures: Like Pompeii, various sections of Herculaneum can be closed unexpectedly.

Visitor Information: Pick up a free, detailed map and excellent booklet at the info desk next to the ticket window. The booklet gives you a quick explanation of each building. There's a bookstore inside the site, next to the audioguide stand.

Tours: The audioguide basically recites the text in the free booklet (€8, €13 for 2, ID required, rent at kiosk near site entry).

Length of This Tour: Allow one hour.

Baggage Storage: Herculaneum is harder than Pompeii for those with luggage, but not impossible. Herculaneum's train station has lots of stairs and no baggage storage, but you can roll wheeled luggage down to the ruins and store it for free in a locked area in the ticket office building (pick up bags at least 30 minutes prior to site closing). To get back to the station, consider splurging on a €5 taxi (ask the staff to call one for you).

Services: There's a free WC in the ticket office building, and another near the site entry.

Eating: Vending machines and café tables are near the entry to the site. There are also several eateries on the way from the train station.

❍ SELF-GUIDED TOUR

Caked and baked by the same A.D. 79 eruption that pummeled Pompeii, Herculaneum is a small community of intact build-

ings with plenty of surviving detail. While Pompeii was initially smothered in ash, Herculaneum was spared at first—due to the direction of the wind—but got slammed about 12 hours after the eruption started by a superheated avalanche of ash and hot gases roaring off the volcano. The city was eventually buried under nearly 60 feet of ash, which hardened into tuff, perfectly preserving the city until excavations began in 1748.

After leaving the ticket building, go through the turnstiles and walk the path below the site to the entrance. Look seaward and note where the shoreline is today; before the eruption, it was where you are standing, a quarter-mile inland. This gives you a sense of how much volcanic material piled up. The present-day city of Ercolano looms just above the ruins. The modern buildings don't look much different from their ancient counterparts.

As you cross the modern bridge into the excavation site, look down into the moat-like **ditch.** On one side, you see Herculaneum's seafront wall. On the other is the wall that you just walked on, a solidified ash layer from the volcano that shows how deeply the town was buried.

After crossing the bridge, stroll straight to the end of the street and find the **College of the Augustali** (Sede degli Augustali, #24). Decorated with frescoes of Hercules (for whom this city was named), it belonged to an association of freed slaves working together to climb their way up the ladder of Roman society. Here and farther on, look around doorways and ceilings to spot ancient wood charred by the pyroclastic flows. Most buildings were made of stone, with wooden floors and beams (which were preserved here by the ash but rarely survive at ancient sites).

Leave the building through the back and go to the right, down the lane. The adjacent *thermopolium* (#19) was the Roman equivalent of a lunch counter or fast-food joint, with giant jars for wine,

oil, and snacks. Most of the buildings along here were shops, with apartments above.

A few steps on, the **Bottega ad Cucumas** wine shop (#14, on the right) still has charred remains of beams, and its drink list remains frescoed on the outside wall (under glass).

Take the next right, go halfway down the street, and on the left find the **House of Neptune and Amphitrite** (Casa di Nettuno e Anfitrite, #7). Outside, notice the intact upper floor and imagine it going even higher. Inside, you'll see colorful mosaics and a unique "frame" made of shells.

Back outside, continue downhill to the intersection, then head left for a block and proceed straight across the street into the don't-miss-it **sports complex** (*palestra;* #4). First you'll see a row of "marble" columns, which (look closer) are actually made of rounded bricks covered with a thick layer of plaster, shaped to

look like carved marble. While important buildings in Rome had solid marble columns, these fakes are typical of ordinary buildings.

Continuing deeper into the complex, look for the hole in the hillside and walk through one of the triangular-shaped entrances to find the highlight: the Hydra of Lerna, a sculpted bronze fountain that features the seven-headed monster defeated by Hercules as one of his 12 labors. If this cavernous space is unlit, go to the second doorway on the left wall and press the light switch.

Return through the sports complex and turn downhill to the **House of the Deer** (Casa dei Cervi, #21). It's named for the statues of deer being attacked by dogs in the garden courtyard (these are copies; the originals are in the Archaeological Museum in Naples). As you wander through the rooms, notice the colorfully frescoed walls. Ancient Herculaneum, like all Roman cities of that age, was filled with color, rather than the stark white we often imagine (even the statues were painted).

You can see more of these colors, this time bright orange, across the street in the **House of Relief of Telephus** (Casa del Rilievo del Telefo, #2).

Continue downhill through the archway. The **Suburban Baths** illustrate the city's devastation (Terme Suburbane, #3; enter near the side of the statue on the terrace, sometimes closed). After you descend into the baths, look back at the steps. You'll see the original wood charred in the disaster, protected by the wooden planks you just walked on. At the bottom of the stairs, in the waiting room to the right, notice where the floor collapsed under the sheer weight of the volcanic debris. (The sunken pavement reveals the baths' heating system: hot air generated by wood-burning furnaces and circulated between the different levels of the floor.) A doorway in front of the stairs is still filled with solidified ash. Despite the damage, elements of refinement remain intact, such as the delicate stuccoes in the *caldarium* (hot bath).

Back outside, make your way down the steps to the sunken area just below. As you descend, you're walking across what was formerly Herculaneum's beach. Looking back, you'll see **arches** that were part of boat storage areas. Archaeologists used to wonder why so few victims were found in Herculaneum. But during excavations in 1981, hundreds of skeletons were discovered here, between the wall of volcanic stone behind you and the city in front of you. Some of Herculaneum's 4,000 citizens tried to escape by sea, but were overtaken by the pyroclastic flows.

Thankfully, your escape is easier. Either follow the sound of water and continue through the tunnel (you'll climb up and pop out near the site entry), or, more scenically, backtrack and exit the same way you entered.

Vesuvius

The 4,000-foot-high Vesuvius, mainland Europe's only active volcano, has been sleeping restlessly since 1944. While Europe has other dangerous volcanoes, only Vesuvius sits in the middle of a three-million-person metropolitan area that would be impossible to evacuate quickly.

Many tourists don't know that you can easily visit the summit. Up top, it's desolate and lunar-like, and the rocks are newly born. Walk the entire accessible part of the crater lip for the most interesting views; the far end overlooks Pompeii. Be still. Listen to the wind and the occasional cascades of rocks tumbling into the crater. Any steam? Vesuvius could blow again. (Don't worry—there'd likely be at least a few hours or days of warning.)

GETTING TO VESUVIUS

By Car or Taxi: Drivers take the exit *Torre del Greco* and follow the signs to *Vesuvio*. Just drive to the end of the road and pay €6 to park. A taxi costs €90 round-trip from Naples, including a 2-hour wait; it's about €70 from Pompeii.

By Private Bus from Pompeii: From the Pompei Scavi train station on the Circumvesuviana line (just outside the main entrance to the Pompeii ruins), you have two bus services to choose from, each taking about three hours (40 minutes up, 40 minutes down, and about 1.5 hours at the summit).

The old-fashioned **Vesuvius Trolley Tram** (Tramvia del Vesuvio) uses the main road up (€12 round-trip plus €10 summit admission, 6/day, tickets sold at and tram departs from Camping

Zeus next to Pompei Scavi train station, tel. 081-861-53__, campingzeus.it).

Busvia del Vesuvio winds you up a bumpy back road to the crater rim (Via Boscotrecase) in a cross between a shuttle bus and a monster truck. The walk up to the rim at the end is about the same, but you approach it from the other direction. It's a fun, more scenic way to go, but not for the easily queasy (€22 includes summit admission, hourly April-Oct Mon-Sat 9:00-15:00, until later June-Aug, rarely Sun or Nov-March, buy tickets at "info point" at Pompei Scavi train station, mobile 340-935-2616, www. busviadelvesuvio.com).

By Private Bus from Herculaneum: The quickest trip up is on the **Vesuvio Express.** These small buses leave from the Ercolano Scavi train station (on the Circumvesuviana line, where you get off for the Herculaneum ruins; €10 round-trip plus €10 summit admission, daily from 9:30, runs every 45 minutes based on demand, 20 minutes each way—about 2.5 hours total, office on square in front of train station, tel. 081-739-3666, www.vesuvioexpress.it).

ORIENTATION TO VESUVIUS

Cost and Hours: €10 covers national park entry and the park guide's orientation; ticket office open daily July-Aug 9:00-18:00, April-June and Sept until 17:00, closes earlier off-season; these are last-entry times—you can stay in the park one hour later. Bad weather can occasionally close the trail.

Information: The ticket office is 200 yards downhill from the parking lot. Tel. 081-865-3911 or 081-239-5653, www.vesuviopark. it (official site) or www.guidevesuvio.it (more helpful site run by guides).

When to Go: Early-morning visitors enjoy the freshest air and snare the best parking spots. The mountain is open all year, but spring and fall are the most comfortable times to visit. Yellow broom flowers blossom in May and June.

VISITING VESUVIUS

Bring sunscreen, water, a light jacket in summer, and a hat and warm coat in winter. By bus, taxi, or private car, you'll reach the volcano crater up a good but windy road from Torre del Greco (between Herculaneum and Pompeii). As you drive up, you'll pass the remnants of the pre-A.D. 79 mountain (on your left, now called Monte Somma) and lava flows from the most recent 1944 eruption. No matter how you travel up, you'll land at the parking lot.

Backtrack 200 yards downhill to buy your ticket at the office. Use the pay WC, as there's none at the summit. From the parking lot, it's a moderately steep half-mile, 20-minute hike (with a 600-foot elevation gain) up a dirt access road to the top. Say "no thank you" to the gentleman passing out walking sticks in return for a tip—you don't need one.

At the rim, a sweeping view of the Bay of Naples is on your right; on your left, fenced off, there's a fearsome drop into the crater. Mountain guides orient you and then set you free.

SORRENTO & CAPRI

Just an hour south of Naples, and without a hint of big-city chaos, serene Sorrento makes an ideal home base for exploring this fascinating region. From this easy-to-enjoy town, you can take day trips to Naples, Pompeii, the Amalfi Coast, the Greek temples at Paestum, and the romantic island of Capri. And every night you can return "home" to Sorrento, to enjoy its elegant strolling scene and sort through its many fine restaurant options.

Sorrento

Wedged on a ledge under the mountains and over the Mediterranean, spritzed by lemon and olive groves, Sorrento is an attractive resort of 20,000 residents and, in summer, just as many tourists. It's as well-located for regional sightseeing as it is a fine place to stay and stroll. The Sorrentines have gone out of their way to create a safe and relaxed place for tourists to come and spend money. As 90 percent of the town's economy is tourism, everyone seems to speak fluent English and work for the Chamber of Commerce. This gateway to the Amalfi Coast has an unspoiled old quarter, a lively shopping street, and a spectacular cliffside setting. Residents are proud of the many world-class romantics who've vacationed here, such as famed tenor Enrico Caruso, who chose Sorrento as the place to spend his last months in 1921.

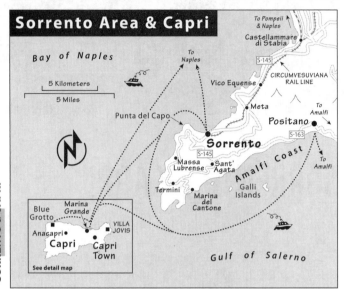

PLANNING YOUR TIME

Sorrento itself has no world-class sights, but it can easily give you a few pleasant hours. More importantly, Sorrento is a fine base for visiting nearby destinations, all reachable within an hour or so: Naples (by boat or train); Pompeii, Herculaneum, and Mount Vesuvius (by train, plus a bus for Vesuvius); the Amalfi Coast (by bus or boat); and the island of Capri (just 30 minutes by boat). Even Paestum's Greek temples, a 2.5-hour train ride away, can be seen from Sorrento in one long day.

Sorrento hibernates in winter. Many places close down in November—others after the New Year—and stay closed until the town reawakens sometime in March.

Orientation to Sorrento

Downtown Sorrento is long and narrow. Piazza Tasso marks the town's center. The congested main drag, Corso Italia, runs paral-

lel to the sea, passing 50 yards below the train station, through Piazza Tasso, and then out toward the cape, where the road's name becomes Via Capo. Nearly everything mentioned here (except Marina Grande and the hotels on Via Capo) is within a 10-minute walk of the station.

The town is perched on a cliff (some hotels have elevators down to sundecks on the water); the best real beaches are a couple of miles away.

Sorrento has two separate port areas: Marina Piccola, below Piazza Tasso, is a functional harbor with boats to Naples and Capri, as well as cruise-ship tenders. (While the big cruise ships dock in Naples, smaller ships drop anchor at Sorrento.) Marina Grande, below the other end of downtown, is a little fishing village, with recommended restaurants and more charm.

TOURIST INFORMATION

The helpful regional TI (labeled *Azienda di Soggiorno*)—located inside the **Foreigners' Club**—hands out a great city map and schedules for boats and buses (Mon-Sat 9:00-19:00, Sun until 18:00 except closed Sun April-May; Nov-March Mon-Fri 8:30-16:00, closed Sat-Sun; Via Luigi de Maio 35, tel. 081-807-4033, www. sorrentotourism.com; Fabiola). If you arrive after the TI closes, look for their useful handouts in the lobby of the Foreigners' Club (open until midnight, closed in winter).

Small "Info Points" are conveniently located around town, where you can get answers to basic questions (open in warm months only). Find them just outside the **train station** in the green caboose; near **Piazza Tasso** at the corner of Via Correale (under the yellow church); at **Marina Piccola,** where cruise-ship tenders and boats from Naples arrive; and at the Achille Lauro **parking garage.**

ARRIVAL IN SORRENTO

By Train or Bus: Sorrento is the last stop on the Circumvesuviana train line from Naples. In front of the train station is the town's main bus stop, as well as taxis waiting to overcharge you (€15 minimum). All recommended hotels—except those on Via Capo—are within a 10-minute walk.

By Boat: Passenger boats and cruise-ship tenders dock at Marina Piccola. As you walk toward town from the marina, go up the big staircase where the pier bends. Standing on the promenade and facing town, you'll see the bus stop directly ahead; a TI kiosk and ticket windows for boats to Capri and Naples in the lower area to your left; and the elevator up to town to the right, about a five-minute walk along the base of the cliff (follow *lift/ acensore* signs).

The elevator (€1; faster, cheaper, and more predictable than a bus) takes you to the Villa Comunale city park. From there, exit through the park's gate and bear left; Piazza Tasso is about four blocks away. Buses take you directly to Piazza Tasso (city bus #B

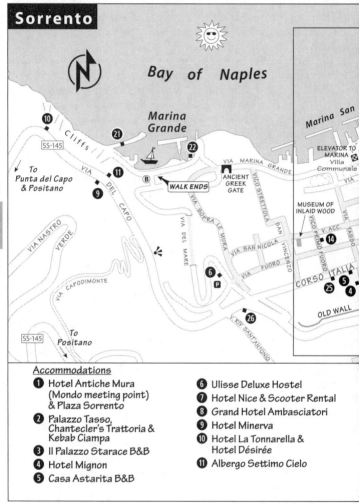

Accommodations

1. Hotel Antiche Mura (Mondo meeting point) & Plaza Sorrento
2. Palazzo Tasso, Chantecler's Trattoria & Kebab Ciampa
3. Il Palazzo Starace B&B
4. Hotel Mignon
5. Casa Astarita B&B
6. Ulisse Deluxe Hostel
7. Hotel Nice & Scooter Rental
8. Grand Hotel Ambasciatori
9. Hotel Minerva
10. Hotel La Tonnarella & Hotel Désirée
11. Albergo Settimo Cielo

or #C, buy €1.20 ticket at newsstand or tobacco shop); for more on buses, see "Getting Around Sorrento," later.

By Car: The Achille Lauro underground parking garage is centrally located, just a couple of blocks in front of the train station (€2/hour, €24/24 hours, on Via Correale).

HELPFUL HINTS

Church Services: The **cathedral** hosts an English-language Anglican service at 17:00 most Sundays from April to October (but not in August). At **Santa Maria delle Grazie** (perhaps the most beautiful Baroque church in town), cloistered nuns

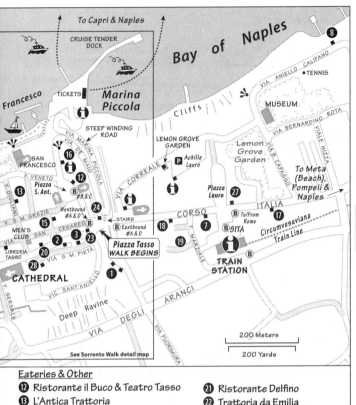

Eateries & Other

12 Ristorante il Buco & Teatro Tasso
13 L'Antica Trattoria
14 Inn Bufalito
15 Rist. Pizzeria da Gigino
16 Foreigners' Club Rest.
17 Pizzeria da Franco
18 Decò Supermarket
19 Gelateria David
20 Gelateria Primavera

21 Ristorante Delfino
22 Trattoria da Emilia
23 The Fauno Bar
24 Daniele's Club
25 The English Inn
26 Launderette
27 Europcar & Scooter Rental
28 Satisfhair Salon

sing from above and out of sight during a Mass each morning at 7:30 (on Via delle Grazie).

Bookstore: Libreria Tasso has a decent selection of books in English, including this one (daily 9:30-22:00, closed in winter, Via San Cesareo 96, one block north of cathedral, near Sorrento Men's Club, tel. 081-807-1639).

Laundry: Sorrento's handy self-service launderette is a couple of long blocks past the station (daily 8:00-24:00, shorter hours off-season, at the corner of Corso Italia and Via degli Aranci, mobile 333-206-2208).

Haircuts: Satisfhair, a fun hair salon for men run by hairless Luca and Tony, makes for a happy memory (€17 for a good cut, closed Sun-Mon, Via S. Maria della Pieta 17, tel. 081-878-3476).

Guided Tours of Pompeii, Naples, the Amalfi Coast, and Capri: Naples-based **Mondo Guide** offers affordable tours of these destinations, including an Amalfi Coast drive that starts from Sorrento (meet in front of the Hotel Antiche Mura). You'll sign up in advance and team up with fellow Rick Steves readers to split the cost.

Local Guides: Giovanna Donadio is a good tour guide for Sorrento and Amalfi (€100/half-day, €160/day, same price for any size group, mobile 338-466-0114, giovanna_dona@hotmail.com) and can also escort up to six people from Sorrento on a well-organized full day of fun on Capri (€160 plus public transportation expenses and admissions). **Giovanni Visetti** is a high-energy nature lover, mapmaker, and orienteer who organizes hikes and has a fine website describing local trails (mobile 339-694-2911, www.giovis.com, giovis@giovis.com).

GETTING AROUND SORRENTO

By Bus: City buses all stop near the main square, Piazza Tasso, and run until at least 20:00 (for info, see www.eavsrl.it). Bus #A (3/hour) takes a long route parallel to the coast, heading east to Meta beach or west to the hotels on Via Capo before continuing to Massa Lubrense; buses #B and #C loop up and down, connecting the port (Marina Piccola) to the town center; and minibus #D heads to the fishing village (Marina Grande). The trip between Piazza Tasso and Marina Piccola (or Marina Grande) costs just €1.20; for other trips, tickets cost €1.60 and are good for up to one hour (purchase at tobacco shops and newsstands). Stamp your ticket upon entering the bus. The €8, 24-hour Costiera SITA Sud pass, good for the entire Amalfi Coast, also covers local buses in Sorrento.

Bus stops can be tricky to find. Buses #A and #D stop where Corso Italia passes through Piazza Tasso. If you're heading west (to Via Capo or Marina Grande), find the stop at the west end of the piazza, across from the statue of Torquato Tasso. If you're heading east (to Meta), catch the bus in front of the yellow church at the east end of the piazza. Buses #B and #C stop at the corner of Piazza Sant'Antonino, just down the hill toward the water.

By Scooter: Several places near the station rent motor scooters for about €35 per day, including **Europcar** (Corso Italia 210p, tel. 081-878-1386, www.sorrento.it) and **Autoservizi De Martino,** in Hotel Nice (Corso Italia 259, tel. 081-878-2801, www.admitaly.com). Don't rent a vehicle in summer unless you enjoy traffic jams.

By Taxi: Taxis charge an outrageous €15 for the short ride from the station to most hotels (more for Via Capo). Because of heavy traffic and the complex one-way road system, you'll get to most central locations faster by walking. If you do use a taxi, even if you agree to a set price, be sure it has a meter (all official taxis have one). I think taxis here are a huge rip-off, since city officials don't have the nerve to regulate them, and hotels are afraid to alienate them. Walk or take the bus instead.

Sorrento Walk

Get to know Sorrento with this lazy self-guided town stroll that ends down by the waterside at the small-boat harbor, Marina Grande.

• *Begin on the main square. Stand under the flags between the sea and the town's main square...*

❶ **Piazza Tasso:** As in any southern Italian town, this "piazza" is Sorrento's living room. It may be noisy and congested, but

locals want to be where the action is...and be part of the scene. The most expensive apartments and top cafés are on or near this square.

Look out at the Bay of Naples. You can see the city of Naples in the distance. The gorge divides the old city (left) and the new (right). It's a

five-minute walk—including 130 stairs—from here to the harbor (cruise-ship tenders, boats to Capri and Naples). On the right side of the gorge, overlooking the bay, is Hotel Excelsior Vittoria. This elegant, 19th-century Grand Tour hotel is where tenor Enrico Caruso (who died in 1921) spent his last months.

Turn to face the square. City buses stop here on their way to Marina Piccola and Via Capo. The train station is a five-minute walk to the left. A statue of St. Anthony, patron of Sorrento, is surrounded by traffic. He faces north as if greeting those coming from Naples (on festival days, he's equipped with an armload of fresh lemons and oranges).

This square bridges the gorge that divides downtown Sorrento. The newer section (now to your left) was farm country just two centuries ago. The older part (to your right) retains its ancient Greek gridded street plan. (Like much of southern Italy, Sorrento was Greek-speaking for centuries before it was Romanized.)

For a better glimpse of the city's gorge-gouged landscape, consider this quick detour: With the water to your back, cross through the square and walk straight ahead a block inland, under a canopy of trees and past a long taxi queue. Belly up to the green railing in front of Hotel Antiche Mura and look down to see steps that were carved centuries before Christ. In more modern times, this was called the "Valley of the Mills" and was busy with river-powered

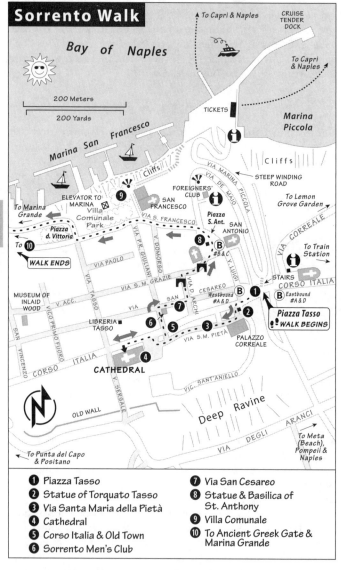

Sorrento Walk

Bay of Naples

To Capri & Naples

CRUISE
TENDER
DOCK

To Capri
& Naples

TICKETS

Marina
Piccola

200 Meters

200 Yards

Marina San Francesco

Cliffs

VIA MARINA PICCOLA

STEEP WINDING
ROAD

VIA DE' MAIO

FOREIGNERS'
CLUB

SAN
FRANCESCO

Piazza
S. Ant.

SAN
ANTONIO

To Lemon
Grove Garden

VIA CORREALE

ELEVATOR TO
MARINA

Villa
Comunale
Park

VIA S. FRANCESCO

B&C

To Marina
Grande

Piazza
d. Vittoria

To 10

WALK ENDS

VIA PAOLO

VIA PR. GIULIANI

VIA D. MORESO

Westbound
#A & D

B

To Train
Station

STAIRS

CORSO ITALIA

Eastbound
#A & D

B

MUSEUM OF
INLAID
WOOD

V. ACC.

VIA S.M. GRAZIE

SAN

VIA D. ARCH.

CESAREO

Piazza Tasso
WALK BEGINS

VICO PRIMO FUORO

VIA

LIBRERIA
TASSO

VIA S.M. PIETA

PALAZZO
CORREALE

SAN VINCENZO

CORSO ITALIA

CATHEDRAL

VIA V. BENSALE

OLD WALL

VIC. SANT'ANIELLO

Deep Ravine

To Punta del Capo
& Positano

VIA

DEGLI

ARANCI

To Meta
(Beach),
Pompeii &
Naples

N

1 Piazza Tasso
2 Statue of Torquato Tasso
3 Via Santa Maria della Pietà
4 Cathedral
5 Corso Italia & Old Town
6 Sorrento Men's Club

7 Via San Cesareo
8 Statue & Basilica of
   St. Anthony
9 Villa Comunale
10 To Ancient Greek Gate &
   Marina Grande

saw- and flour-mills, along with a public laundry, until well into the 19th century.

The combination of the gorge and the seaside cliffs made Sorrento easy to defend. A small section of wall closed the landward gap in the city's defenses (you can still see a surviving piece of it a few blocks away, near Hotel Mignon).

Sorrento's name may come from the Greek word for "siren,"

the legendary half-bird, half-woman who sang an intoxicating lullaby. According to Homer, the sirens lived on an island near here. All those who sailed by the sirens succumbed to their incredible musical charms...and to death. But Homer's hero Ulysses was determined to hear the song and restrain his manhood. He put wax in his oarsmen's ears and had himself lashed to the mast of his ship. The sirens, thinking they had lost their powers, threw themselves into the sea, and the place became safe to inhabit. Ulysses' odyssey was all about the westward expansion of Greek culture, and to the ancient Greeks, places like Sorrento were the wild, wild west.

• *Back at Piazza Tasso, head to the far-left inland corner of the square. You'll find a...*

❷ **Statue of Torquato Tasso:** The square's namesake, a Sorrento native, was a lively Renaissance poet—but today he seems only to wonder which restaurant to choose for dinner. Directly behind the statue, pop into the **Fattoria Terranova** shop, one of many fun, family-run, and touristy boutiques. Susy sells regional goodies and offers free biscuits and tastes of liqueurs at this shop that makes all of its entirely organic products on its *agriturismo* outside the city. The gifty edibles spill into the courtyard of **Palazzo Correale,** which gives you a feel for an 18th-century aristocratic palace's courtyard, its walls lined with characteristic tiles from 1772.

• *As you're leaving the courtyard, on your immediate left you'll see the narrow...*

❸ **Via Santa Maria della Pietà:** Here, just a few yards off the noisy main drag, is a street that goes back centuries before Christ. About 100 yards down the lane, at #24 (on the left), find a 13th-century palace (no balconies back then...for security reasons), now an elementary school. A few steps farther on, you'll see a tiny shrine across the street. Typical of southern Italy, it's where the faithful pray to their saint, who contacts Mary, who contacts Jesus, who contacts God. This shrine is a bit more direct—it starts right with Mary.

• *Continue down the lane (passing a recommended kebab shop and trattoria, and under the clock tower) to reach the delightful...*

❹ **Cathedral:** Walk alongside this long church (free, daily 8:00-12:30 & 16:30-21:00) until you reach the doors facing the street, halfway down. Step inside the outer door and examine the impressive *intarsio* (inlaid-wood) interior doors. They show scenes of the town and its industry, as well as an old-town map (find Piazza Tasso, trace the fortified walls, and notice the Greek street-grid plan). These doors were made to celebrate Pope John Paul II's visit in 1992. Now enter the church for a cool stroll around the ambulatory, checking out the intricate inlaid Stations of the Cross. Notice the fine inlaid-marble seat of the bishop and how the church's elegance matches that of the town. Work your way toward the back door. Before exiting, on the right find the *presepe* (manger scene) with its lovingly painted terracotta figures, each with an expressive face. This takes Bethlehem on that first Christmas and sets it in Naples—with pasta, mozzarella, salami, and even Mount Vesuvius in the background. Exiting through the back door, notice that these doors are also finely inlaid wood.

• *Backtrack 10 yards down Via Santa Maria della Pietà, turn left at the passage under the covered arcade, and cross busy Corso Italia.*

❺ Corso Italia and the Old Town: In the summer, this stretch of road is closed to traffic each evening, when it hosts a wonderful *passeggiata*. Look back at the bell tower, with the scavenged ancient Roman columns at its base. Now go straight down Via P. Reginaldo Giuliani, following the old Greek street plan. Locals claim the ancient Greeks laid out the streets east-west for the most sunlight and north-south for the prevailing and cooling breeze. Pause at the poster board on your right to see who's died lately.

• *One block ahead, on your right, the 14th-century loggia (called Sedil Dominova) is home to the...*

❻ Sorrento Men's Club: Once the meeting place of the town's nobles, for generations now the Sedil Dominova has been a retreat for retired working-class men. Strictly no women—and no phones.

Italian men venerate their mothers. (Italians joke that Jesus must have been a southern Italian because his mother believed her son was God, he believed his mom was a virgin, and he lived at home with her until he was 30.) But Italian men have also built into their culture ways to be on their own. Here, men play cards and gossip under an historic emblem of  the city and a finely frescoed 16th-century dome, with its marvelous 3-D scenes.

• *Turn right for a better view of the Men's Club and a historical marker describing the building. Then continue along...*

❼ Via San Cesareo: This touristy pedestrian-only shopping street leads back to Piazza Tasso. It's lined with competitive little shops where you can peruse (and sample) lemon products. Notice the huge ancient doorways with their tiny doors—to let the right people in, carefully, during a more dangerous age.

• *After a block, take a left onto Via degli Archi, go under the arch, and then hang a right (under another arch) to the square with the...*

❽ Statue and Basilica of St. Anthony (Antonino): Sorrento's town saint humbly looms among the palms, facing the basilica of

St. Anthony. Step inside and descend into the crypt (free, stairs beside main altar) where you'll find a chapel and reliquary containing a few of Anthony's bones surrounded by lots of votives. Locals have long turned to St. Anthony when faced with challenges and hard times. Exploring the room, you'll find countless tokens of appreciation to the saint for his help.

Before tourism, fishing was the big employer. The back walls feature paintings of storms with Anthony coming to the rescue. Circle behind the altar with Anthony's relics and study the shiny ex-votos (religious offerings) thanking the saint for healthy babies, good employment, surviving heart attacks and lung problems, and lots of strong legs.

SORRENTO & CAPRI

• *Exit the square at the bottom-left (following Lift to the Port signs; don't go down the street with the line of trees and Porto signs). Watch on the left for The Corner Shop, where Giovanni sells a wide variety of wines, limoncello, pastas, and other foods, specializing in high-quality gifty edibles from the Campania region. (Across the street is a travel agency that sells train tickets for a 10 percent commission—handy if you're heading to Rome.) Soon after, on the right you'll see the trees in front of the Imperial Hotel Tramontano, and to their right a path leading to the...*

❾ **Villa Comunale:** This fine public park overlooks the harbor. Belly up to the banister to enjoy the view of Marina Piccola and the

Bay of Naples. Notice Naples' skyline and the boats that commute from here to there in 35 minutes. Imagine the view in A.D. 70 when Vesuvius blew its top and molten mud flowed down the mountain, burying Pompeii. From here, steps zigzag down to the harbor, where lounge chairs, filled by vacationers working on tans, line the sundecks (there's also the elevator to the harbor). The Franciscan church fronting this square faces a fine modern statue of Francis across the street.

Next to the church is a dreamy little cloister. Pop inside to see local Gothic—a 13th-century mix of Norman, Gothic, and Arabic styles, all around the old pepper tree. This is an understandably popular spot for weddings and concerts.

At the far side of the cloister, stairs lead to a **photo exhibit:** *The Italians* shows off the work of local photographer Raffaele Celentano, who artfully captures classic Italian scenes from 1990 to 2016 in black and white (€2.50, daily 10:00-22:00, great prints for sale, fun photo-op through the grand tree on their deck, adjacent music box exhibit is free).

• *From here, you can quit the walk and stay in the town center, or continue another few minutes downhill to the waterfront at Marina Grande.*

❿ To continue to **Marina Grande,** return to the road and keep going downhill. At the next square (Piazza della Vittoria, with a dramatic WWI memorial and another grand view), cut over to the road closest to the water. After winding steeply down for a few minutes, it turns into a wide stairway, then makes a sharp and steep switchback (take the right fork to continue downhill). Farther down, just before reaching the waterfront, you pass under an...

Ancient Greek Gate: This gate fortified the city of Sorrento. Beyond it was Marina Grande, technically a separate town with its own proud residents—it's said that even their cats look different. Because Marina Grande dwellers lived outside the wall and were more susceptible to rape, pillage, and plunder, Sorrentines believe that they come from Saracen (Turkish pirate) stock. Sorrentines still scare their children by saying, "Behave—or the Turks will take you away."

• *Now go all the way down the steps into Marina Grande, Sorrento's "big" small-boat harbor.*

Marina Grande: Until recently, this little community was famously traditional, with its economy based on its fishing fleet.

To this day, fathers pass their houses and fishing-boat stalls down to their sons. Locals recall when women wore black when a relative died (1 year for an uncle, aunt, or sibling; 2-3 years for a husband or parent). Men got off easy, just wearing a black memorial button.

Two recommended restaurants are on the harbor. **Trattoria da Emilia** has an old newspaper clipping, tacked near the door, about Sophia Loren filming here. On the far side of the harbor, **Ristorante Delfino** boasts a delightful sundeck for a lazy drink before or after lunch (free access for those with this book).

• *From here, where the road hits the beach, buses return to the center at Piazza Tasso every hour (pay the driver). Or you can walk back up.*

Sights in Sorrento

▲▲Strolling

Each balmy evening Sorrento offers one of Italy's most enchanting *passeggiata* scenes. Take time to explore the surprisingly pleasant old city between Corso Italia and the sea. The views from Villa Comunale, the public park next to Imperial Hotel Tramontano, are worth the detour. Each night in summer (May-Oct at 19:30; Nov-April weekends only), the police close off Corso Italia to traffic, and Sorrento's main drag becomes a thriving people scene. The *passeggiata* peaks at about 22:00.

Lemon Products Galore

Via San Cesareo is lined with hardworking rival shops selling a mind-boggling array of lemon products and offering samples of lots of sour goodies. You'll find *limoncello,* lemon biscuits, lemon pasta, lemon drops, lemon chocolate, lemon perfume, lemon soap, and on and on. Poke around for a pungent experience (and read the "Lemons" sidebar, later). A few produce stands are also mixed in.

▲Lemon Grove Garden (Agruminato)

This lemon-and-orange grove, lined with shady, welcoming paths, was rescued from development by the city of Sorrento and turned into a park. The family that manages it has seasoned green thumbs and descends from the family that started working here decades ago, when the grove was still in private hands. The garden is dotted with benches, tables, and an inviting little tasting (and buying) stand. You'll get a chance to sniff and taste the varieties of lemons and enjoy free samples of *limoncello* along with other homemade liqueurs made from mandarins, licorice, or fennel. Check out how they've grafted orange-tree branches onto a lemon tree so that both fruits grow on the same tree.

Cost and Hours: Free, daily 10:00-sunset, closed in rainy weather, tel. 081-878-1888, www.igiardinidicataldo.it. Enter the garden on Corso Italia (100 yards north of the train station—where painted tiles show lemon fantasies) or at the intersection of Via Capasso and Via Rota (next to Hotel La Meridiana).

Eating: For a cheap and relaxing meal, get a big-enough-to-split *saltimbocca* sandwich to-go from the recommended **Pizzeria da Franco** (across the street on Corso Italia) and enjoy it in the lemon grove.

Lemons

Around here, *limoni* are ubiquitous: screaming yellow painted on ceramics, dainty bottles of *limoncello,* and lemons the size of softballs at the fruit stand.

The Amalfi Coast and Sorrento area produce several different kinds of lemons. The gigantic, bumpy "lemons" are actually citrons, called *cedri,* and are more for show—they're pulpier than they are juicy, and make a good marmalade. The juicy *sfusato sorrentino,* grown only in Sorrento, is shaped like an American football, while the *sfusato amalfitano,* with knobby points on both ends, is less juicy but equally aromatic. These two kinds of luscious lemons are used in sweets such as *granita* (shaved ice doused in lemonade), *limoncello* (a candy-like liqueur with a big kick, called *limoncino* on the Cinque Terre), *delizia* (a dome of fluffy cake filled and slathered with a thick whipped lemon cream), *spremuta di limone* (fresh-squeezed lemon juice), and, of course, gelato or *sorbetto al limone.*

Nearby: The entrepreneurial family's small "factory"—where you can see how they use the lemons, and buy a tasty gelato, *granita,* or lemonade—is just past the parking garage along the road below the garden (Via Correale 27). They also have a small shop across from the Corso Italia entrance (at #267).

Museum of Inlaid Wood
(Museobottega della Tarsialignea)

Sorrento doesn't have much in the way of museums, but if you want to get out of the heat and crowds, this is a good place to do it. It's not only a collection of inlaid wood, but also a painting gallery featuring scenes of 19th-century Sorrento, antique maps, and portraits, and a fine decorative arts collection. The basement displays modern examples of inlaid wood. While pricey, it's serious, thoughtfully presented, and bursting with local pride.

Cost and Hours: €8, daily 10:00-18:30, Nov-March until 17:30, Via San Nicola 28, tel. 081-877-1942, www.museomuta.it.

▲Swimming and Sunbathing

If you require immediate tanning, you can rent a chair on a pier by the port. There are no great beaches in Sorrento—the gravelly, jam-packed private beaches of **Marina Piccola** are more for partying than pampering, and there's just a tiny spot for public use. The elevator in Villa Comunale city park (next to the Church of San

Francesco) gets you down for €1. There's another humble beach at **Marina Grande,** and Ristorante Delfino has a pier lined with rentable lounge chairs (€10 but free for those with this book).

The classic, sandy Italian beach two miles away at **Meta** is generally overrun by teenagers from Naples. Bus #A goes directly from Piazza Tasso to Meta beach (last stop, schedule posted for hourly returns; you can also get there on the Circumvesuviana but the Meta stop is a very long walk from the beach). At Meta, you'll find pizzerias, snack bars, and a little free section of beach, but the place is mostly dominated by several prawling private-beach complexes—if you go, pay for a spot in one of these, such as Lido Metamare (lockable changing cabins, lounge chairs, tel. 081-532-2505). It's a very Italian scene—locals complain that it's "too local" (i.e., inundated with riffraff)—with light lunches, a playground, a manicured beach, loud pop music...and no international tourists.

More relaxing beaches are west of Sorrento. Tarzan might take Jane to the wild and stony beach at **Punta del Capo,** a 15-minute bus ride from Piazza Tasso (the same bus #A explained above, but in the opposite direction from Meta; 2/hour, get off at stop in front of the American Bar, then walk 10 minutes past ruined Roman Villa di Pollio).

Another good choice is **Marina di Puolo,** a tiny fishing town popular in the summer for its sandy beach, surfside restaurants, and beachfront disco (to get here, stay on bus #A a bit farther—ask driver to let you off at Marina di Puolo—then follow signs and hike down about 15 minutes).

More Activities

Tamara's Sorrento Food Tour: Run by a US expat, this outfit offers an information-filled, fast-paced food tour. Tamara and colleagues dish up a parade of local edibles interspersed with lots of food history, stopping at eight places in three hours (€75, 15 percent discount for Rick Steves readers, use code "ricksteves"; departures at 10:30 and 16:00 with demand, maximum 12 people; mobile 331-304-5666, www.sorrentofoodtours.com).

Tennis: The Sorrento Sport Snack Bar has two tennis courts open to the public (long hours daily, pay to use the court and rent equipment, call to reserve, across from recommended Grand Hotel Ambasciatori at Via Califano 5, tel. 081-807-1616).

Snorkeling and Scuba Diving: To snorkel or scuba dive in the Mediterranean, contact Futuro Mare for details on a one-hour boat ride to the protected marine zone between Sorrento and Capri (options for snorkelers, beginners, and experienced certified divers; about 3 hours round-trip, call 1-2 days in advance to reserve, mobile 349-653-6323, www.sorrentodiving.it, info@futuromare.it).

Motorboat Rental: You can rent motorboats big enough for four people (with your back to the ferry-ticket offices, it's to the left around the corner at Via Marina Piccola 43; tel. 081-807-2283, www.nauticasicsic.com).

Nightlife in Sorrento

PUBS AND CLUBS

Sorrento is a fun place to enjoy a drink or some dancing after dinner. The crowd is older, and the many local English expats seem to have paved the way for you.

The Fauno Bar, which dominates Piazza Tasso with tables spilling onto the square, is a fine place to make the scene over a drink any time of day.

Daniele's Club is run by DJ Daniele, who tailors music to the audience (including karaoke, if you ask nicely). The scene, while sloppy, is generally comfortable for the 30- to 60-year-old crowd. If you're alone, there's a pole you can dance with (no cover charge, try their signature cocktail, "Come Back to Sorrento," a mojito made with *limoncello;* no food, nightly from 21:30, down the steps from the flags at Piazza Tasso 10).

The English Inn offers both a streetside sports pub and a more refined-feeling garden out back—at least until the evening, when the music starts blaring. English vacationers come to Sorrento in droves (many have holidayed here annually for decades). The menu includes fish-and-chips, all-day English breakfast, baked beans on toast, and draft beer (daily, Corso Italia 55, tel. 081-878-2570).

The Foreigners' Club offers live Neapolitan songs, Sinatra-style classics, and jazzy elevator music nightly at 20:00 throughout the summer. It's just right for old-timers feeling frisky (in the center).

THEATER SHOW

At **Teatro Tasso,** a hardworking troupe puts on *The Sorrento Musical,* a folk-music show that treats visitors to a schmaltzy dose of Neapolitan Tarantella music and dance—complete with "Funiculì Funiculà" and "Santa Loo-chee-yee-yah." The 75-minute Italian-language extravaganza features a cast of 14 playing guitar, mandolin, saxophone, and tambourines, and singing operatically from Neapolitan balconies...complete with Vesuvius erupting in the background. Your €25 ticket (€50 with 4-course dinner) includes a drink before and after the show. Maurizio promises my readers a €5 discount if you buy directly from the box office and show this book (2 tickets/book, 3-5 nights/week mid-April-Oct at 21:30, bar opens 30 minutes before show, dinner starts at 20:00 and must be reserved in advance—in person or by email, box office open virtually all day long, theater seats 500, facing Piazza Sant'Antonino

in the old town, tel. 081-807-5525, www.teatrotasso.com, info@
teatrotasso.com).

Sleeping in Sorrento

Given the location, hotels here often have beautiful views, and
many offer balconies. At hotels that offer sea views, ask for a room
"con balcone, con vista sul mare" (with a balcony, with a sea view).
"Tranquillo" is taken as a request for a quieter room off the street.

Hotels listed are either near the train station and city center
(where balconies overlook city streets) or on cliffside Via Capo
(with sea-view balconies). Via Capo is a 20-minute walk—or short
bus ride—from the station.

You should have no trouble finding a room any time except in
August, when the town is jammed with Italians and prices often
rise above the regular high-season rates.

The spindly, more exotic, and more tranquil Amalfi Coast
town of Positano is also a good place to spend the night.

IN THE TOWN CENTER

$$$$ Hotel Antiche Mura, with 50 rooms and four stars, is sophisticated, elegant, and plush. It offers all the amenities, including an impressive breakfast buffet. Surrounded by lemon trees, the
pool and sundeck are a peaceful oasis. Just a block off the main
square, it's quieter than some central hotels because it's perched
on the ledge of a dramatic ravine (RS%, some rooms with balconies, family rooms, air-con, elevator, pay parking, closed in winter,
a block inland from Piazza Tasso at Via Fuorimura 7, tel. 081-807-
3523, www.hotelantichemura.com, info@hotelantichemura.com,
Michele). Meet in front of the hotel for the Mondo Guide full-day
Amalfi Coast Minibus tour.

$$$$ Palazzo Tasso, nicely located near the center, has 11
small, sleek, fashionably designed modern rooms; there's no public
space except for the breakfast room (some rooms with balconies,
air-con, elevator, Via Santa Maria della Pietà 33, tel. 081-878-
3579, www.palazzotasso.com, info@palazzotasso.com, Valentina).

$$$$ Plaza Sorrento is a contemporary-feeling, upscale refuge in the very center of town (next-door to Antiche Mura but
not as elegant). Its 65 rooms mix mod decor with wood grain, and
the rooftop swimming pool is inviting (RS%, some rooms with
balconies, air-con, elevator, closed in winter, Via Fuorimura 3, tel.
081-878-2831, www.plazasorrento.com, info@plazasorrento.com).

$$$ Il Palazzo Starace B&B, conscientiously run by Mas-
simo, offers seven tidy, modern rooms in a little alley off Corso
Italia, one block from Piazza Tasso (RS%, use code "RS2018,"
some rooms with balconies, family room, air-con, lots of stairs, no

elevator but a luggage dumbwaiter, ring bell around corner from Via Santa Maria della Pietà 9, tel. 081-807-2633, mobile 366-950-5377, www.palazzostarace.com, info@palazzostarace.com).

$$$ Hotel Mignon rents 22 soothing blue rooms with beautiful, tiled public spaces, a rooftop sundeck, and a small garden surrounded by a lemon grove (RS%, most rooms have balconies but no views, air-con, closed in winter; from the cathedral, walk a block farther up Corso Italia and look for the hotel up a small gated lane to your left; Via Sersale 9, tel. 081-807-3824, www.sorrentohotelmignon.com, info@sorrentohotelmignon.com, Paolo).

$$$ Casa Astarita B&B, hiding upstairs in a big building facing the busy main street, has a crazy-quilt-tiled entryway and eight bright, tranquil, creatively decorated, air-conditioned rooms (three with little balconies). Thin doors, echoey tile, and a buzzing location can result in noise...bring earplugs (air-con, open year-round, 50 yards past the cathedral on Corso Italia at #67, tel. 081-877-4906, www.casastarita.com, info@casastarita.com, Annamaria and Alfonso). If there's no one at reception, ask at Hotel Mignon (described above)—the same family runs both hotels.

$$ Hotel Nice rents 29 simple, cramped, cheap rooms with high ceilings 100 yards in front of the train station on the noisy main drag. This overpriced last resort is worth considering only for its very handy-to-the-train-station location. Alfonso promises a quiet room—critical given the thin windows and busy location—if you request it when you book by email (RS%, air-con, elevator, rooftop terrace, closed Nov-March, Corso Italia 257, tel. 081-878-1650, www.hotelnice.it, info@hotelnice.it).

$ Ulisse Deluxe Hostel is the best budget deal in town. This "hostel" is actually a hotel, with 56 well-equipped, marble-tiled rooms and elegant public areas, but it also has two single-sex dorm rooms with bunks (RS%, family rooms, breakfast buffet extra, air-con, elevator, spa and pool use extra, pay parking, closed Jan-mid-Feb, Via del Mare 22, tel. 081-877-4753, www.ulissedeluxe.com, info@ulissedeluxe.com, Chiara). It's a five-minute walk from the old-town action: From Corso Italia, walk down the stairs just beyond the hospital *(ospedale)* to Via del Mare. Go downhill along the right side of the big parking lot to find the entrance.

AT THE EAST END OF TOWN

$$$$ Grand Hotel Ambasciatori is a sumptuous five-star hotel with 100 rooms, a cliffside setting, a sprawling garden, and a pool. This is Humphrey Bogart land, with plush public spaces, a relaxing stay-awhile ambience, and a free elevator to its "private beach"—actually a sundeck built out over the water (RS%, some view rooms, balconies in all rooms, air-con in summer, elevator, pay parking, closed Nov-March, Via Califano 18, tel. 081-878-2025, www.

ambasciatorisorrento.com, ambasciatori@manniellohotels.com). It's a short walk from the town center (10-15 minutes from the train station or Piazza Tasso).

WITH A VIEW, ON VIA CAPO

These cliffside hotels are outside of town, toward the cape of the peninsula (from the train station, go straight out Corso Italia, which turns into Via Capo). Once you're set up, commuting into town by bus or on foot is easy. Hotel Minerva is my favorite Sorrento splurge, while Hotel Désirée is a super budget bet with comparable views. If you're in Sorrento to stay put and luxuriate, especially with a car, these accommodations are perfect (although I'd rather luxuriate in Positano).

Getting to Via Capo: From the city center, it's a gradually uphill 15-minute walk (20 minutes from train station, last part is a bit steeper), a €20 taxi ride, or a cheap bus ride. If you're arriving with luggage, you can wait at the train station for one of the long-distance SITA buses that stop on Via Capo on their way to Massa Lubrense (about every 40 minutes; some buses heading for Positano/Amalfi also work—check with the driver). Frequent Sorrento city buses leave from Piazza Tasso in the city center, a five-minute walk from the station (go down a block and turn left on Corso Italia; from far side of the piazza, look for bus #A, about 2-3/hour). Tickets for either bus are sold at the station newsstand and tobacco shops (€1.60). Get off at the Hotel Belair stop for the hotels listed here.

Getting from Via Capo into Town: Buses work great once you get the hang of them (and it's particularly gratifying to avoid the taxi racket). To reach downtown Sorrento from Via Capo, catch any bus heading downhill from Hotel Belair (2-3/hour, buses run all day and evening).

$$$$ Hotel Minerva is a sun-worshipper's temple. The road-level entrance (on a busy street) leads to an elevator that takes you to the fifth-floor reception. Getting off, you'll step onto a spectacular terrace with outrageous Mediterranean views. Bright common areas, a small rooftop swimming pool, and a cold-water Jacuzzi complement 60 large, tiled, colorful rooms with views, some with balconies (3-night peak-season minimum, air-con, pay parking, closed Nov-March, Via Capo 30, tel. 081-878-1011, www.minervasorrento.com, info@minervasorrento.com).

$$$$ Hotel La Tonnarella is an old-time Sorrentine villa-turned-boutique-hotel, with several terraces, stylish tiles, and indifferent service. Eighteen of its 24 rooms have views of the sea, and you can pay extra for a terrace (air-con, pay parking, small beach with private elevator access, closed Nov-March, Via Capo 31, tel. 081-878-1153, www.latonnarella.it, info@latonnarella.it).

$$$ Albergo Settimo Cielo ("Seventh Heaven") is an old-fashioned, family-run cliffhanger sitting 300 steps above Marina Grande. The reception is just off the waterfront side of the road, and the elevator passes down through four floors with 50 clean but spartan rooms—all with grand views, and many with balconies. The rooms feel dated for the price—you're paying for the views (family rooms, air-con in summer, parking, inviting pool, sun terrace, closed Nov-March, Via Capo 27, tel. 081-878-1012, www. hotelsettimocielo.com, info@hotelsettimocielo.com; Giuseppe, sons Stefano and Massimo, and daughter Serena).

$ Hotel Désirée is a modest affair, with reasonable rates, humbler vistas, and no traffic noise. The 22 basic rooms have high, ravine-facing or partial-sea views, and half come with balconies (all the same price). There's a fine rooftop sunning terrace and a lovable cat, Tia. Owner Corinna (a committed environmentalist), daughter Cassandra, and receptionist Antonio serve an organic breakfast and are hugely helpful with tips on exploring the peninsula (family rooms, most rooms have fans, lots of stairs and no elevator, laundry services, free parking, shares driveway and beach elevator with La Tonnarella, closed early-Nov-Feb except open at Christmas—rare for this area, Via Capo 31, tel. 081-878-1563, www. desireehotelsorrento.com, info@desireehotelsorrento.com).

Eating in Sorrento

GOURMET SPLURGES DOWNTOWN

In a town proud to have no McDonald's, consider eating well for a few extra bucks. Both of these places are worthwhile splurges run by a hands-on boss with a passion for good food and exacting service. The first is gourmet and playful. The second is classic. Both are romantic. Be prepared to relax and stay awhile.

$$$$ Ristorante il Buco, once the cellar of an old monastery, is now a small, dressy restaurant—with spacious seating—that serves delightfully presented, playful, and creative modern Mediterranean dishes under a grand, rustic arch. Peppe holds a Michelin star, and he and his staff love to explain exactly what's on the plate—often sophisticated dishes with an emphasis on seafood, but a good vegetarian selection as well. They offer lots of fine wines by the glass. Reserve ahead (extravagant-tasting €75-100 fixed-price meal, 10 percent discount when you show this book, Thu-Tue 12:30-14:30 & 19:30-22:30, closed Wed and Jan; just off Piazza Sant'Antonino—facing the basilica, go under the grand arch on the left and immediately enter the restaurant at II Rampa Marina Piccola 5; tel. 081-878-2354, www.ilbucoristorante.it).

$$$$ L'Antica Trattoria enjoys a sedate, *romantico,* candlelit ambience, tucked away in its own little world. The cuisine is traditional but with modern flair, and the inviting menu is fun to peruse (though pricey). Run by the same family since 1930, the restaurant has a trellised garden outside and intimate nooks inside. Aldo and sons will take care of you while Vincenzo—the Joe Cocker-esque resident mandolin player—entertains. Readers who show this book can choose a 10 percent discount on a fixed-price meal or a free *limoncello* if ordering à la carte. Reservations are smart (good vegetarian options, daily 12:00-23:30, closed Jan-Feb, air-con, Via Padre R. Giuliani 33, tel. 081-807-1082, www.lanticatrattoria.it).

MIDPRICED RESTAURANTS DOWNTOWN

$$$ Inn Bufalito specializes in all things buffalo: *mozzarella di bufala* (and other buffalo-milk cheeses), steak, sausage, salami, carpaccio, and buffalo-meat pasta sauce on homemade pasta. The smartly designed space has a modern, borderline-trendy, casual atmosphere and a fun indoor-outdoor vibe (don't miss the seasonal specialties on the blackboard, Wed-Mon 12:00-23:00, closed Tue and Jan-March, Vico I Fuoro 21, tel. 081-365-6975).

$$ Ristorante Pizzeria da Gigino, lively and congested with a sprawling interior and tables spilling onto the street, makes huge, tasty Neapolitan-style pizzas in their wood-burning oven. Their *linguine gigino* and the seafood salad are favorites (daily 12:00-24:00, closed Jan-Feb, just off Piazza Sant'Antonino at Via degli Archi 15, tel. 081-878-1927, Antonino).

$$ Chantecler's Trattoria is a hole-in-the-wall, family-run place with delicious food, a casual familial interior, and a long string of tables outside; it's on the narrow lane that leads to the cathedral. Their lunch menu is very affordable; at dinner, prices are slightly higher but still easy on the budget (good vegetarian dishes, take out or eat in, Tue-Sun 12:00-15:00 & 18:30-23:00, closed Mon, Via Santa Maria della Pietà 38, tel. 081-807-5868; Luigi, Francesco, and family).

With a Sea View: $$$ The **Foreigners' Club Restaurant** has some of the best sea views in town (with a sprawling terrace under breezy palms), live music nightly at 20:00 (May-mid-Oct), and affordable—if uninspired—meals. It's a good spot for dessert or an after-dinner *limoncello* ("snack" menu with light meals, daily, bar opens at 9:30, meals served 11:00-23:00, Via Luigi de Maio 35, tel. 081-877-3263). If you'd enjoy eating along the water (rather than just with a water view), see "Harborside in Marina Grande," later.

CHEAP EATS DOWNTOWN

Pizza: $ Pizzeria da Franco is Sorrento's favorite place for basic, casual pizza in a fun, untouristy atmosphere. There's nothing fancy about this place—just locals on benches eating hot sandwiches and great pizzas served on waxed paper in a square tin. It's packed to the rafters with a youthful crowd that doesn't mind the plastic cups. Consider their *saltimbocca,* a baked sandwich with top-quality prosciutto and mozzarella on pizza bread—splittable and perfect to-go (daily 8:00-late, just across from Lemon Grove Garden on busy Corso Italia at #265, tel. 081-877-2066).

Kebabs: $ Kebab Ciampa, a little hole-in-the-wall, has a passionate following among eaters who appreciate Andrea's fresh bread, homemade sauces, and ethic of buying meat fresh each day (and closing when the supply is gone). This is your best cheap, non-Italian meal in town. Choose beef or chicken—locals don't go for pork—and garnish with fries and/or salad (Thu-Tue from 17:00, closed Wed, before the cathedral off Via Santa Maria della Pietà, at Vico il Traversa Pietà 23, tel. 081-807-4595).

Picnics: Get groceries at the **Decò** supermarket (Mon-Sat 8:30-20:00, shorter hours Sun, Corso Italia 223) or at the **Carrefour** supermarket underneath Hotel Mignon (daily 8:00-22:00).

Gelato: Near the train station, **Gelateria David** has many repeat customers (so many flavors, so little time; they make 155 different flavors, but have about 30 at any one time). In 1957, Augusto Davide opened a *gelateria* in Sorrento, and his grandson Mario proudly carries on the tradition today, still making the gelato on-site. Before choosing a flavor, sample *Profumi di Sorrento* (an explosive sorbet of mixed fruits), "Sorrento moon" (white almond with lemon zest), or lemon crème (daily 9:00-24:00, shorter hours off-season, closed Dec-Feb, a block below the train station at Via Marziale 19, tel. 081-807-3649). Mario also offers gelato-making classes (€12/person, 5-person minimum, 1 hour, call or email ahead to reserve, www.gelateriadavidsorrento.it, info@gelateriadavidsorrento.it). Don't mistake this place for the similarly named Gelateria Davide, in the town center.

At **Gelateria Primavera,** Antonio and Alberta whip up 70 exotic flavors...and still have time to make pastries for the pope and other celebrities—check out the nostalgic photos in their inviting back room, proving this is a Sorrento institution (daily 9:00-24:00, just west of Piazza Tasso at Corso Italia 142, tel. 081-807-3252).

HARBORSIDE IN MARINA GRANDE

For a decent dinner *con vista,* head down to either of these restaurants by Sorrento's small-boat harbor, Marina Grande. To get to Marina Grande, follow the directions from Villa Comunale on my self-guided Sorrento walk, earlier. It's about a 15-minute stroll from downtown. You can also take minibus #D from Piazza Tasso. Be prepared to walk back (last bus leaves at 20:00) or spring for a pricey taxi.

$$$ Ristorante Delfino serves fish in big portions to hungry locals in a quiet and bright, Seattle-style pier restaurant. The cooking, service, and setting are all top-notch. The restaurant is lovingly run by Luisa, her brothers, Andrea and Roberto, and her husband/chef, Antonio. Show this book for a free glass of *limoncello* to cap the meal. If you're here for lunch, take advantage of the sundeck—travelers with this book are welcome to relax and digest on the lounge chairs for free (daily 12:00-14:30 & 18:30-21:30, closed Nov-March, reservations recommended for dinner; at Marina Grande, facing the water, go all the way to the left and follow signs; tel. 081-878-2038).

$$ Trattoria da Emilia, at the opposite end of the tranquil Marina Grande waterfront, is considerably more rustic, less expensive, and good for straightforward, typical Sorrentine home-cooking, including fresh fish, lots of fried seafood, and *gnocchi di mamma*—potato dumplings with meat sauce, basil, and mozzarella (daily 12:00-15:00 & 19:00-22:30, closed Nov-Feb, no reservations taken, indoor and outdoor seating, tel. 081-807-2720).

Sorrento Connections

It's impressively fast to zip by boat from Sorrento to many coastal towns and islands during the summer—in fact, it's quicker and easier for residents to get around by fast boat than by car or train (see "By Boat," later).

BY TRAIN AND BUS

From Sorrento to Naples, Pompeii, and Herculaneum by Circumvesuviana Train: This commuter train runs twice hourly between Naples and Sorrento (www.eavsrl.it). The schedule is available at the TI: Pompeii (30 minutes, €2.20); Herculaneum (50 minutes, €2.70); and Naples (70 minutes, €3.60). If there's a line at the train station, you can also buy tickets at the snack bar (across from the main ticket office) or downstairs at the newsstand. To confirm the latest departures, look for the electric schedule above the ticket window. Note that the risk of theft on this train is mostly limited to suburban Naples. Going between Sorrento and Pompeii or Herculaneum is generally safer.

From Sorrento to Naples Airport: Six Curreri buses run daily to the airport (€10, pay driver, daily at 6:30, 8:30, 10:30, 12:00, 14:00, and 16:30, likely 2 additional departures in summer, 1.5 hours, departs from in front of train station, tel. 081-801-5420, www.curreriviaggi.it). From Naples Airport to Sorrento, the bus departs at 9:00, 11:00, 12:00, 13:00, 14:30, 16:30, 18:00, and 19:30.

From Sorrento to Rome: Most people ride the Circumvesuviana 70 minutes to Naples, then catch the Frecciarossa or Italo express train to Rome. Another option is the Sorrento-Rome bus: It's direct, comfortable, cheaper, and all on one ticket—although the departure times can be inconvenient (Mon-Sat at 6:00 and 17:00, Sun at 17:00; off-season Mon-Sat at 6:00, Fri-Sun at 17:00; 4 hours; departs Sorrento from Corso Italia 259B, by Bar Kontatto, a block from the train station, and runs to Tiburtina bus station in Rome; buy tickets at www.marozzivt.it—in Italian only, at some travel agencies, or on board for a surcharge; tel. 080-579-0111).

BY BOAT

The number of boats that run per day varies: The frequency indicated here is for roughly mid-May through mid-October, with more boats per day in the peak of summer and fewer off-season. The specific companies operating each route also tend to change from season to season. Check all schedules locally with the TI, your hotel, or online (use the individual boat-company websites—see below—or visit www.capritourism.com, select English, and click "Shipping timetable"). Although some ferry-company websites sell tickets online, for ease, and to keep your departure options open, you can always buy tickets at the port (especially if you're watching the weather); next-day tickets typically go on sale starting the evening before. All boats take several hundred people each and (except for the busiest days) rarely fill up.

From Sorrento to Capri: Boats run at least hourly. Your options are a fast **ferry** (*traghetto* or *nave veloce*, takes cars, 4/day, 30 minutes, Caremar, tel. 081-807-3077, www.caremar.it) or a slightly faster and pricier **hydrofoil** (*aliscafi*, up to 20/day, 20 minutes, Gescab, tel. 081-807-1812, www.gescab.it). To visit Capri when it's least crowded, it's best to buy your ticket at 8:00 and take the 8:30 hydrofoil (try to depart by 9:45 at the very latest). If you make a reservation, it's not changeable. These early boats can be jammed, but it's worth it once you reach the island.

From Sorrento to Other Points: Naples (6/day, more in summer, departs roughly every 2 hours starting at 7:20, few or no boats on winter weekends, arrives at Molo Beverello, 35 minutes), **Positano** (mid-April-mid-Oct only, 4-6/day, 35 minutes), **Amalfi** (mid-April-mid-Oct only, 4-6/day, 1 hour).

Getting to Sorrento's Port (Marina Piccola): To walk, either hike steeply down directly from Piazza Tasso (find the stairs under the flags, 5-minute walk), or walk to the Villa Comunale public park (see my self-guided Sorrento Walk, earlier), where you can pay €1 to ride the elevator down (from the bottom, it's a 5-minute walk to the port). Otherwise, catch bus #B or #C from Piazza Sant'Antonino (buy ticket at tobacco shop and specify that you're going to the *porto;* pay driver, buses cost €1.20 and run 3/hour).

Capri

Capri was made famous as the vacation hideaway of Roman emperors Augustus and Tiberius. In the 19th century, it was the haunt of

Romantic Age aristocrats on their Grand Tour of Europe. Later it was briefly a refuge for Europe's artsy gay community: Oscar Wilde, D. H. Lawrence, and company hung out here back when being gay could land you in jail...or worse. And these days, the island is a world-class tourist trap, packed with gawky, nametag-wearing visitors searching for the rich and famous—and finding only their prices.

About 12,000 people live on Capri (although many winter in Naples) and during any given day in high season, the island hosts another 20,000 tourists. The "Island of Dreams" is a zoo in July and August—overrun with tacky, low-grade group tourism at its worst. At other times of year, though still crowded, it can provide a relaxing and scenic break from the cultural gauntlet of Italy. Even with its crowds, commercialism, fame, and glitz, Capri is a flat-out gorgeous place: Chalky white limestone cliffs rocket boldly from the shimmering blue-and-green surf, and the Blue Grotto sea cave glows with reflected sunlight. Strategically positioned gardens, villas, and viewpoints provide stunning vistas of the Sorrento Peninsula, Amalfi Coast, Vesuvius, and Capri itself. And, if you study this chapter carefully, you'll find that it's very well-organized for its many visitors.

PLANNING YOUR TIME

This is the best see-everything-in-a-day plan from Naples or Sorrento:

- Take an early hydrofoil to Capri (from Sorrento, buy ticket at 8:00, boat leaves around 8:30 and arrives around 8:50—smart).
- At the port, decide among three boating options: Enjoy the scenic circle-the-island tour with a visit to the Blue Grotto (1.5-2 hours); circle the island without Blue Grotto stop (1 hour); or just visit the Blue Grotto. (There are generally spaces available for departures every few minutes.)
- Arriving back at Marina Grande, catch a bus to Anacapri, which has two or three hours' worth of sightseeing.
- In Anacapri, see the town, ride the chairlift to Monte Solaro

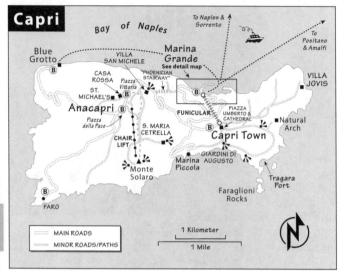

and back (or hike down), stroll out from the base of the chair-lift to Villa San Michele for the view, and eat lunch.

- Afterward, catch a bus to Capri town, which is worth an hour of browsing.
- Finally, ride the funicular from Capri town down to the harbor and laze on the free beach or wander the yacht harbor while waiting for your boat back to Sorrento.

If you're heading to Capri specifically to see the Blue Grotto, be sure to check the weather and sea conditions. If the tide is too high or the water too rough, the grotto can be closed. Ask the TI or your hotelier. If the Blue Grotto is closed or you're not keen on seeing it, you can still enjoy a leisurely day on the island seeing the sights in Anacapri and Capri town. Or, for the same amount of time and less money, you can skip the Blue Grotto and enjoy circling the entire island by boat (an experience I find even more fun than the famed grotto).

Efficient travelers can see Capri on the way between destinations: Sail from Sorrento, check your bag at the harbor, see Capri, and take a boat directly from there to Naples or to the Amalfi Coast (or vice versa).

If you buy a one-way ticket to Capri (there's no round-trip discount), you'll have maximum schedule flexibility and can take any convenient hydrofoil or ferry back. (Check times for the last return crossing upon arrival with any TI on Capri, or at www.capritourism.com; the last return trips usually leave between 18:30 and 19:30.) During July and August, however, it's wise to get a round-trip boat ticket (ensuring you a spot). On busy days, be 20 minutes early for the boat, or you can be bumped.

Starting your day as early as is reasonably possible is key to an enjoyable trip to Capri. Legions of day-trippers on big bus tours come down from as far as Rome, combining with cruise-ship excursion groups to create a daily rush hour in each direction (arriving between 10:00-11:00, leaving around 17:00) and packing the island through the early afternoon. If you arrive before them, the entire trip to and into the Blue Grotto might take just a half-hour (10 minutes there, 10 minutes in the dingy going inside, and 10 minutes back); arrive later and you might face a two-hour delay.

GETTING TO CAPRI

For instructions on getting to Capri by **scheduled ferry,** see the "Connections" sections of the Sorrento and Naples chapters, and the "Getting Around the Amalfi Coast" section of the Amalfi Coast chapter.

Another option is to visit Capri by **tour boat. Mondo Guide** offers my readers a great-value, no-stress, all-day itinerary for €90: You'll be picked up at your Sorrento hotel around 8:00 and driven to the port, where you'll board a small boat (maximum 12 people, shared with other Rick Steves readers) and be taken across to Capri to visit the Blue Grotto (optional entry fee to hop in one of the little rowboats to go in). Then you'll continue to Marina Grande for about four hours of free time on the island—just enough to head to Anacapri for sightseeing and the Monte Solaro chairlift (island transportation and admissions on your own). Finally, you'll reboard the boat for a lightly narrated circle around the island and pass through the iconic Faraglioni Rocks (includes drinks, a snack, and—conditions permitting—a chance to swim from the boat). Considering the expense and hassle of doing all this on your own, the tour is a good value—you're basically paying about €20-30 extra for a less stressful, more personalized experience. The trip only goes if enough people sign up, and reservations are required—book online at www.mondoguide.com. **Tempio Travel**—based at the Sorrento train station—offers a similar trip at a similar price (tel. 081-878-2103, www.tempiotravel.com, or drop by their office).

Orientation to Capri

First thing—pronounce it right: Italians say KAH-pree, not kah-PREE like the song (or the pants). The island is small—just four miles by two miles—and is separated from the Sorrentine Peninsula by a five-mile-wide strait. Home to 12,000 people, Capri has only two towns to speak of: Capri and Anacapri. The island also has some scant Roman ruins and a few interesting churches and villas. But its chief attraction is its famous Blue Grotto, and its best activity beyond the boat rides is the chairlift from Anacapri up the island's Monte Solaro ("the sunny mount").

TOURIST INFORMATION

Capri's efficient English-speaking TI has branches in Marina Grande, Capri town, and Anacapri. Their well-organized website has schedules and practical information in English (www.capritourism.com). At any TI, pick up the free map or pay for a better one if you'll be venturing to the outskirts of Capri town or Anacapri.

The **Marina Grande TI** is by the Motoscafisti Capri tourboat dock (Mon-Sat 9:00-13:30 & 15:30-18:00, Sun 9:00-13:00, shorter hours off-season, tel. 081-837-0634).

The **Capri town TI** fills a closet under the bell tower on Piazza Umberto I and is less crowded than its sister at the port (same hours as Marina Grande TI, WC and baggage storage downstairs behind TI, tel. 081-837-0686).

The tiny **Anacapri TI** is on the main pedestrian/shopping street, Via Orlandi, at #59 (Mon-Sat 9:00-15:00, closed Sun, shorter hours Nov-Easter, tel. 081-837-1524).

ARRIVAL IN CAPRI

Get oriented on the boat before you dock, as you near the harbor with the island spread out before you. The port is a small community of its own, called **Marina Grande,** connected by a funicular and buses to the rest of the island. **Capri town** fills the ridge high above the harbor. The ruins of Emperor Tiberius' palace, **Villa Jovis,** cap the peak on the left. To the right, the dramatic *"Mamma mia!"* road arcs around the highest mountain on the island **(Monte Solaro),** leading up to **Anacapri** (the island's second town, just out of sight). Notice the old zigzag steps below that road. Until 1874, this was the only connection between Capri and Anacapri. (Though it's quite old, it's nowhere near as old as implied by its nickname, "The Phoenician Stairway.") The white house on the ridge above the zigzags is **Villa San Michele** (where you can go later for a grand view).

Arrival at Marina Grande: Upon arrival, get your bearings. Find the base of the **funicular railway** (signed *funicolare*) that runs up to Capri town, and stand facing it, with your back to the water.

The fourth little clothing-and-souvenir shop to the right of the funicular provides **baggage storage** (€3/bag, look inside for *left luggage* sign on far back wall, daily 9:00-18:00, tel. 081-837-4575, shorter hours or closed in winter).

The ferry-terminal building facing the funicular has ticket

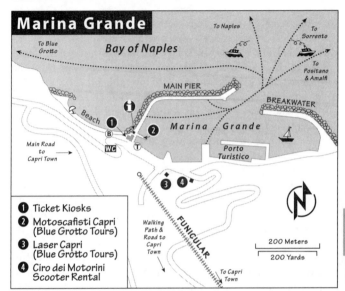

Marina Grande

To Naples

To Sorrento

To Blue Grotto

Bay of Naples

To Positano & Amalfi

MAIN PIER

BREAKWATER

Beach

Marina Grande

Main Road to Capri Town

Porto Turistico

WC

T

B

1

2

3 **4**

Walking Path & Road to Capri Town

FUNICULAR

To Capri Town

N

1 Ticket Kiosks

2 Motoscafisti Capri (Blue Grotto Tours)

3 Laser Capri (Blue Grotto Tours)

4 Ciro dei Motorini Scooter Rental

200 Meters

200 Yards

SORRENTO & CAPRI

windows with counters for **funicular and bus tickets** (same price for both—don't line up without one) and for **boat tickets** to Naples and Sorrento. (Notice the grand electronic departure board on the terminal building listing all boats leaving in the next couple of hours.) Adjacent is the **stop for buses** to the rest of the island. Notice how long the line is for your destination, and how small the buses are—and line up accordingly: to Anacapri or San Costanzo (for Capri town). Across the street is a pay **WC,** and a little farther on is Marina Grande's pebbly public beach.

Two companies offer **boat trips** around the island and to the Blue Grotto: **Laser Capri** and **Motoscafisti Capri.** Motoscafisti Capri's ticket shed is along the pier; Laser Capri's office is halfway down the waterfront to the left at Via Cristoforo Colombo 69. Both offer similar services (see "Sights in Capri," later).

From the port, you can take a boat to the Blue Grotto or around the island, the funicular to Capri town, or a bus to various destinations on Capri. The steep paved footpath that connects the port area with Capri town starts a block inland from the ferry dock (follow the signs to *Capri centro;* I've heard it takes 30 minutes).

HELPFUL HINTS

Cheap Tricks: A cheap day trip to Capri is tough, as you'll pay about €20 each way just to get there and about €30 to see the Blue Grotto. That's €70 already. But if you picnic and ride buses rather than enjoying restaurants and taxis, you'll find your time on the island itself to be relatively inexpensive. Many of Capri's greatest pleasures are free.

Best Real Hike: Serious hikers love the peaceful and scenic three-hour Fortress Hike, which takes you entirely away from the tourists. You'll walk under ruined forts along the rugged coast, from the Blue Grotto to the *faro* (lighthouse). From there, you can take a bus back to Anacapri (3/hour). The TI has a fine map/brochure.

Free Beach: Marina Grande has a free pebbly beach (pay at the bar for a shower).

Local Guides: Anna Bilardi Leva lives on Capri and is licensed to guide both on the island and elsewhere around the region. She seems to know everybody and every trick on the island (groups of up to six people: €150/half-day, €220/day, mobile 339-712-7416, www.capritourinformation.com, annaleva@hotmail.it).

GETTING AROUND CAPRI

By Bus and Funicular: Tickets for the island's buses and funicular cost €2 per ride and are available at newsstands, tobacco shops, or official ticket offices. Validate your ticket when you board. The €10 all-day pass (available only at official ticket offices) isn't a good value for most visitors.

Schedules are clearly posted at all bus stations. Public buses are orange, while gray and blue buses are for private tour groups. Public buses from the port to Capri town, and from Capri town to Anacapri, are frequent (4/hour, 10 minutes). The direct bus between the port and Anacapri runs less often (2/hour, 25 minutes). From Anacapri, branch bus lines run to the parking lot above the Blue Grotto and to the lighthouse (3/hour). Buses are teeny (because of the island's narrow roads) and often packed, the aisles filled with people standing. At most stops, you'll see ranks for passengers to line up in (locals feel free to cut the line). If the driver changes the bus's display to read *completo* (full), you'll need to wait for the next one.

By Taxi: Taxis have fixed rates, listed at www.capritourism. com (Marina Grande to Capri town-€17; Marina Grande to Anacapri-€28). You can hire a taxi for about €70 per hour—negotiate.

By Scooter: If you're an experienced scooter rider, this is the perfect way to have the run of the island. (For novice riders, Capri's steep and narrow roads aren't a good place to start.) **Capri Scooter** proudly rents bright-yellow scooters with 50cc engines—strong enough to haul couples. Rental includes a map and instructions with parking tips and other helpful information (€15/hour, €55/day, 10 percent discount with this book for 2 hours or more; includes helmet, gas, and insurance; daily April-Oct 9:30-18:00, may open in good weather off-season, at Via Don Giobbe Ruocco 55, Marina Grande, mobile 338-360-6918, www.capriscooter.com).

Sights in Capri

ON THE WATER

You have three boat-tour options: circle the island with a stop at the Blue Grotto, circle only, or Blue Grotto only.

▲▲▲Capri Boat Circle (Giro dell'Isola)

For me, the best experience on Capri is to take the scenic boat trip around the island. It's cheap, comes with good narration and lots of curiosities, and there are plenty of departures from Marina Grande.

Both **Laser Capri** and **Motoscafisti Capri** run trips that circle the island and pass stunning cliffs, caves, and views that most miss when they go only to the Blue Grotto (€18, no one-way discount; Motoscafisti Capri—tel. 081-837-7714, www.motoscafisticapri.com; Laser Capri—tel. 081-837-5208, www.lasercapri.com). The circular tour comes with a live guide and takes about an hour (1.5-2 hours with Blue Grotto stop). As you circle the dramatic limestone rock called Capri, you'll see quirky sights (a solar-powered lighthouse, tiny statues atop desolate rocks, holes in the cliffs with legends going back to Emperor Tiberius' times), pop into various caves and inlets, power through a tiny hole in the famed Faraglioni Rocks, hear stories of celebrity-owned villas, and marvel at a non-stop parade of staggering cliffs.

With both companies, you can combine the boat trip with a stop at the Blue Grotto at no extra charge (this adds about an hour; check schedules to find out which tours include the optional Blue Grotto stop). As the 10-minute ride just to the grotto costs €15 (no one-way discount), the island circle is well worth the extra three euros.

All boats leave daily from 9:00 until at least 13:00 (or later, depending on when the Blue Grotto rowboats stop running—likely 16:00 in summer).

▲▲Blue Grotto

Three thousand tourists a day visit Capri's Blue Grotto (Grotta Azzurra). I did—early (when the light is best), without the frustration of crowds, and with choppy waves nearly making entrance impossible...and it was great.

The actual cave experience isn't much: a five-minute dinghy ride through a three-foot-high entry hole to reach a 60-yard-long cave, where the sun reflects brilliantly blue on its limestone bottom. But the experience—getting there, getting in, and getting back—is a scenic hoot. You get a fast ride and scant narration on a 30-foot boat partway around the gorgeous island; along the way, you see bird life and dramatic limestone cliffs. You'll understand why Roman emperors appreciated the invulnerability of the island—it's surrounded by cliffs, with only one good access point, and therefore easy to defend.

Just outside the grotto, your boat idles as you pile into eight-foot dinghies that hold up to four passengers each. Next, you'll be taken to a floating ticket counter to pay the grotto entry fee. From there, your ruffian rower will elbow his way to the tiny hole, then pull fast and hard on the cable at the low point of the swells to squeeze you into the grotto (keep your head down and hands in the boat). Then your man rows you around, spouting off a few descriptive lines and singing "O Sole Mio." Depending upon the strength of the sunshine that day, the blue light inside can be brilliant.

The grotto was actually an ancient Roman *nymphaeum*—a retreat for romantic hanky-panky. Many believe that, in its day, a tunnel led here directly from the palace, and that the grotto experience was enlivened by statues of Poseidon and company, placed half-underwater as if emerging from the sea. It was ancient Romans who smoothed out the entry hole that's still used to this day.

When dropping you off, your boatman will fish for a tip—it's optional, and €1 is enough (you've already paid plenty). If you don't want to return by boat, ask to be let off at the little dock, where stairs lead up to a café and the Blue Grotto bus stop.

Cost: The €14 entry fee (separate from the €15 ride from Marina Grande and back) includes €10 for the rowboat service plus €4 for admission to the grotto itself. Though some people swim in for free from the little dock after the boats stop running (about 17:00), it's illegal and can be dangerous.

Timing: When waves or high tide make entering dangerous, the boats don't go in—the grotto can close without notice, sending tourists (flush with anticipation) home without a chance to squeeze through the little hole. (If this happens to you, consider the one-hour boat ride around the island instead.)

If you're coming from Capri's port (Marina Grande), allow 1-2 hours for the entire visit, depending on the chaos at the caves. Going with the first trip (around 9:00) will get you there at the same time as the boatmen in their dinghies—who hitch a ride behind your boat—resulting in less chaos and a shorter wait at the entry point.

If you arrive on the island later in the morning—when the Blue Grotto is already jammed—you could try waiting to visit until about 15:00, when most of the tour groups have vacated. But this may only work by bus (not boat). Confirm that day's closing time with a TI before making the trip.

Getting There: You can take the **boat** from Marina Grande (either as part of a longer circle-the-island tour-€18, or directly-€15, 10 minutes; see details on both options earlier), as most people do, or save money by taking the **bus** via Anacapri. You'll save almost €8, lose time, and see a beautiful, calmer side of the island (roughly 3/hour, 10 minutes; buses depart only from the Anacapri bus station at Piazza della Pace—not from the bus stop at Piazza Vittoria 200 yards away). If you're coming from Marina Grande or Capri town and want to transfer to the Blue Grotto buses, don't get off when the driver announces "Anacapri." Instead, ride one more stop to Piazza della Pace. If in doubt, ask the driver or a local. At the Piazza della Pace bus station, notice the two lines: "Grotta Azzurra" for the Blue Grotto, and "Faro" for the lighthouse.

Getting Back from the Blue Grotto: You can take the boat back or ask your boatman to drop you off on the small dock next to the grotto entrance (for a small tip), from where you climb up the stairs to the stop for the bus to Anacapri (if you came by boat, you'll still have to pay the full round-trip boat fare).

CAPRI TOWN AND NEARBY

This is a cute but extremely clogged and touristy shopping town. It's worth a brief visit, including the Giardini di Augusto, before moving on to more interesting parts of the island.

Piazza Umberto I

The funicular drops you just around the corner from Piazza Umberto I, the town's main square. With your back to the funicular, the bus stop is 50 yards straight ahead down Via Roma. The **TI** is under the bell tower on Piazza Umberto (see "Tourist Information," earlier). The footpath to the port starts just behind the TI (follow signs to *Il Porto*, 15-minute walk).

Capri town's main square is dedicated to the second king of Italy. Enjoy what's considered the "Living Room of Capri." Imagine the days when, rather than fancy cafés, the square was filled with a public market. Today, Capri town is traffic-free with only electric service minitrucks scooting here and there. While a coffee costs €1 at any bar, it's €5 at a table on the square.

To the left of City Hall (Municipio, lowest corner), a narrow, atmospheric lane leads into the medieval part of town, which has plenty of eateries and is the starting point for the 45-minute hike to Villa Jovis.

Cathedral

Capri town's multidomed Baroque cathedral, which faces the square, is worth a quick look. Its multicolored marble floor at the altar dates from the 1st century A.D.—it was scavenged from Emperor Tiberius' villa and laid here in the 19th century.

"Rodeo Drive"

The lane to the left of the cathedral (past Bar Tiberio, under the wide arch) is a fashionable shopping strip that's justifiably been dubbed "Rodeo Drive" by residents.  Walk a few minutes down the street (past Gelateria Buonocore at #35, with its tempting fresh waffle cones— you'll smell them as you approach) to Quisisana Hotel, the island's top old-time hotel (formerly a 19th-century sanitorium). From there, head left for fancy shops and villas, and right for gardens and views. Between the lane and the sea is a huge monastery (Certosa di San Giacomo, described below; access to the left).

Giardini di Augusto

To the right and downhill, a five-minute walk leads to this lovely public garden (€1, daily 9:00-19:30, Nov-March until 17:30, free to enter off-season, no picnicking). While the garden itself is modest, it boasts great views over the famous Faraglioni Rocks—handy if you don't have the time, money, or interest to access the higher vantage points near Anacapri (Monte Solaro, Villa San Michele).

Monastery of San Giacomo

One of the most historic buildings on the island is the Certosa di San Giacomo (€4, €3 combo-ticket with Giardini di Augusto at the garden entry, Tue-Sun 10:00-17:00, later in summer, closed Mon). The stark monastery has an empty church and sleepy cloister. But the finest piece of art on Capri is over the church's front entrance: an exquisite 14th-century fresco of Mary and the baby Jesus by the Florentine Niccolo di Tommaso. Today, the monastery hosts the **Museo Diefenbach,** a small collection of dark and moody paintings by eccentric German artist Karl Wilhelm Diefenbach, who walked around naked in Capri in the early 1900s, when this was a gay, political, and avant-garde place.

Villa Jovis and the Emperor's Capri

Even before becoming emperor, Augustus loved Capri so much that he traded the family-owned Isle of Ischia to the (then-independent) Neapolitans in exchange for making Capri his personal property. Emperor Tiberius spent a decade here, A.D. 26-37. (Some figure he did so in order to escape being assassinated in Rome.)

Emperor Tiberius' ruined villa, Villa Jovis, is reachable only by a scenic 45-minute hike from Capri town. You won't find any statues or mosaics here—just an evocative, ruined complex of terraces clinging to a rocky perch over a sheer drop to the sea...and a lovely view. You can make out a large water reservoir for baths, the foundations of servants' quarters, and Tiberius' private apartments (fragments of marble flooring still survive). The ruined lighthouse dates from the Middle Ages.

Cost and Hours: €4, Wed-Mon 10:00-18:00, closed Tue, shorter hours and closed off-season—check at Capri TI.

ANACAPRI TOWN AND NEARBY

Capri's second town has two or three hours' worth of interesting sights. Though Anacapri sits higher up on the island ("ana" means "upper" in Greek), there are no sea views at street level in the town center.

When visiting Anacapri by bus, note that there are two stops: Piazza Vittoria, in the center of town at the base of the Monte Solaro chairlift; and 200 yards farther along at Piazza della Pace (pronounced "PAH-chay"), a larger bus station near the cemetery. Piazza Vittoria gets you closer to the main sights (chairlift and Villa San Michele), while Piazza della Pace is where you transfer to the Blue Grotto bus. When leaving Anacapri for Capri town or Marina Grande (marked *San Costanzo*), buses can be packed. Your best chance of getting a seat is to catch the bus from Piazza della Pace (the first stop).

Via Orlandi

Anacapri's pedestrianized main drag takes you through the charming center of town. It's just a block or so from either bus stop. (From Piazza Vittoria, the street is right there—just go down the lane to the right of the Anacapri statue. From Piazza della Pace, cross the street and go down the small pedestrian lane called Via Filietto.) Anacapri's **TI** is at Via Orlandi 59, near Piazza Vittoria.

To see the town, stroll along Via Orlandi for 10 minutes or so. Signs propose a quick circuit that links the Casa Rossa, St. Michael's Church, and peaceful side streets. You'll also find shops and eateries, including good choices for quick, inexpensive pizza, *saltimbocca* (prosciutto and mozzarella on baked pizza bread—great for a filling picnic), *panini,* and other goodies. These two are both open daily in peak season: **$ Sciué Sciué** (same price for informal seating or takeaway, 50 yards below the TI at #73, tel. 081-837-2068) and **$ Pizza e Pasta** (takeaway only, just before the church at #157, tel. 328-623-8460).

Of the sights below, the first two are in the heart of town (on or near Via Orlandi), while the next two are a short walk away.

Casa Rossa (Red House)

This "Pompeiian-red," eccentric home, a hodgepodge of architectural styles, is the former residence of John Clay MacKowen, a Louisiana doctor and ex-Confederate officer who moved to Capri in the 1870s and married a local girl. (MacKowen and the Villa San Michele's Axel Munthe—see later—loathed each other, and even tried to challenge each other to a duel.) Its small collection of 19th-century paintings of scenes from around the island recalls a time before mass tourism. Don't miss the second floor, with more paintings and four ancient, sea-worn statues, which were recovered from the depths of the Blue Grotto in the 1960s and 1970s.

Cost and Hours: €3.50; discounted to €1 with ticket stub from Blue Grotto, Villa San Michele, or Monte Solaro chairlift; Tue-Sun 10:00-13:30 & 17:30-20:00; shorter hours April-May and Oct; closed Nov-March and Mon year-round, Via Orlandi 78, tel. 081-838-2193.

▲Church of San Michele

This Baroque church in the village center has a remarkable majolica floor showing paradise on earth in a classic 18th-century Neapolitan style. The entire floor is ornately tiled, featuring an angel (with flaming sword) driving Adam and Eve from paradise. The devil is wrapped around the trunk of a beautiful tree. The animals—happily ignoring this momentous event—all have human expressions. For the best view, climb the spiral stairs from the postcard desk. Services are held only during the first two weeks of Advent, when the church is closed to visitors.

Cost and Hours: €2, daily 9:00-19:00, Nov and mid-Dec-March usually 10:00-14:00, closed late-Nov-mid-Dec, in town center just off Via Orlandi—look for *San Michele* signs, tel. 081-837-2396, www.chiesa-san-michele.com.

▲Villa San Michele and Grand Capri View

This is the 19th-century mansion of Axel Munthe, Capri's grand personality, an idealistic Swedish doctor who lived here until

1946 and whose services to the Swedish royal family brought him into contact with high society. Munthe was gay at a time when that could land you in jail. He enjoyed the avant-garde and permissive scene at Capri, during an era when Europe's leading artists and creative figures could gather here and be honest about their sexual orientation.

At the very least, walk the path from Piazza Vittoria past the villa to a superb, free viewpoint over Capri town, Marina Grande, and—in the distance—Mount Vesuvius and Sorrento. Paying to enter the villa lets you see a few rooms with period furnishings (follow the one-way route, good English descriptions); an exhibit on Munthe; and one of this region's most delightful gardens, with a chapel, the Olivetum (a tiny museum of native birds and bugs), and a view that's slightly better than the free one outside. Throughout the gardens and the house, you'll see a smattering of original ancient objects unearthed here—and lots and lots of copies. A café (also with a view) serves affordable sandwiches.

Cost and Hours: €8, daily 9:00-18:00, closes earlier Oct-April, tel. 081-837-1401, www.villasanmichele.eu.

Getting There: From Piazza Vittoria, walk up the grand staircase and turn left onto Via Capodimonte. At the start of the shopping street, on your right, pass the deluxe Capri Palace Hotel—venture in if you can get past the treacherously eye-catching swimming pool windows (behind the pillars). After lots of overpriced shops, just before the villa, notice the Swedish consulate. In honor of Munthe, Swedes get into the villa for free.

▲▲Chairlift up to Monte Solaro

From Anacapri, you can ride the chairlift *(seggiovia)* to the 1,900-foot summit of Monte Solaro for a commanding view of the Bay of Naples. Work on your tan as you float over hazelnut, walnut, chestnut, apricot, peach, kiwi, and fig trees, past a montage of tourists (mostly from cruise ships; when the grotto is closed—as it often is—they bring passengers here instead). Prospective smoochers should know

that the lift seats are all single. As you ascend, consider how Capri's real estate has been priced out of the locals' reach. The ride takes 13 minutes each way, and you'll want at least 30 minutes on top, where there are picnic benches and a café with WCs.

Cost and Hours: €8 one-way, €11 round-trip, daily 9:30-17:00, last run down at 17:30; March-April until 16:00, Nov-Feb until 15:30, tel. 081-837-1438, www.capriseggiovia.it. Note that the lift gets more crowded with tour groups in the afternoon.

Getting There: From the Piazza Vittoria bus stop, just climb the steps and look right.

At the Summit: You'll enjoy the best panorama possible: lush cliffs busy with seagulls enjoying the ideal nesting spot. Find the Faraglioni Rocks—with tour boats squeezing through every few minutes—which are an icon of the island. The pink building nearest the rocks was an American R&R base during World War II. Eisenhower and Churchill met here. On the peak closest to Cape Sorrento, you can see the distant ruins of Emperor Tiberius' palace, Villa Jovis. Pipes from the Sorrento Peninsula bring water to Capri (demand for fresh water here long ago exceeded the supply provided by the island's three natural springs). The Galli Islands mark the Amalfi Coast in the distance. Cross the bar terrace for views of Mount Vesuvius and Naples.

Hiking Down: A highlight for hardy walkers (provided you have strong knees and good shoes) is the 40-minute down-hill hike from the top of Monte Solaro, through lush vegetation and ever-changing views, past the 14th-century Chapel of Santa Maria Cetrella (at the trail's only intersection, it's a 10-minute detour to the right), and back into Anacapri. The trail starts downstairs, past the WCs

(last chance). Down two more flights of stairs, look for the sign to *Anacapri e Cetrella*—you're on your way. While the trail is well established, you'll encounter plenty of uneven steps, loose rocks, and few signs.

Lighthouse near Anacapri

The lighthouse *(faro)*, at the rocky, arid, and desolate southwestern corner of the island, is a favorite place to enjoy the sunset. This area has a private beach, pool, small restaurants, and a few fishermen. Reach it by bus from Anacapri (3/hour, departs from Piazza della Pace stop).

Capri Connections

From Capri's Marina Grande by Boat to: Sorrento (ferry: 4/day, 30 minutes, www.caremar.it; hydrofoil: up to 20/day, 20 minutes, www.gescab.it), **Naples** (roughly hourly, more in summer, hydrofoil: 45 minutes, arrives at Molo Beverello; ferries: 50-80 minutes, arrive at Calata Porta di Massa), **Positano** (mid-April-mid-Oct, 4-6/day, 30-60 minutes), **Amalfi** (mid-April-mid-Oct, 4-6/day, 1.5 hours). Confirm the schedule carefully at TIs or www.capritourism.com (under "Shipping Timetable")—the last boats back to the mainland usually leave around 18:00-20:00. For a steep price, you can always hire a water taxi (weather permitting).

AMALFI COAST & PAESTUM

With its stunning scenery, hill- and harbor-hugging towns, and historic ruins, Amalfi is Italy's coast with the most. The breathtaking trip from Sorrento to Salerno is one of the world's great bus or taxi rides. It will leave your mouth open and your camera's memory card full. You'll gain respect for the 19th-century Italian engineers who built the roads—and even more for the 21st-century drivers who squeeze past each other here daily. Cantilevered garages, hotels, and villas cling to the vertical terrain, and beautiful but out-of-reach coves tease from far below. As you hyperventilate, notice how the Mediterranean, a sheer 500-foot drop below, really twinkles. All this beautiful scenery apparently inspires local Romeos and Juliets, with the latex evidence of late-night romantic encounters littering the roadside turnouts. Over the centuries, the spectacular scenery and climate have been a siren call for the rich and famous, luring Roman Emperor Tiberius, Richard Wagner, Sophia Loren, Gore Vidal, and others to the Amalfi Coast's special brand of *la dolce vita*.

The two main Amalfi Coast towns (Positano and Amalfi) are pretty, but they're also touristy, congested, and overpriced. (Many visitors prefer side-tripping in from Sorrento.) Most beaches here are private, pebbly, and expensive. Check and understand your bills in this greedy region.

In Paestum, farther south, you can see one of the world's best collections of ruined Greek temples, a worthwhile museum with artifacts from the site, and the remains of a Roman town.

Amalfi Coast

The Amalfi Coast is one of those places with a "must see" reputation. Staggeringly picturesque and maddeningly touristy, it can be both rewarding and frustrating. As if an antidote to intense Naples, it is the perfect place for a romantic break, if done right and if you can afford it. These towns are the big three sights of the Amalfi Coast: Positano is like a living Gucci ad; Amalfi evokes a day when small towns with big fleets were powerhouses on the Mediterranean; and Ravello is fun for that tramp-in-a-palace feeling.

PLANNING YOUR TIME

On a quick visit, use Sorrento as your home base and do the Amalfi Coast as a day trip (skipping Paestum). But for a small-town vacation from your vacation, spend a few more days on the coast, sleeping in Positano.

Trying to decide between staying in Sorrento or Positano? Sorrento is larger, with useful services and the best transportation connections and accommodations. Tiny Positano is more touristy, but also more chic and picturesque, with a decent beach.

Naples or Paestum can also work as a base for an Amalfi Coast day trip, if you get an early start and the timetables align. From Naples, you have two options by public transport: train to Salerno, then bus (or boat) to Amalfi town; or, Circumvesuviana train to Sorrento, then bus to Positano and/or Amalfi. (You can go out one way and return the other.) From Paestum, you can take the train to Salerno, then the bus (or boat) to Amalfi.

GETTING AROUND THE AMALFI COAST

The real thrill here is the scenic drive between Sorrento and Salerno. The stretch from Positano to Amalfi is the best. This is treacherous stuff—even if you have a car, you may want to take the bus or hire a driver. Brave souls enjoy seeing the coast by scooter or motorbike (rent in Sorrento).

Next, I've outlined your options by bus, boat, and taxi. Many travelers do the Amalfi Coast as a round-trip by bus, but a good strategy is to go one way by bus and return by boat. For example, instead of bussing from Sorrento to Salerno (end of the line) and back again, consider taking the bus along the coast to Positano and/or Amalfi, then catching the ferry back. Ferries run

AMALFI COAST

AMALFI COAST

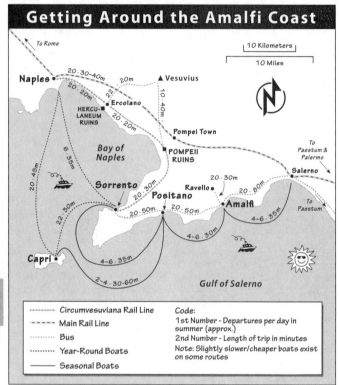

Getting Around the Amalfi Coast

To Rome

10 Kilometers

10 Miles

Naples   20·30-40m   2.0m   ▲ Vesuvius

20·20m

Ercolano

HERCU-   20·20m
LANEUM
RUINS   20·20m

10·40m

Pompei Town

Bay of
Naples   ■ POMPEII
RUINS

6·35m   20·30m   Ravello •   To
Paestum &
Palermo

Salerno

20·45m   **Sorrento**   20·30m   20·30m   20·80m   Salerno
Positano   **Amalfi**   To
Paestum

22·30m   20·50m   20·50m   4-6·35m

4-6·30m

Capri •   4-6·35m

2-4·30-60m   *Gulf of Salerno*

······· Circumvesuviana Rail Line   Code:
----- Main Rail Line   1st Number - Departures per day in
summer (approx.)
········· Bus   2nd Number - Length of trip in minutes
········· Year-Round Boats   Note: Slightly slower/cheaper boats exist
on some routes
——— Seasonal Boats

less often in spring and fall, and some don't run at all off-season (mid-Oct-mid-April). Boats don't run in stormy weather at any time of year. If boats aren't running between Amalfi and Sorrento, you can change boats in Capri.

Looking for exercise? Consider an Amalfi Coast hike. Numerous trails connect the main coastal towns with villages on the hills. Get a good map before you venture out.

By Public Bus

SITA buses from Sorrento to Amalfi, via Positano, are the most common, inexpensive way to see the coast (for schedules, see www.sitabus.it or—easier to read—www.positano.com). In Sorrento, buses depart from in front of the train station beginning at 6:30; from 8:30 they run roughly every half hour until 16:00, then hourly until 22:00 in summer, until 19:00 in winter (50-minute trip to Positano; another 50 minutes to Amalfi). To reach Ravello (the hill town beyond Amalfi) or Salerno (at the far end of the coast), transfer in Amalfi.

Individual tickets are inexpensive (€2-4). All rides are covered by the 24-hour Costiera SITA Sud pass (€8), which may not save you money but does save time buying tickets. Tickets are sold at tobacco shops and newsstands, not by drivers; in Sorrento, buy them at an outdoor stand by the bus stop or in train station shops.

Line up under the *Bus Stop SITA* sign across from the train station (10 steps down, look for the sales desk under an umbrella). When checking the schedule, carefully note the lettered codes that differentiate daily buses from weekend-only buses. *Giornaliero (G)* means daily; *Feriale (F)* denotes Monday-Saturday departures; and *Festivo (H)* is for Sundays and holidays.

Leaving Sorrento, grab a seat on the right for the best views. If you return by bus, it's fun to sit directly behind the driver for a box seat with a view over the twisting hairpin action. Sitting toward the front will also help minimize carsickness.

Avoiding Crowded Buses: Amalfi Coast public buses are routinely unable to handle demand during summer months and holidays (perhaps because the fares are so cheap). Generally, if you don't get on one bus, you're well positioned to catch the next one (in 20 minutes). From Sorrento, aim to leave on the 8:30 bus at the latest—earlier if possible. Departures between 9:00 and 11:00 can be frustratingly crowded.

Note that an eight-seater minibus and driver costs about €300 for the day: If you can organize a small group, €40 per person is a very good deal. (For options, see "By Taxi," later.)

When to Stop in Positano: Summer congestion can be so bad—particularly in July and August—that Amalfi-Sorrento buses don't even stop in Positano (because they fill up in Amalfi). Those trying to get back from Positano to Sorrento are stuck taking an extortionist taxi or hopping a boat...if one's running. When day-tripping from Sorrento to Amalfi, it's safest to make your Positano stop on the outbound leg, then come straight home from Amalfi, where the bus originates. Or, you can consider the hop-on, hop-off bus as an alternative.

By Hop-On, Hop-Off Bus

CitySightseeing Sorrento's bright red buses travel from Sorrento to Positano to Amalfi and back. While more expensive than public buses, they can be much less crowded and come with a recorded commentary. You'll pay €10 for your outgoing ride (buy tickets onboard), then €6 for the return trip (on the same day). Buses run hourly all day April-October, leaving the Sorrento train station at :45 past each hour starting at 8:45. Return trips from Amalfi leave at :15 past each hour (until 19:15—but confirm). The trip takes about 1.5 hours, with a stop in Positano each way. Check out www.sorrento.city-sightseeing.it (but don't be confused by their "two bays" tour of the Cape of Sorrento, which is not worth considering).

By Boat

A few passenger boats per day link Positano and Amalfi with Sorrento, Capri, and Salerno (generally April-Oct only). The last daily departure can be as early as midafternoon and is never much later than 18:00. Check schedules carefully: Frequency varies from month to month, and boats may be suspended without notice in bad weather (especially at Positano, where there's no real pier). The companies operating each route change frequently, compete for passengers, and usually claim to know nothing about their rivals' services. The best sources for timetables are www.capritourism.com (under "Shipping Timetable") and www.positano.com (under "Ferry Schedules"). You can also check individual company websites (such as www.travelmar.it, www.alicost.it, and www.gescab.it). It's smartest to confirm locally: The region's TIs hand out flyers with current schedules. Buy tickets on the dock.

If you're going to Capri from Positano or Amalfi, check whether there's a boat that goes directly to the Blue Grotto (rather than dropping you in the port to catch another boat from there—saving you time and money). Here's another useful trick: If no boats are going directly between Sorrento and Positano/Amalfi, you can usually still connect the two sides of the peninsula via Capri.

By Taxi

Given the hairy driving, impossible parking, crowded public buses, and potential fun, you might consider splurging to hire your own car and driver for your Amalfi day.

The **Monetti family** car-and-driver service—Raffaele, brother-in-law Tony, cousin Lorenzo, and daughter Carolina—have taken excellent care of my readers' transit needs for decades. Sample trips and rates: all-day Amalfi Coast (Positano, Amalfi, Ravello), 8 hours, €280; Amalfi Coast and Paestum, 10 hours, €400; transfer to Naples airport or train station to Sorrento, €110. These prices are for up to four people; you'll pay more for a larger eight-seater van. Though based in

Sorrento, they also do trips from Naples. Payment is cash only (as with most of the car services listed). Their reservation system is simple and reliable (Raffaele's mobile 335-602-9158 or 338-946-2860, "office" run by his English-speaking Finnish wife, Susanna, www.monettitaxi17.it, monettitaxi17@libero.it). Don't just hop into any taxi claiming to be a Monetti—call first. If you get into any kind of serious jam in the area, you can call Raffaele for help.

Francesco del Pizzo is another smooth and honest Sorrento-based driver. A classy man who speaks English well, Francesco enjoys explaining things as he drives (9 hours or so in a car with up to 4 passengers, €280; up to 8 passengers in a minibus, €320; mobile 333-238-4144, francescodelpizzo@yahoo.it).

Anthony Buonocore, based in Amalfi, specializes in cruise shore excursions, as well as transfers anywhere in the region in his eight-person Mercedes van (rates vary, tel. 349-441-0336, www.amalfitransfer.com, buonocoreanthony@yahoo.it).

Rides Only: If you're hiring a cabbie off the street for a ride and not a tour, here are sample fares from Sorrento to Positano: up to four people one-way for about €80 in a car, or up to six people for €90 in a minibus. Figure on paying 50 percent more to Amalfi. While taxis must use a meter within a city, a fixed rate is OK elsewhere. Negotiate—ask about a round-trip.

By Shared Minibus

While hiring your own driver is convenient, it's also expensive. To bring the cost down, split the trip—and the bill—with other travelers using this book. Naples-based **Mondo Guide** offers a nine-hour minibus trip that departs from Sorrento and heads down the Amalfi Coast, with brief stops in Positano, Amalfi, and Ravello, before returning to Sorrento (€50/person). They also offer Rick Steves readers shared tours in Pompeii and Naples.

Amalfi Coast Tour

The wildly scenic Amalfi Coast drive from Sorrento to Salerno, worth ▲▲▲, is one of the all-time great white-knuckle rides, whether you tackle it by bus, taxi, or shared minibus.

Gasp from the right side of the car or bus as you go out and from the left as you return to Sorrento. (Those on the wrong side really miss out.) Traffic is so heavy that private tour buses are only allowed to go in one direction (southbound from Sorrento). Summer traffic is infuriating. Fluorescent-vested police are posted at tough bends during peak hours to help fold in side-view mirrors and keep things moving. Here's a loose, self-guided tour of what you're seeing as you travel from west to east.

○ Self-Guided Tour: Leaving **Sorrento,** the road winds up into the hills past lemon groves and hidden houses. The gray-green trees are olives. (Notice the green nets slung around the trunks; these are unfurled in October and November, when the ripe olives drop naturally, for an easy self-harvest.) Dark, green-leafed trees planted in dense groves are the source of the region's lemons (many destined to become *limoncello* liqueur) and big, fat citrons (*cedri,* mostly used for marmalade). The black nets over the orange and lemon groves create a greenhouse effect, trapping warmth and humidity for maximum tastiness, while offering protection from extreme weather (preserving the peels used for *limoncello*).

Atop the ridge outside Sorrento, look to your right: The two small islands are the **Li Galli Islands,** where some say the sirens in Homer's *Odyssey* lived. The largest of these islands was once owned by the famed ballet dancer Rudolf Nureyev; it's now a luxury residence, rented to wealthy visitors for upward of $100,000 per week (bring your own yacht or arrive by helicopter).

When Nureyev bought the island, the only building standing was the stony watchtower—the first of many you'll see all along the coast. These were strategically placed within sight of one another so that a relay of rooftop bonfires could quickly spread word of a Saracen (Turkish pirate) attack.

The limestone cliffs that plunge into the sea were traversed by a hand-carved trail that became a modern road in the mid-19th century. Fruit stands sell produce from farms and orchards just over the hill. Limestone absorbs the heat and rainwater, making this south-facing coastline a fertile suntrap, with temperatures as much as 10 degrees higher than in nearby Sorrento. The chalky, reflective limestone, which extends below the surface, accounts for the uniquely colorful blues and greens of the water. With the favorable climate, bougainvillea, geraniums, oleander, and wisteria grow like weeds here in the summer. Notice the nets pulled tight against the cliffs—they're designed to catch rocks that often tumble loose after heavy rains.

The dramatic, exotic-looking town of **Positano** is the main stop along the coast. The town is built on a series of man-made terraces, which were carefully carved out of the steep rock, then filled with fertile soil carried here from Sorrento on the backs of donkeys. You can read the history of the region in Positano's rooftops—a mix of Roman-style red terracotta tiles and white domes inspired by the Saracens.

If you're getting off here, stay on through the first stop by the round-domed yellow church (Chiesa Nova), which is a very long walk above town. Instead, get off at the second stop, Sponda, then head downhill toward the start of my self-guided Positano Walk.

Sponda is also the best place to catch the onward bus to Amalfi. If you're coming on a smaller minibus, you'll twist all the way down—seemingly going in circles—to the start of the walk.

Just south of Positano, **St. Peter's Hotel** (Il San Pietro di Positano, camouflaged below the tiny St. Peter's church) is just about the poshest stop on the coast. In the adjacent gorge, notice the hotel's terraced gardens (where produce is grown for their restaurant) above an elevator-accessible beach and dock.

Just around the bend, **Praiano** comes into view. Less ritzy or charming than Positano or Amalfi, it's notable for its huge Cathedral of San Gennaro, with a characteristic majolica-tiled roof and dome—a reminder of this region's respected ceramics industry. In spindly Praiano, most of the homes are accessible only by tiny footpaths and staircases. Near the end of town, just before the big tunnel, watch on the left for the big *presepe* (manger scene) embedded into the cliff face. This Praiano-in-miniature was carved by one local man over several decades. At Christmastime, each house is filled with little figures and twinkle lights.

Just past the tunnel, look below and on the right to see another Saracen watchtower. (Yet another caps the little point on the horizon.)

A bit farther along, look down to see the fishing hamlet of **Marina di Praia** tucked into the gorge *(furore)* between two tun-

nels. If you're driving—or being driven—consider a detour down here for a coffee break or meal. This serene, tidy nook has its own little pebbly beach with great views of the stout bluffs and watchtower that hem it in. A seafront walkway curls around the bluff all the way to the tower.

Just after going through the next tunnel, watch for a jagged rock formation on its own little pedestal. Locals see the face of the Virgin Mary in this natural feature and say that she's holding a flower (the tree growing out to the right). Also notice several caged, cantilevered parking pads sticking out from the road. This stretch of coastline is popular for long-term villa rentals—Italians who want to really settle in to Amalfi life.

Look down and left for the blink-or-you'll-miss-it fishing village that's aptly named **Fiordo** ("fjord"), filling yet another gorge. You'll see humble homes burrowed into the cliff face, tucked so far into the gorge that they're entirely in shadow for much of the year. Today these are rented out to vacationers; the postage-stamp beach is uncrowded and inviting.

After the next tunnel, in the following hamlet, keep an eye out

AMALFI COAST

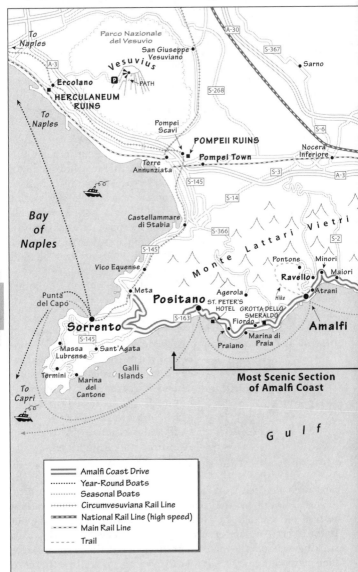

Legend:

- ═══ Amalfi Coast Drive
- ·········· Year-Round Boats
- ·········· Seasonal Boats
- ++++++++ Circumvesuviana Rail Line
- ▭▭▭▭ National Rail Line (high speed)
- ─·─·─ Main Rail Line
- ─ ─ ─ Trail

for donkeys with big baskets on their backs—the only way to make heavy deliveries to homes high in the rocky hills.

Soon you'll pass the big-for-Amalfi parking lot of the **Grotta dello Smeraldo** ("Emerald Grotto"), a cheesy roadside attraction that wrings the most it can out of a pretty, seawater-filled cave. Passing tourists park here and pay to take an elevator down to sea level, pile into big rowboats, and get paddled around a genuinely

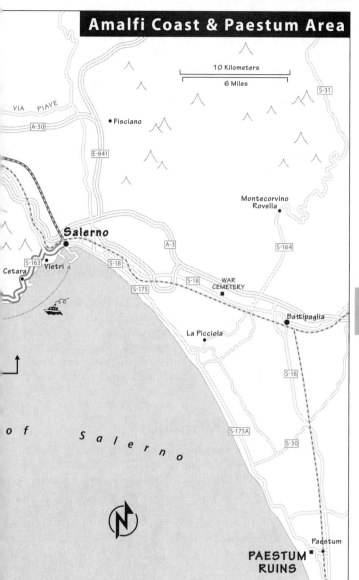

Amalfi Coast & Paestum Area

10 Kilometers

6 Miles

VIA PIAVE

A-30

E-841

• Fisciano

S-31

Montecorvino
Rovella •

Salerno

A-3

S-164

S-163

Cetara • Vietri

S-18

WAR
CEMETERY ■

S-18

S-175

Battipaglia •

La Picciola •

S-18

o f   *S a l e r n o*

S-175A

S-30

Paestum ■

PAESTUM ■
RUINS

AMALFI COAST

impressive cavern while the boatman imparts sparse factoids. Unless you've got time to kill, skip it.

Now you're approaching what might be the most dramatic watchtower on the coast, perched atop a near-island. This tower guarded the harbor of the Amalfi navy until the fleet was destroyed in 1343 by a tsunami caused by an earthquake, which also led to Amalfi's decline (it was once one of Italy's leading powers).

Around the next bend you're treated to stunning views of the coastline's namesake town—**Amalfi.** The white villa sitting on the low point between here and there (with another watchtower at its tip) once belonged to Sophia Loren. Now look up to the very top of the steep, steep cliffs overhead. The hulking former Monastery of Santa Rosa occupies this prime territory. Locals proudly explain that the *sfogliatella* dessert so beloved throughout the Campania region was first created at this monastery. (Today it's a luxury resort, where you can pay a premium to sleep in a tight little former monk's cell.)

The most striking stretch of coastline ends where the bus pulls to a halt—at the end of the line, the waterfront of Amalfi town. Spend some time enjoying this once-powerful, now-pleasant city, with its fine cathedral, fascinating paper museum, and fun-to-explore tangle of lanes (covered later in this chapter).

From Amalfi, you can transfer to another bus to head up to **Ravello** (described later), capping a cliff just beyond Amalfi, or onward to the big city of **Salerno.** Alternatively, buses and boats take you back to Positano and Sorrento.

If you're continuing the trip southward (on the bus to Salerno or Ravello), look up to the left as you leave Amalfi—the white house that clings to a cliff (Villa Rondinaia) was home for many years to writer Gore Vidal. Soon you'll pass through the low-impact, pleasantly untouristy town of **Atrani.** From here, you'll enjoy fine (though slightly less thrilling) scenery all the way to Salerno.

Positano

Specializing in scenery and sand, the easygoing town of Positano hangs halfway between Sorrento and Amalfi town on the most

spectacular stretch of the coast. According to legend, the Greek god Poseidon created Positano for Pasitea, a nymph he lusted after. History says the town was founded when ancient Greeks at Paestum decided to move out of the swamp (to escape the malaria carried by its mosquitoes).

In antiquity, Positano was famed for its bold sailors and hearty fleet. But after a big 1343 tsunami and the pirate raids of the Middle Ages, its wealth and power declined. It flourished again as a favorite under the Bourbon royal family in the 1700s, when many of its fine mansions were built. Until the late 1800s, the only access was by donkey path or by sea. In the 20th century, Positano became a haven for artists and writers escaping Communist Russia and Nazi Germany. In 1953, American writer John Steinbeck's essay on the town popularized Positano among tourists, and soon after it became a trendy Riviera stop. That was when the town gave the world "Moda Positano"—a leisurely *dolce vita* lifestyle of walking barefoot; wearing bright, happy, colorful clothes; and sporting skimpy bikinis.

Today, the village, a breathtaking ▲▲▲ sight from a distance, is a pleasant gathering of cafés and expensive stores draped over an almost comically steep hillside. Terraced gardens and historic houses cascade downhill to a stately cathedral and a broad, pebbly beach. Positano is famous for its fashions—and 90 percent of its shops are women's clothing boutiques (linen is a particularly popular item).

The "skyline" looks like it did a century ago. Notice the town's characteristic Saracen-inspired rooftop domes. Filled with sand, these provide low-tech insulation—to help buildings, in the days before central air, stay cool in summer and warm in winter. Traditionally, they were painted white in summer and black in winter.

For more than 25 years, it's been practically impossible to get a building permit in Positano. Landowners who want to renovate can't make external changes. Endless staircases are a way of life for the hardy locals. Only one street in Positano allows motorized traffic; the rest are narrow pedestrian lanes. While Positano has 4,000 residents, an average of 12,000 tourists visit daily from Easter through October. But because hotels don't take large groups (bus access is too difficult), this town—unlike Sorrento—has been spared the worst ravages of big-bus tourism. In winter, hotels shut down and the town once again belongs to the locals.

Consider seeing Positano as a day trip from Sorrento: Take the bus out and the afternoon ferry home, but be sure to check boat schedules when you arrive—the last ferry often leaves before 18:00 and doesn't always run in spring and fall. Or spend the night to enjoy the magic of Positano after dark. The town has a local flavor at night, when the grown-ups stroll and the kids play soccer on the church porch.

Orientation to Positano

Squished into a ravine, with narrow alleys that cascade down to the harbor, Positano requires you to stroll, whether you're going up or heading down. The center of town has no main square (unless you count the beach). There's little to do here but eat, window shop, and enjoy the beach and views...hence the town's popularity.

TOURIST INFORMATION

The TI is a block from the beach, in the red building a half-block beyond the bottom of the church steps (Mon-Sat 9:00-19:00, Sun until 14:00, shorter hours off-season, Via Regina Giovanna 13, tel. 089-875-067, www.aziendaturismopositano.it).

Local Guide: Positano native **Lucia Ferrara** (a.k.a. "Zia Lucy") brings substance to this glitzy town. During the day, she leads guided hiking tours, including the "Path of the Gods" above Amalfi town (up to 10 people, about 4 miles, 5 hours, €55/person, includes picnic). In the evening, if there's enough demand, she leads a Positano town walking tour (3 hours, departs at 17:00, €30/person). Also ask about her food tours (mobile 339-272-0971, www.zialucy.com).

ARRIVAL IN POSITANO

The main coastal highway winds above the town. Regional SITA buses stop at two scheduled bus stops located at either end of town: **Chiesa Nuova** (at Bar Internazionale, near the Sorrento end of town; use this one only if you're staying at Brikette Hostel) and **Sponda** (nearer Amalfi town). Although both stops are near roads leading downhill through the town to the beach, Sponda is closer and less steep; from this stop, it's a scenic 20-minute downhill stroll/shop/munch to the beach (and TI).

Neither bus stop has easy **baggage storage.** Positano does have porter services: A porter can meet you at the Sponda bus stop and watch your bags for €5 apiece—but you have to call them in advance (try Blu Porter, tel. 089-811-496). Another option is to get off at Chiesa Nuova and head for the Brikette Hostel, which offers day privileges for €10, including luggage storage, Wi-Fi, and showers. A last resort is to get off at the Sponda stop and roll your bags all the way down to Piazza dei Mulini, where the porters tend to hang out.

If you're catching the SITA bus from Positano, be aware that it may leave from the Sponda stop five minutes before the printed departure time. There's simply no room for the bus to wait, so in case the driver is early, you should be, too. Buy tickets at the tobacco shop in the town center (on Piazza dei Mulini).

If the walk up to the stop is too tough, take the dizzy little orange-and-white **shuttle bus** (marked *Interno Positano*), which constantly loops through Positano, connecting the lower town with the highway's two bus stops (2/hour, €1.30 at tobacco shop on Piazza dei Mulini, €1.70 on board, catch it at convenient stop at the corner of Via Colombo and Via dei Mulini, heads up to Sponda). Collina Bakery, located off Piazza dei Mulini (as close as cars, taxis, and the shuttle bus can get to the beach), is just across from the shuttle bus stop, with a fine, breezy terrace to enjoy while you wait.

Drivers must go with the one-way flow, entering the town only at the Chiesa Nuova bus stop (closest to Sorrento) and exiting at Sponda (a 20-minute one-way loop). Driving is a headache here. Parking is even worse.

Positano Walk

While there's no real sightseeing in Positano, this short, self-guided stroll downhill will help you get your bearings from top to bottom.
• *Start at...*

Piazza dei Mulini: This is the upper-town meeting point—as close to the beach as vehicles can get—and the lower stop for the little orange-and-white shuttle bus. Collina Bakery is a local hangout (in this small town, gossiping is a big pastime). Older people tend to gather inside, while the younger crowd congregates on the wisteria-draped terrace across the street.

Dip into the little yellow Church of the Holy Rosary (by the road), with a serene 12th-century interior. Up front, to the right of the main altar, find the delicately carved fragment of a Roman sarcophagus (first century B.C.). Positano sits upon the site of a sprawling Roman villa, and we'll see a scant few reminders of that age as we walk.

At the top of the town lane (across from the church) is a popular *granita* (lemon slush) stand, where the family has been following the same secret recipe for generations.

Now continue downhill into town, passing a variety of shops—many selling linen and ceramics. These industries boomed when tourists discovered Positano in the 1970s. The beach-inspired Moda Positano fashion label was born as a break from the rigid dress code of the '50s. (For tips on shopping for linen, see "Shopping," later, under "Sights in Positano.") Positano also considers itself an artists' colony, and you'll see many galleries featuring the work of area artists.
• *Wander downhill to the "fork" in the road (stairs to the left, road to the right). You've reached...*

Midtown: At Enoteca Cuomo (#3), butchers Pasquale and Rosario stock fine local red wines and are happy to explain their virtues. They also make homemade sausages, salami, and *panini*— good for a quick lunch. The smaller set of stairs leads to the recommended Delicatessen grocery store, where Emilia can fix you a good picnic (see "Eating in Positano," later).

La Zagara (across the lane from the steps, at #10, with a leafy terrace) is a pricey pastry shop by day and a cocktail bar by night. Tempting pastries such as the rum-drenched *babà* (a southern Italian favorite) fill the window display. A bit farther downhill, Brunella (on the right, at #24) is respected for traditional quality, and Positano-made linens.

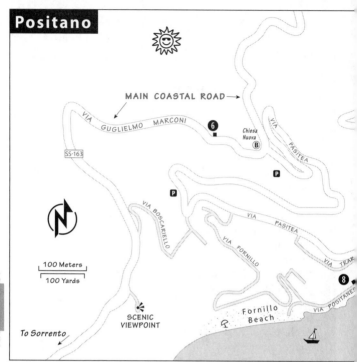

Positano

MAIN COASTAL ROAD →

VIA GUGLIELMO MARCONI

Chiesa Nuova Ⓑ

SS-163

VIA PASITEA

Ⓟ

VIA BOSCARIELLO

Ⓟ

VIA PASITEA

VIA FORNILLO

VIA TRAR

❽

SCENIC VIEWPOINT

Fornillo Beach

VIA POSITANES

100 Meters
100 Yards

To Sorrento

AMALFI COAST

Across the street, the ritzy Hotel Palazzo Murat fills what was once a grand Benedictine monastery. Napoleon, fearing the power of the Church, had many such monasteries closed during his rule here. This one became a private palace, named for his brother-in-law, who was briefly the King of Naples. Step into the plush courtyard to enjoy the scene, with great views of the cathedral's majolica-slathered dome below. Continuing on, under a fragrant wisteria trellis, you'll pass "street merchants' gulch," where artisans display their goodies.

• *Continue straight down. You'll run into a fork at the big church. For now, turn right and go downstairs to Piazza Flavio Gioia, facing the big...*

Church of Santa Maria Assunta: This church, which sits upon Roman ruins, was once the abbey of Positano's 12th-century Benedictine monastery. Originally Romanesque, it was eventually abandoned (along with the entire lower town) out of fear of pirate attacks. When the coast was clear in the 18th century, the church was given an extreme Baroque makeover.

Step **inside** and find these items: In the first chapel on the left is a fine manger scene *(presepe)*. Its original 18th-century figurines give you an idea of the folk costumes of the age. Above the main altar is the Black Madonna, an icon-like Byzantine painting likely

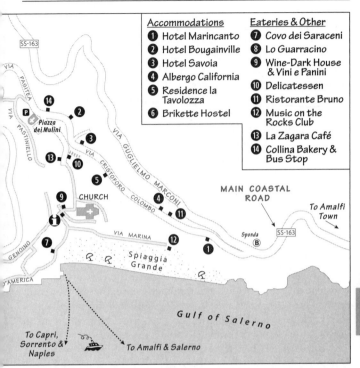

Accommodations
1 Hotel Marincanto
2 Hotel Bougainville
3 Hotel Savoia
4 Albergo California
5 Residence la Tavolozza
6 Brikette Hostel

Eateries & Other
7 Covo dei Saraceni
8 Lo Guarracino
9 Wine-Dark House & Vini e Panini
10 Delicatessen
11 Ristorante Bruno
12 Music on the Rocks Club
13 La Zagara Café
14 Collina Bakery & Bus Stop

AMALFI COAST

brought here from Constantinople by monks in the 12th century. But locals prefer a more romantic origin story for the painting: Saracen pirates had it on their ship as plunder. A violent storm hit—sure to sink the evil ship. The painting of Mary spoke, saying, *"Posa, posa"* (lay me down), and the ship glided safely to this harbor. The pirates were so stricken they became Christians. Locals kept the painting, and the town became known as *Posa-tano* (recalling Mary's command).

To the right of the altar, a small freestanding display case holds a silver-and-copper bust of St. Vitus (along with his bones, now holy relics). He's the town patron, who brought Christianity here in about A.D. 300. In the adjacent niche (on the right) is a rare 1599 painting by Fabrizio Santafede of Baby Jesus being circumcised, considered the finest historic painting in town.

Back outside, you'll see the **bell tower,** dating from 1707. Above the door, it sports a Romanesque relief scavenged from the original church. The scene—a wolf mermaid with seven little fish—was a reminder to worshippers of how integral the sea was to their livelihood. Nicknamed "our pagan protector," it's a good example of how early Christians incorporated pagan elements into their worship. Notice the characteristic shallow, white "insulation domes" on rooftops in front of the church.

• *Backtrack up the steps, circling around the church. You'll likely see the entry to an underground Roman exhibit.*

The entire town center of today's Positano—from this cathedral all the way up to the Piazza dei Mulini, where we started this walk—sits upon the site of a huge **Roman villa complex,** buried when Mount Vesuvius erupted in A.D. 79. Positano recently excavated one small part of the villa, and a small museum provides views of a surviving fragment of a large Roman fresco. Take the stairs down to two glass doors that offer a peek into the church's crypt—originally the early church's altar. According to local legend, the Benedictines sat their dead brothers on the stone choir chairs here to decompose and remind all of their mortality.

• *Continue climbing down the steps arcing to the right (following* beach/ spiaggia *signs). You'll eventually come to the little square, with concrete benches, facing the beach.*

Piazzetta: This is the town gathering point in the evening, as local boys hustle tourist girls into the nearby nightclub. Step down to beach level. Residents traded their historic baptistery font with Amalfi town for the two iron lions you see facing the beach. Around the staircase, you'll also see some original Roman columns, scavenged from the buried villa. Look up and admire the colorful majolica tiles so typical of church domes in this region.

The Positano **beach,** called Spiaggia Grande, is half public (straight ahead) and half private (to the left, behind the little fence). It's atmospherically littered with a commotion of fishing boats and recreational craft. The big kiosk on the beach straight ahead sells excursions to Capri and elsewhere.

Looking out over the beach from this point, you can see three of the **watchtowers** built centuries ago to protect the Amalfi Coast from Saracen pirates: one on the far-left horizon, just below Praiano; a small one on the Li Galli Islands, straight ahead; and the rectangular one far to the right, marking the end of Fornillo Beach. (The round tower in the foreground is modern.) Defenders used these towers—strategically situated within sight of each other—to relay smoke signals. In more recent times, the tower on the right (near Fornillo Beach) was a hangout for artists, who holed up inside for inspiration. (The people of Positano pride themselves on being artists rather than snazzy jet-setters like those in Capri.)

As you face out to sea, on the far-left side of the beach (below Rada Restaurant) is **Music on the Rocks,** a chic club that's the only remaining piece of the 1970s scene, when Positano really rocked. While it's dead until very late, you're welcome to peek in at the cool troglo-disco interior, or go upstairs to the Fly Bar for the priciest cocktails in town.

• *Now turn right and wander across the beach. Behind the kiosks that sell boat tickets, find the steps to the path that climbs up and over, past a*

13th-century lookout fort from Saracen pirate days, to the next beach. It's a worthwhile little five-minute walk to...

Fornillo Beach: This is where locals go for better swimming and to escape some of the tourist crowds. Via Positanesi d'America is the lane (lit at night) leading to the beach. It's named for the more than 50 percent of Positano's population that emigrated to America between the 1860s and the 1940s. (Locals remember when priests used to say at Mass, "And now, let's pray for Positanesi Americani.") The walk offers a welcome change of scene, as the path winds through a shady ravine.

• *Our walk is over. Time to relax.*

Sights in Positano

Beaches

Positano's pebbly and sandy primary beach, **Spiaggia Grande,** is colorful with umbrellas as it stretches wide around the cove. It's mostly private (pay about €12 to enter, includes lounge chair and umbrella), with a free section near the middle, close to where the boats take off. Look for the pay showers. The nearest WC is beneath the steps to the right (as you face the water).

Fornillo Beach, a less-crowded option just around the bend (to the west) of Spiaggia Grande, is favored by residents, with more affordable chair/umbrella rentals (€8). It has a mellow Robinson Crusoe vibe, with a sturdy Saracen tower keeping watch overhead. This beach has a few humble snack bars and lunch eateries. Note that its position, tucked back in the rocks, means it gets shade earlier in the day than the main beach.

Boat Trips

Boats serving Positano pull up to the dock at the west end of Spiaggia Grande (to the right as you face the sea; booths sell tickets). Also consider renting a rowboat, or see whether they can talk you into taking a boat tour. Passenger boats run to Amalfi, Capri, Salerno, and Sorrento.

Shopping

Linen: Garments made of **linen** (especially women's dresses) are popular items in Positano. To find a good-quality piece that will last, look for "Made in Positano" (or at least "Made in Italy") on the label, and check the percentage of linen; 60 percent or more is good quality and 100 percent is best. Two companies with top reputations and multiple outlets are **Brunella** and **Pepito's** (each has shops on Via Colombo, near the top of town; along Via Pasitea, the main drag; and along claustrophobic Saraceno lane, near the bottom of town, parallel to the beach).

Ceramics: Ceramica Assunta, one of the oldest ceramics stores in Positano, carries colorful Solimene dinnerware and more at two locations (Via Colombo 97 and Via Colombo 137).

Custom Sandals: Positano has a tradition of handmade sandals, crafted to your specifications while you wait (prices start at about €50). One good shop, La Botteguccia, faces the tranquil little square just up from the TI; around the corner, in front of the Capricci restaurant, you'll see Carmine Todisco, who loves to explain how his grandfather shod Jackie O.

Nightlife

The big-time action in the old town center is the impressive club **Music on the Rocks,** literally carved into the rocks on the beach (opens at 23:00 mid-April-Oct, but party starts even later, there's often a €15-30 cover charge on weekends and in summer, which includes a drink, closed off-season, Via Grotte Dell'Incanto 51, tel. 089-875-874, www.musicontherocks.it). For a more low-key atmosphere, café/pastry shop **La Zagara** morphs into a cocktail bar with music nightly in summer (Via dei Mulini 10, tel. 089-875-964, www.lazagara.com).

Sleeping in Positano

These hotels—with the exception of the hostel—are all on or near Via Cristoforo Colombo, which leads from the Sponda bus stop down into the village (ideal for arrival by bus). Outside high season (May-Sept), prices go soft. Most places close in the winter (Dec-Feb or longer). Expect to pay more than €20 per day to park, except at Albergo California.

$$$$ Hotel Marincanto is a recently restored, somewhat impersonal four-star hotel with 32 beautiful rooms and a bright breakfast terrace practically teetering on a cliff. Suites seem to be designed for a *luna di miele*—honeymoon (air-con, elevator, pool, stairs down to a private beach, pay parking, closed Nov-March, 50 yards below Sponda bus stop at Via Cristoforo Colombo 50, reception on bottom floor, tel. 089-875-130, www.marincanto.it, info@marincanto.it).

$$$$ Hotel Bougainville rents 16 comfortable rooms, half with balconies. Everything's bright, modern, and tasteful (rooms without views are cheaper, air-con, small elevator, closed Nov-March, Via Cristoforo Colombo 25, tel. 089-875-047, www.bougainville.it, info@bougainville.it, friendly Marella).

$$$ Hotel Savoia, run by the friendly D'Aiello family, has 39 sizeable, breezy, bright, simple, tiled rooms (some cheaper non-view rooms, some rooms with balcony or terrace, air-con, elevator, closed Nov-March, Via Cristoforo Colombo 73, tel. 089-875-003, www.savoiapositano.it, info@savoiapositano.it).

$$$ Albergo California has 15 spacious rooms (all with lofty views), a grand terrace draped with vines, and full breakfasts. The Cinque family—including Maria, Bronx-born son John, and grandchildren Giuseppe and Maria—will welcome you (air-con, free parking, closed Nov-Easter, Via Cristoforo Colombo 141, tel. 089-875-382, www.hotelcaliforniapositano.it, info@hotelcaliforniapositano.it).

$$ Residence la Tavolozza is an attractive six-room hotel, warmly run by Celeste (cheh-LEHS-tay) and daughters Francesca (who speaks English) and Paola. Each cheerily tiled room comes with a view, a terrace, and silence (lavish à la carte breakfast extra, families can ask for sprawling "Royal Apartment," air-con, confirm by phone if arriving late, closed Dec-Feb, Via Cristoforo Colombo 10, tel. 089-875-040, www.latavolozzapositano.it, info@latavolozzapositano.it).

$ Brikette Hostel offers your best budget option in this otherwise ritzy town. Its 35 dorm beds are pricey by hostel standards, but you're in Positano. It has a great sun and breakfast terrace and a youthful ambience (private and family rooms available, breakfast extra, cheap dinners, air-con; day privileges for day-trippers, including luggage storage-€10; closed Nov-March but a few apartments without breakfast are available all year long; leave bus at Chiesa Nuova/Bar Internazionale stop and backtrack uphill 500 feet to Via G. Marconi 358, www.hostel-positano.com, hostelpositano@gmail.com, Cristiana). The hostel isn't reachable by phone; email instead.

Eating in Positano

On the Beach: At the waterfront, several interchangeable restaurants with view terraces leave people fat and happy, albeit with skinnier wallets (figure €15-20 pastas and *secondi,* plus pricey drinks and sides, and a cover charge). Little distinguishes one place from the next; all are scenic, convenient, and overpriced. **$$$ Covo dei Saraceni** offers the best value on the beach, with good pizza and tables overlooking the ac-

tion (daily, on the far right as you face the sea, where Via Positanesi d'America starts).

Near the Beach: $$$ Lo Guarracino, hidden on the path

to Fornillo Beach, is a local favorite for its great views and good food at prices similar to the beachfront places (daily 12:00-15:30 & 19:00-23:00, closed Nov-Easter, follow path behind the boat-ticket kiosks 5 minutes to Via Positanesi d'America 12, tel. 089-875-794).

$$ Wine-Dark House, tucked around the corner from the beach (and the TI), fills a cute little piazzetta at the start of Via del Saraceno. They serve good pastas and *secondi*, have a respect for wine (several local wines), and are popular with Positano's youngsters for their long list of sandwiches (closed Tue, Via del Saraceno 6, tel. 089-811-925).

Picnics: If a picnic dinner on your balcony or the beach sounds good, sunny Emilia at the **Delicatessen** grocery store can supply the ingredients: *antipasto misto,* pastas, home-cooked dishes, and sandwiches made to order. She'll heat it up for you and throw in the picnic ware. Come early for the best selection (all sold by weight, daily 7:00-22:00, shorter hours off-season, just below car park at Via del Mulini 5, tel. 089-875-489). **Vini e Panini** (a.k.a. "The Wine Shop"), another small grocery, is a block from the beach a few steps above the TI. Daniela, the fifth-generation owner, speaks English and happily makes sandwiches to order. Choose from the "Caprese" (mozzarella and tomato), the "Positano" (mozzarella, tomato, and prosciutto), or create your own. They also have a nice selection of well-priced regional wines (daily 8:00-20:00, until 22:00 in summer, closed mid-Nov-mid-March, just off church steps, tel. 089-875-175).

"Uptown": The unassuming, family-run **$$$ Ristorante Bruno** is handy to my listed hotels. While expensive, it has nice views and is worth considering if you want a meal without hiking down into the town center (daily 12:30-23:00, closed Nov-Easter, near the top of Via Cristoforo Colombo at #157, tel. 089-875-179).

Amalfi Town

After Rome fell, the town of Amalfi was one of the first to trade goods—coffee, carpets, and paper—between Europe and points east. Its heyday was the 10th and 11th centuries, when it was a powerful maritime republic—a trading power with a fleet that controlled this region and rivaled Pisa, Genoa, and Venice. The Republic of Amalfi founded a hospital in Jerusalem and claims to have founded the Knights of Malta order—even giving them the Amalfi cross, which became the famous Maltese cross. Amalfi minted its own coins and established "rules of the sea"—the basics of which survive today.

In 1343, this little powerhouse was suddenly destroyed by a tsunami caused by an undersea earthquake. That disaster, compounded by devastating plagues, left Amalfi a humble backwater. Much of the culture of this entire region was driven by this town—but because it fell from power, Amalfi doesn't always get

the credit it deserves. Today its 5,000 residents live off tourism. The coast's namesake is not as picturesque as Positano or as well-connected as Sorrento, but it has a real-life feel and a vivacious bustle.

Though less touristy than Positano, Amalfi is still packed during the day with big-bus tours (whose drivers pay €50 an hour to park while their groups shop for *limoncello* and ceramics). Amalfi's charms reveal themselves early and late in the day, when the crowds dissipate.

Orientation to Amalfi Town

Amalfi's waterfront is the coast's biggest transport hub. Right next to each other are the bus station, ferry docks, and a parking lot (€5/hour; if the lot is full, park in the huge Lunarossa garage, burrowed into the hillside just past town and just before the tunnel leading into Atrani). The waterfront hub is overlooked by a statue of local boy Flavio Gioia, the purported inventor of the magnetic compass.

Amalfi's **TI** is just up the main road, right before the post office and overlooking the beach (Mon-Sat 8:30-13:00 & 14:00-18:00, Nov-March Mon-Sat 8:30-13:00, closed Sun year-round, pay WC in same courtyard, Corso della Repubbliche Marinare 27—about 100 yards from the bus station and ferry dock, next to the post office; facing the sea, it's to the left; tel. 089-871-107, www.amalfitouristoffice.it).

HELPFUL HINTS

Don't Get Stranded: If you're day-tripping to Amalfi from elsewhere in the region, check locally to confirm when the last return bus to Sorrento or Salerno leaves in the evening (in winter this can be as early as 19:00). Don't plan to leave on the last bus of the day; if that bus is full, your only option might be a €100 taxi ride.

Baggage Storage: You can store your bag safely for €5 at the **Divina Costiera Travel Office** facing the waterfront square, across from the bus parking area (daily 8:00-13:00 & 14:00-19:00, closed mid-Nov-March, tel. 089-872-467).

Speedboat Charters: To hire your own boat for a tour of the coast-

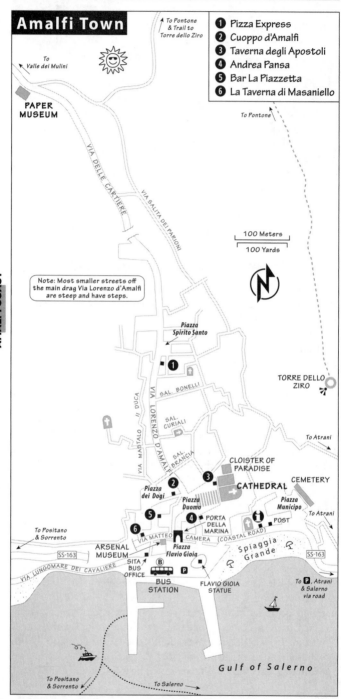

Amalfi Town

1. Pizza Express
2. Cuoppo d'Amalfi
3. Taverna degli Apostoli
4. Andrea Pansa
5. Bar La Piazzetta
6. La Taverna di Masaniello

Note: Most smaller streets off the main drag Via Lorenzo d'Amalfi are steep and have steps.

line from Amalfi (or to Capri), consider **Charter La Dolce Vita** (mobile 335-549-9365, www.amalficoastyacht.it).

Sights in Amalfi Town

AMALFI TOWN

Amalfi's one main street runs up from the waterfront through a deep valley, with stairways to courtyards and houses on either side. It's worth walking uphill to the workaday upper end of town. Super-atmospheric, narrow, stepped side lanes branch off, squeezing between hulking old buildings. If you hear water under a grate in the main street, it's the creek that runs through the ravine—a reminder that the town originally straddled the stream but later paved over it to create a main drag.

Before you enter the town, notice the colorful tile above the Porta della Marina gateway, showing off the trading domain of the maritime Republic of Amalfi. Just to the left, along the busy road, a series of arches marks the long, narrow, vaulted halls of Amalfi's arsenal—where ships were built in the 11th century. One of these is now the little Arsenal Museum.

Venture into town, and you'll quickly come to Piazza Duomo, the main square, with the cathedral—the town's most important sight—and a spring water-spewing statue of St. Andrew.

As you get farther away from the water, Amalfi becomes less glitzy and more traditional. The Paper Museum is a 10-minute walk up Via Lorenzo d'Amalfi, the main drag. On the way up to the museum, don't miss the huge, outdoor *presepi* (Nativity scenes) on your left. From the museum, the road narrows and you can turn off onto a path leading to the shaded Valle dei Mulini; it's full of paper-mill ruins that recall this once proud and prosperous industry. The ruined castle clinging to the rocky ridge above Amalfi is Torre dello Ziro, a good lookout point for intrepid hikers (see "Hikes," later).

As you return downhill, be sure to explore up the winding and narrow lanes and arcaded passages on either side of the main street.

Arsenal Museum

This small, underground museum just across the road from the bus station tells a bit about Amalfi's maritime glory years. Stepping into the single long room under the dramatic vaulted stone ceiling, you can just tell that 1,000 years ago, they made ships here.

Cost and Hours: €2, Tue-Sun 10:00-14:00 & 16:00-20:00, closed Mon and Feb, Piazza Flavio Gioia, mobile 334-917-7814.

Performances: Half of the arsenal space is a venue for performances of *Amalfi Musical,* a 1.5-hour musical bonanza loosely based on local history (English subtitles, 2/week in summer, www.amalfimusical.it).

Cathedral

This church is "Amalfi Romanesque" (a mix of Moorish and Byzantine flavors, built c. 1000-1300), with a fanciful Neo-Byzantine facade from the 19th century. Climb the imposing stairway, which functions as a mini Spanish Steps-style hangout zone and a handy outdoor theater. The 1,000-year-old bronze door at the top was given to Amalfi by a wealthy local merchant who had it made in Constantinople. Visitors are directed on a one-way circuit through the cathedral complex with four stops: the cloister, original basilica, crypt, and cathedral.

Cost and Hours: €3, daily 9:00-18:45, July-Sept until 19:45, Nov-Feb 10:00-13:00 & 14:30-16:30. The cathedral—but not the rest of the complex—can be entered free for prayer or discreet visits daily 7:30-10:00 & 17:00-19:30; it's closed 10:00-17:00 except as part of the paid visit; tel. 089-871-324, www.parrocchiaamalfi.com. There's a fine, free WC at the top of the steps (through unmarked green door, just a few steps before ticket booth, ask for key at desk).

Visiting the Cathedral: You'll follow a self-guided, one-way tour of the complex, beginning in a courtyard of 120 graceful columns—the **"Cloister of Paradise."** This was the cemetery for nobles in the 13th century (note their stone sarcophagi). Don't miss the fine view of the bell tower and its majolica tiles.

The original ninth-century church, known as the **Basilica of the Crucifix,** boasts a fine 13th-century wooden crucifix. Today the basilica is a museum filled with the cathedral's art treasures. The Angevin Mitre (Mitra Angioina), with a "pavement of tiny pearls" setting off its gold and gems, has been worn by bishops since the 14th century. Also on display (waist-high, facing the altar) is a carved wooden decoration from a Saracen pirate ship that wrecked just outside of town in 1544 during a freak storm. The church is dedicated to St. Andrew, whom believers credit with causing the storm and saving the town from certain Turkish pillage and plunder.

Down the stairs to the right of the basilica's altar is the **Crypt of St. Andrew.** Just as Venice needed St. Mark to get on the pilgrimage map, Amalfi needed St. Andrew—one of the apostles who, along with his brother Peter, left their fishing nets to become the original "fishers of men." Under the huge bronze statue, you'll see a reliquary holding what are believed to be Andrew's remains. These were brought here from Constantinople in 1206 during the Crusades—an indication of the wealth and importance of Amalfi back then.

Climb the stairs up into the **cathedral** itself. Behind the main altar is a painting of St. Andrew martyred on an X-shaped cross flanked by two Egyptian granite columns supporting a triumphal arch. Before leaving, check out the delicate mother-of-pearl crucifix (right of door in back).

▲Paper Museum

This excellent little museum—worth ▲▲▲ for engineers—makes for a good excuse to break free from the crowds and walk up the main drag to a quieter, more local part of town. Paper has been an important industry here since Amalfi's glory days in the Middle Ages. Millworkers would pound rags into pulp in a big vat, pull it up using a screen, and air-dry each sheet (the same technique used to make artisan paper today—look for it at shops in town). At this cavernous, cool 13th-century paper mill-turned-museum, a multilingual guide collects groups at the entrance (no particular times) for a 25-minute tour. The guide recounts the history and process of papermaking and turns on the museum's vintage machinery. You'll see how the Amalfi River (which you can still hear rumbling underfoot) powered this important industry, and learn the origins of the term "watermark." Kids can dip a screen into the rag pool and make a sheet of paper. It's amazing to think this factory produced paper through 1969 (when it was replaced by a modern facility up the valley).

Cost and Hours: €4; daily 10:00-18:30; Nov-Feb Tue-Wed and Fri-Sun until 15:30, closed Mon and Thu; a 10-minute walk up the main street from the cathedral, look for signs to *Museo della Carta;* tel. 089-830-4561, www.museodellacarta.it.

HIKES

Amalfi is the starting point for several fine hikes, two of which I've described here. The TI hands out photocopies of Giovanni Visetti's trail maps (or download them from his engaging website, www. giovis.com). The best book on local hikes is Julian Tippett's *Sorrento Amalfi Capri Car Tours and Walks* (2015), with useful color-coded maps and info on public transportation to the trailheads. Lucia Ferrara, a great guide based in Positano, leads hikes around Amalfi.

Hike #1: Pontone

This loop trail leads up the valley past paper-mill ruins, ending in the tiny town of Pontone; you can get lunch there, and head back

AMALFI COAST

down to the town of Amalfi (allow 3 hours total). Bring a good map, since it's easy to veer off the main route. Start your hike by following the main road (Via Lorenzo d'Amalfi) away from the sea.

After the Paper Museum, jog right, then left to join the trail, which runs through the shaded woods along a babbling stream. Heed the signs that warn people to stay away from the ruins of paper mills (no matter how tempting they look), since many are ready to collapse on unwary hikers. Continue up to Pontone, where Trattoria l'Antico Borgo offers wonderful cuisine and a great view (Via Noce 4, tel. 089-871-469). After lunch, return to Amalfi via a steep stairway.

If you're feeling ambitious, before you head back to Amalfi, add a one-hour detour (30 minutes each way) to visit the ridge-hugging **Torre dello Ziro** (ask a local how to find the trail to this tower). You'll be rewarded with a spectacular view.

Hike #2: Atrani

For an easier stroll, head to the nearby town of Atrani. This village, just a 15-minute stroll beyond Amalfi town, is a world apart; its 1,500 residents consider themselves definitely *not* from Amalfi. Leave Amalfi via the main road and stay on the water side until the promenade ends. Cross the street, continue a few more yards, then go up the whitewashed staircase just past the pizzeria. From here, twist up through old lanes to a paved route that takes you over the hill and drops you into Atrani in about 15 minutes.

With relatively few tourists, a delightful town square, and a free, sandy beach (if you drive here, pay for parking at harbor), Atrani has none of Amalfi's trendy resort feel. Piazza Umberto is the core of town, with cafés, restaurants, and little grocery stores that can make sandwiches. A whitewashed staircase leads up to the serene and beautiful town church (under the clock face).

To save time and sweat on the return walk, follow the promenade just above water level toward Amalfi. Then walk up through the restaurant terrace and find the big, long tunnel next to the parking garage—this will deposit you in the middle of Amalfi.

From Atrani, you could theoretically continue up to **Ravello** (described later). But unless you're part mountain goat, you'll probably prefer catching the bus to Ravello from Amalfi town instead.

Eating in Amalfi Town

Quick Bites: Walk five minutes up the main drag; on the right, past the first archway, is **$ Pizza Express,** with honest pies, calzones, and heated sandwiches to go (Mon-Sat 9:00-21:00, closed Sun, Via

Capuano 46, mobile 339-581-2336). The **Cuoppo d'Amalfi** fried-fish stand at Piazza dei Dogi (described below) is another good option.

On the Main Square, Piazza Duomo: Several pricey places face the cathedral steps. The best of the bunch is tucked just around the left side of the grand staircase, up a smaller flight of stairs: **$$ Taverna degli Apostoli,** with colorful outdoor tables and cozy upstairs dining room in what was once an art gallery. The menu is brief but thoughtful, going beyond the old standbys, and everything is well executed (daily 12:00-16:00 & 19:00-24:00, Supportico San Andrea 6, tel. 089-872-991). For dessert, the **Andrea Pansa** pastry shop and café, to the right as you face the cathedral steps, is the most venerable place in town—a good spot to try *sfogliatella* (the delicate pastry invented at a nearby monastery) and other desserts popular in southern Italy.

Near the Main Square, on Piazza dei Dogi: If you walk straight ahead from the cathedral stairs, go up the little covered lane, and hook right at the fork, you'll pop out in atmospheric little Piazza dei Dogi. Slightly less trampled and more neighborhood-feeling than Piazza Duomo, this has several decent (if forgettable) restaurants aimed squarely at pleasing tourists. The **$ Cuoppo d'Amalfi** fried-fish shop, on the right as you enter the square, fills cardboard cones with all manner of deep-fried sea life. **$$ Bar La Piazzetta** has good prices at its tables right in the middle of the square. And tucked at the corner of the square leading to the port, **$$ La Taverna di Masaniello** is a bit pricier, with good food.

Ravello

The Amalfi Coast's version of a hill town, Ravello (a 30-minute bus ride from Amalfi town) sits atop a lofty perch 1,000 feet above the sea. It boasts an interesting church, two villas with stunning gardens, and breathtaking views that have attracted celebrities for generations. Gore Vidal, Richard Wagner, D. H. Lawrence, M. C. Escher, Henry Wadsworth Longfellow, and Greta Garbo all succumbed to Ravello's charms and called it home.

The town is like a lush and peaceful garden floating in a world all its own. It seems to be made entirely of cafés, stonework, old villas-turned-luxury hotels, tourists, and grand views. Ravello feels like a place to convalesce.

Sights in Ravello

To see the sights listed here, start at the bus stop and walk through the tunnel to the main square, where you'll find the Villa Rufolo on the left, the church on the right, and the **TI** down the street past the church (TI open daily 10:00-18:00, closes earlier Nov-April, 100 yards from the square—follow signs to Via Roma 18, tel. 089-857-096, www.ravellotime.it). Villa Cimbrone is a 10-minute walk from the square (follow the signs).

If you have time for only one villa, consider this: Villa Rufolo is easier to reach (facing the main square) and has a stunning terrace garden. Villa Cimbrone requires an up-and-down hike, but it's bigger and more rugged and offers even grander views in both directions along the coast.

Piazza Duomo

The town's entry tunnel deposits you on the main square. Though Ravello is perfectly peaceful today, the weathered watchtower of Villa Rufolo—which once kept an eye out for fires and invasions—is a reminder that it wasn't always postcards and *limoncello*.

The fine umbrella pines on the square provide a shady meeting place for strollers ending up here on the piazza. Opposite the church is a fine view of the terraced hillside and the community of Scala (which means "steps"—historically a way of life there). The terraces—supporting grapevines and lemon trees—mostly date from the 16th century. Viale Wagner climbs to the top of town for sea views and ruined villas that are now luxury hotels. The town is essentially traffic-free.

Duomo

Ravello's cathedral, overlooking the main square, feels stripped-down and Romanesque. The facade of the cathedral is plain because the earlier, fancy west portal was destroyed in a 1364 earthquake. The front door is locked; to enter, go through the museum on Viale Wagner, around the left side. Inside, you'll find tastefully restrained decoration and a floor that slopes upward. The key features of this church are its 12th-century bronze doors (from Constantinople), with 54 Biblical scenes; the carved marble pulpit supported by six lions; and the chance to get a close-up look at the relic of holy blood (in the chapel left of main altar). The geometric designs show Arabic influence. The humble cathedral museum, through which you'll enter, is two rooms of well-described carved marble that evoke the historical importance of the town.

Cost and Hours: €3 for the museum—which also gets you into the church, daily 9:00-19:00, Nov-April until 18:00.

Villa Rufolo

The villa, built in the 13th-century ruins of a noble family's palace, presents wistful gardens among stony walls, with oh-my-God views. The Arabic/Norman gardens seem designed to frame commanding coastline vistas (you can enjoy the same view, without the entry fee, from the bus parking lot just below the villa). It's also one of the venues for Ravello's annual arts festival (July-Sept, www.ravellofestival.com) and music society performances (April-June and Sept-Oct, www.ravelloarts.org). Musicians perch on a bandstand on the edge of the cliff for a combination of wonderful music and dizzying views. Wagner visited here and was impressed enough to set the second act of his opera *Parsifal* in the villa's magical gardens. By all accounts, the concert on the cliff is a sublime experience.

Cost and Hours: €7, daily 9:00-21:00, Oct-April 9:00 until sunset, may close earlier for concerts, tel. 089-857-621, www.villarufolo.it.

Visiting the Villa: From Piazza Duomo, enter through the stout watchtower to buy your ticket and pick up the English booklet explaining the sight. Then, walk through part of the sprawling villa ruins. Check out the short video in the tiny theater at the base of the tower and the exhibit upstairs. The palace itself has little to show, but the gardens and views are magnificent and invite exploration.

▲Villa Cimbrone

This villa offers another romantic garden, this one built upon the ruins of an old convent. Located at the opposite end of Ravello, it was created in the 20th century by Englishman William Beckett. His mansion is now a five-star hotel. It's a longish walk to the end of town, where you explore a bluff dreamily landscaped around the villa. At the far end, above a sublime café on the lawn, "the Terrace of Infinity" dangles high above the sea.

Cost and Hours: €7, daily 9:00-sunset, tel. 089-857-459, www.villacimbrone.com.

Getting There: Facing the cathedral on Piazza Duomo, exit the square to the right and follow signs. You'll climb up and down (and up and down) some stair-step lanes, enjoying a quieter side of Ravello, before reaching the villa at the point.

Visiting the Villa: Buy your ticket and pick up the free map/guide of the gardens. Across from the ticket booth, duck into the old monastery. Then pass the rose-garden terrace and head up the "main boulevard," which leads straight to the stunning Terrace of Infinity, with 360-degree views up and down the coast. If you have the interest and energy, loop back along the more rugged downhill slope (facing the adjacent town of Scala). Tiny lizards scurry underfoot, while mythological statues (Mercury's Seat, Temple of Bacchus, Eve's Grotto) strike their poses before a stunning and serene backdrop.

▲Hike to Amalfi Town from Villa Cimbrone

To walk downhill from Ravello's Villa Cimbrone to the town of Amalfi (a path for hardy hikers only—follow the TI's map), retrace your steps back toward town. Take the first left, which turns into a stepped path winding its way below the cliff. Pause here to look back up at the rock with a big white mansion—Villa La Rondinaia, where Gore Vidal lived for many years. Continue down the fairly steep path about 40 minutes to the town of Atrani, where several bars on the main square offer well-deserved refreshments. From here, it's about a 15-minute walk back to Amalfi.

Eating in Ravello

Several no-brainer, interchangeable restaurants face Piazza Duomo and line the surrounding streets. To enjoy this fine setting, just take your pick. You can also grab a takeaway lunch at one of the little groceries and sandwich shops that line Via Roma (between Piazza Duomo and the TI). Enjoy your meal at the panoramic benches at the far end of Piazza Duomo (facing the cathedral), or facing even better views just outside of town, near the bus stop and Ristorante Da Salvatore. (Picnicking isn't allowed inside the two villas.)

$$$ Ristorante Da Salvatore, near the Ravello bus stop (at the other end of the little tunnel from the Duomo), serves a serious sit-down lunch with great views. Pino, the English-speaking owner of this formal restaurant, serves nicely presented, traditional Amalfi cuisine from a fun, if pricey, menu. Their pasta with potatoes and calamari is a favorite. Be adventurous when ordering and share dishes. Pato, the parakeet, is learning English (Tue-Sun 12:30-15:00 & 19:30-22:00, closed Mon, Via della Repubblica 2, tel. 089-857-227, reservations smart, www.salvatoreravello.com).

Ravello Connections

Ravello and the town of **Amalfi** are connected by bus along a very windy road. Coming from Amalfi town, buy your bus ticket at the bar on the waterfront, and ask where the stop for Ravello is (normally by the statue on the waterfront, just to the statue's left as you face the water). When returning from Ravello, line up early, since the buses are often crowded (at least every 40 minutes, 30-minute trip, €1.20, buy ticket in tobacco shop; catch bus 100 yards off main square, at other end of tunnel). Coming from Positano or Sorrento, you'll change buses in Amalfi. From Naples or Paestum, you have to change twice (in Salerno and Amalfi), making for a long day.

Paestum

The ruins at Paestum (PASTE-oom) include one of the best collections of Greek temples anywhere—and certainly the most accessible to Western Europe. Serenely situated, Paestum (worth ▲▲) is surrounded by fields and wildflowers. It

also has a functional zone with a bus stop, train station, church, and a straggle of houses and cafés that you could barely call a village.

This town was founded as Poseidonia by Greeks in the sixth century B.C. and became a key stop on an important trade route. In the fifth century B.C., the Lucanians, a barbarous inland tribe, conquered Poseidonia and tried to adopt the cultured ways of the Greeks. By the time of the Romans, who took over in the third century B.C., the name Poseidonia had been simplified to Paestum. The final conquerors of Paestum, malaria-carrying mosquitoes, kept the site wonderfully deserted for nearly a thousand years. The temples were never buried—just ignored. Rediscovered in the 18th century, Paestum today offers the only well-preserved Greek ruins north of Sicily.

While most visitors do Paestum as a day trip (it's 1.5 hours south of Naples by convenient direct train), it's not a bad place to overnight. Accommodations offer great value, and though it's a bit far, you could use Paestum as a base for day trips to Naples or the Amalfi Coast. There's a beach nearby, and hotels can help arrange visits to local buffalo-milk dairies.

Tourist Information: There's a small TI window at the train station (daily 8:30-18:30) and a bigger one next to the Paestum Archaeological Museum (daily 9:00-13:00 & 15:00-17:00, tel. 0828-811-016, www.infopaestum.it).

GETTING THERE

Direct trains to Paestum run from Naples and Salerno; from elsewhere, you'll need to transfer at one of those two points. For those transferring in Salerno, see the map on next page, which shows

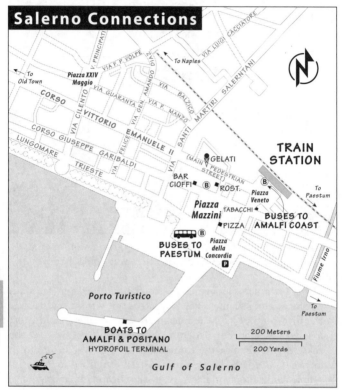

train, bus, and boat stops as well as a few handy takeaway places if you need to grab a bite.

From Naples: Direct **trains** run from Naples' Centrale Station to Paestum for €6 (10/day, 1.5 hours, direction: Sapri). Buy tickets from the ticket windows or machines at the station (stamp before boarding). For a day trip from Naples, it's wise to get an early start—especially in warm weather. Most recently, trains left at 6:50, 7:25, 7:55, and 8:55, then not until 12:07 (confirm schedule at station or www.trenitalia.it).

From Amalfi Town: First take a 75-minute bus ride (or possibly a boat) to Salerno, where you can catch the **train** on its way from Naples (30-40 minutes from Salerno to Paestum). You'll need to leave Amalfi early—8:00 at the latest—to make the last morning train. In Salerno, buy your train ticket at the ticket machines, ticket office, or the newsstand in the train station (stamp before boarding). Buses from Amalfi terminate at the Salerno train station, but if you arrive in Salerno from the Amalfi Coast by boat, you'll walk from the boat dock a few short blocks up to the train station (about 10 minutes, mostly level; see map).

If you're in a pinch—for example, you've arrived in Salerno during the midday lull in the train schedule—you could take **local CSTP bus #34** from Salerno to Paestum (about hourly, fewer on Sun, 1-hour trip). It seems convenient to the port (it departs from Piazza della Concordia—look for bus shelter between the big parking lot and the main road, no posted schedule), but you can't buy tickets nearby—the closest sales point is the tobacco shop a block in front of the train station. In Paestum, this bus drops you only slightly closer to the ruins than does the train.

From Positano: The extra 50 minutes by road to Amalfi, plus time spent changing buses there, makes a day trip from Positano to Paestum more difficult than from Amalfi town. It's possible, though (take a crack-of-dawn bus to Amalfi or the first ferry of the day to Salerno), especially in summer, when return buses from Amalfi run until late in the evening.

From Sorrento: The smart (if dull) approach is to go by Circumvesuviana train to Naples (70 minutes), catch the direct Naples-Paestum train, and return the same way. While it's technically possible to do one leg of the trip via an Amalfi Coast bus, this makes for a very long day marred by worry about making connections back. Other options are to rent a car or hire a taxi for the day. From Sorrento, Paestum is 60 miles and at least 3 hours (depending on traffic) via the Amalfi Coast road, but a smooth 2 hours by autostrada. To reach Paestum from Sorrento via the autostrada, drive toward Naples, catch the autostrada (direction: Salerno), skirt Salerno (direction: Reggio), exit at Battipaglia, and drive straight through the roundabout.

If you drive to Paestum, you'll see signs for *mozzarella di bufala*, cheese made from the milk of water buffalo. Try it here—it couldn't be any fresher.

Arrival at Paestum: If you arrive by train, cross under the tracks, exit the tiny station, and walk through the ancient city gate; the ruins are a 10-minute walk straight ahead, up a dusty road. When you hit the street with hotels and shops, turn right to find the museum and site entrance. Buses from Salerno stop near a corner of the ruins (at a little bar/café). There's no official baggage storage at the train station or museum. If you're desperate, you can try nicely asking one of the bars along the main road (they may want a small payment).

ORIENTATION TO PAESTUM

Cost: €7, €10 with special exhibits, includes site and museum. The site alone is €6 on days when the museum is closed; the museum alone is €4 after dark on winter evenings, when the site is closed.

Hours: Museum open daily 8:30-19:30 (last ticket sold at 18:50), except closed the first and third Mon of each month. Site open daily 8:30 to one hour before sunset (as late as 19:30 June-July, as early as 16:00 in late Nov-Dec, last site ticket sold 40 minutes before closing).

Information: Tel. 0828-811-023, www.museopaestum.beniculturali.it.

Getting In: The site and museum have separate entrances. The museum, just outside the ruins, is in a cluster with the TI and a small early-Christian basilica. Most visitors buy tickets at the museum and use the entrance across the street, but another ticket office and entrance are near the recommended Ristorante Nettuno (at the south end of the site). On days when the museum is closed, you have to buy tickets at the site entrances.

Local Guide: Silvia Braggio specializes in Paestum and gives a fine two-hour walk of the site and museum (special rate with this book-€100, arrange in advance, mobile 347-643-2307, www.silviaguide.it, silvia@silviaguide.it). She also offers walking tours of Pompeii and Herculaneum.

Eating: Several cafés and bars cluster around the museum (all open long hours daily in summer). **$ La Basilica Café,** facing a pretty little garden between the parking lot and TI, is the most straightforward and reasonable option, with good pizzas and other lunch fare (Via Magna Grecia 881, tel. 0828-811-301). **Ristorante Nettuno,** with quality food and good temple views, is at the south entrance to the site. They have a fine little glassed-in **$$** café facing the ruins (affordable light food, including a fixed-price lunch) and a dressier, more expensive **$$$** restaurant across the path (Via Nettuno 2, tel. 0828-811-028).

Length of This Tour: Allow two hours to see the ruins and the museum. Which one you see first depends on your interest and the heat: You'll enjoy the coolest temperatures in the morning, but the best light and smallest crowds late in the day.

BACKGROUND

While Paestum is famous for its marvelous Greek temples, most of the structures you see are Roman. Five elements of Greek Paestum survive: three misnamed temples, a memorial tomb, and a circular meeting place (the Ekklesiasterion). The rest, including the wall that defines the site, is Roman.

Paestum was once a seaport (the ocean is now about a mile away—the wall in the distance, which stretches about three miles, is about halfway to today's coastline). Only about a fifth of the site has been excavated. The Greek city, which archaeologists figure had a population of about 13,000, was first conquered by Lucanians (distant relatives of the Romans, who spoke a language related

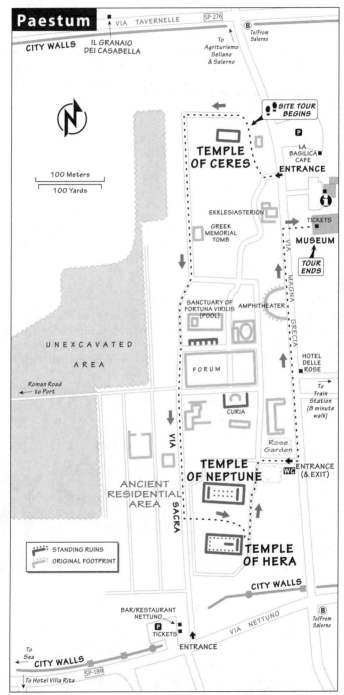

to Latin), and then by the Romans (who completely made it over and built the wall you see today).

The remaining Greek structures survive because the Romans were superstitious—they respected sacred areas and didn't mess with temples and tombs. While most old Christian churches are built upon Roman temples (it tends to be what people do when they conquer another culture), no Roman temple is built upon a Greek temple. Romans appreciated how religion could function as the opiate of the masses. As long as people paid their taxes and obeyed the emperor's dictates, the practical Romans had no problem with any religion. The three Greek temples that you'll see here today have stood for about 2,500 years.

⊙ SELF-GUIDED TOURS

Although there are only scant descriptions at the site, the following self-guided tours provide all the information you need for both the site and the museum. Skip the museum bookshop's mediocre guidebooks and dull audioguide.

Paestum Archaeological Site

This part of the tour starts at the entrance by the museum, visits the Temple of Ceres, goes through the center of the Roman town past the Greek Memorial Tomb, circles around the other two Greek temples, and then leaves the site to walk down the modern road to the Ekklesiasterion (which faces the museum).

• *Buy your ticket at the museum, then head to the right to find the site's north entrance. Once inside, stand in front of the...*

Temple of Ceres: All three Paestum temples have inaccurate names, coined by 19th-century archaeologists who based their "discoveries" on wishful thinking. (While the Romans made things easy by leaving lots of inscriptions, the Greeks did not.) Those 1800s archaeologists  wanted this temple to be devoted to Ceres, the goddess of agriculture. However, all the little votive statues found later, when modern archaeologists dug here, instead depicted a woman with a big helmet: Athena, goddess of wisdom and war. (The Greeks' female war goddess was also the goddess of wisdom—thinking...strategy... female. The Romans' masculine war god was Mars—just fighting.) Each temple is part of a sanctuary—an open, sacred space around the temple. Because regular people couldn't go into the temple, the altar logically stood outside.

The Temple of Ceres dates from 500 B.C. It's made of locally quarried limestone blocks. Good roads and shipping didn't come along until the Romans, so the Greeks' buildings were limited to local materials. The wooden roof is long gone. Like the other two temples, this one was once painted white, black, and red, and has an east-west orientation—facing the rising sun. This temple's *cella* (interior room) is gone, cleared out when it was used as a Christian church in the sixth century. In medieval times, Normans scavenged stones from here; chunks of these temples can be found in Amalfi's cathedral.

Walk around to the back side of the Temple of Ceres. The capitals broke in a modern earthquake, so a steel bar provides necessary support. Each of the Paestum temples is Doric style—with three stairs, columns without a base, and shafts that narrow at the top to a simple capital of a round, then a square, block. While there were no carved reliefs, colorful frescoes once decorated the pediments.

As you walk away, look back at the temple. Traditionally, Greeks would build a sanctuary of Athena on a city's highest spot (like the Parthenon in Athens, on the Acropolis). Paestum had no hill, so the Greeks created a mound. The hill was more impressive in its time because the level of the Greek city was substantially lower than the Roman pavement stones you'll walk on today.

• *Continue all the way past the temple, follow the path down, and turn left to walk on the paving stones of Via Sacra toward the other Greek temples. After about 100 yards, to the left of the road, you'll see a little half-buried house with a tiled roof.*

Greek Memorial Tomb (Heroon): This tomb (from 500 B.C.) also survived because the Romans respected religious buildings. But the tomb was most inconveniently located, right in the middle of their growing city. So the practical Romans built a perimeter wall around it (visible today), added a fine tiled roof, and then buried the tomb.

There's a mystery here. Greeks generally buried their dead outside the city (as did Romans)—there are over a thousand ancient tombs outside Paestum's walls—yet this tomb was parked smack-dab in the center of town. When it was uncovered in 1952, no bodies were found inside. The tomb instead held nine perfectly preserved vases (now in the museum). Archaeologists aren't sure what the tomb's purpose was. Perhaps it was a memorial dedicated to some great hero (like a city founder). Or perhaps it was a memorial to those lost when a neighboring community had to evacuate and settle as refugees here.

• *Continue walking down Via Sacra, the main drag of...*

Roman Paestum: Roman towns were garrison towns: rectangular with a grid street plan and two main streets cutting north-south and east-west, dividing the town into four equal sections.

They were built by military engineers with a no-nonsense standard design. New excavations (on the left) have uncovered Roman-era lead piping. City administration buildings were on the left, and residential buildings were on the right.

Shortly after the road turns into a dirt path, you'll come to a big **Roman pool** (on the left) that archaeologists believe was a sanctuary dedicated to Fortuna Virilis, goddess of luck and fertility. The strange stones likely supported a wooden platform for priests and statues of gods. Imagine young women walking down the ramp at the far end and through the pool, hoping to conceive a child.

The next big square on the left was the **Roman forum** and ancient Paestum's main intersection. The road on the right led directly (and very practically) to the port. It made sense to have a direct connection to move freight between the sea and the center of town.

Until 2007, the vast field of ruins on the right (between the forum and the next temple) was covered in vegetation. It's since been cleared and cleaned of harmful lichen, which produce acids that dissolve limestone. Study the rocks: Yellow lichen is alive, black is dead. Even the great temples of Paestum were covered in this destructive lichen until 2000, when a two-year-long project cleaned them for the first time.

• *Ahead on the left are the so-called...*

Temples of Neptune and Hera: The **Temple of Neptune** dates from 450 B.C. and employs the Greek architectural trick where the

base line is curved up just a tad to overcome the illusion of sagging caused by a straight base. The Athenians built their Parthenon (with a similar bowed-up base line) just 30 years after this. Many think this temple could have been their inspiration.

The adjacent **Temple of Hera,** dating from 550 B.C., is the oldest of Paestum's three temples and one of the oldest Greek temples still standing anywhere. Notice the change 100 years makes in the architectural styles: Archaic Doric in 550 B.C. versus Classic Doric in 450 B.C.

Archaeologists now believe the "Temple of Neptune" was actually devoted to a different god. Votive statues uncovered here suggest that Hera was the focus (perhaps this was a new-and-improved version of the adjacent, simpler, and older Temple of Hera). Or perhaps it was a temple to Zeus, Hera's husband, to honor the couple together.

Together, the two temples formed a single huge sanctuary

with altars on the far (east) side. Walk between the temples, then hook right to get a good look at the front of the Temple of Hera. Notice how overbuilt this temple appears. Its columns and capitals are closer together than necessary, as if the builders lacked confidence in their ability to span the distance between supports. Square pillars mark the corners of the *cella* inside. Temples with an odd number of columns (here, nine) had a single colonnade crossing in the center inside to support the wooden roof. More modern temples (such as the Temple of Neptune) had six columns, with two colonnades passing through the *cella*. This left a line of vision open through the middle so that worshippers could see the big statue of the god.

By the way, in 1943, Allied paratroopers dropped in near here during the famous "Landing of Salerno," when the Allies (who had already taken Sicily) invaded mainland Italy. Paestum was part of their first beachhead. The Temple of Hera served as an Allied military tent hospital. From here, the Allies pushed back the Nazis, marching to Naples, Cassino, and finally to Rome.

• Leave the site (using the exit straight ahead from the Temple of Neptune and a bit to the left) and turn left on the modern road...

Via Magna Grecia: The king of Naples had this Naples-to-Paestum road built in 1829 to inspire his people with ancient temples. While he was modern in his appreciation of antiquity, his road project destroyed a swath of the ancient city, as you'll see as you pass by half of the small amphitheater.

• Just past the amphitheater, you'll find the...

Ekklesiasterion: Immediately across the street from the museum is what looks like a sunken circular theater. This rare bit of ancient Greek ruins was the Ekklesiasterion, a meeting place where the Greeks would get together to discuss things and vote. Archaeologists believe that the agora (market) would also have been located here.

• Across the street is the...

Paestum Archaeological Museum

Paestum's museum offers the rare opportunity to see artifacts—dating from prehistoric to Greek to Roman times—at the site where they were discovered. These beautifully crafted works (with good English descriptions throughout) help bring Paestum to life. Not everything you see here is from Paestum, though, as the museum also collects artifacts from other nearby sites.

Before stepping into the museum, notice the proud fascist architecture. Though the building dates from 1954, it was designed in 1938. It seems to command that you *will* enjoy this history lesson.

The exhibit is on several levels. You'll find mostly Greek pieces on the ground floor (artifacts from the Temple of Hera in front, frescoes from tombs in the back), Paleolithic to Iron Age artifacts on the mezzanine level, and Roman art on the top floor (statues, busts, and inscriptions dating from the time of the Roman occupation). While Roman art is not unique to Paestum, the Greek collection is—so that's what you should focus on. Here are the highlights:

Temple Reliefs: The museum's first room is designed like a Greek temple, with an inner *cella* used for temporary exhibitions. The large carvings overhead that wrap around this inner sanctum once adorned a sanctuary of the goddess Hera (wife of Zeus) five miles away. This sanctuary, called Heraion del Sele, was discovered and excavated in 1934. Some of the carvings show scenes from the life of Hercules.

• *Along the back wall of this room, find the glass case holding nine perfectly preserved...*

Vases: One ceramic and eight bronze, with artistic handles, these vases were found in Paestum's Greek Memorial Tomb (if these vases are off-view for restoration, look for the similar bronze vases upstairs, at the end of this tour). Greek bronzes are rare because Romans often melted them down to make armor. These were discovered in 1952, filled with still-liquid honey and sealed with beeswax. The honey (as you can see in the display cases below) has since crystallized. Honey was a standard part of a funeral because, to ancient Greeks, honey symbolized immortality...it lasts forever.

• *Enter the room at the far end of the main hall, filled with ancient Greek...*

Votive Offerings: These were dug up at Heraion del Sele (not at Paestum). Such offerings are a huge help to modern archaeologists, since the figures that worshippers brought to a temple are clues as to which god the temple honored. These votives depict a woman with a crown on a throne—clearly Hera. The clay votives were simple, affordable, and accessible to regular people.

• *Now enter the large room (broken up by pillars and interior walls) that holds...*

Relics from the Temples at Paestum: This room displays smaller pieces. Displays (mostly in Italian) tell in which temple each relic was found. The Temple of Ceres is often referred to as the Temple of Athena or as the northern *(settentrionale)* sanctuary. The Temples of Neptune and Hera are spoken of as the southern *(meridionale)* sanctuaries. Before exploring the collection, notice the display case near the entrance with the **huge book** turned to a page with a fine drawing by the Italian artist Giovanni Piranesi, showing his visit to Paestum in 1777.

Across the room, look for the short fragment of a **frieze** with lion heads. Paestum's three temples were once adorned with decorations, such as these ornamental spouts that spurted rainwater out of lions' mouths. Notice the bits of the surviving black, red, and white paint. Reconstructions on the adjacent wall show archaeologists' best guesses as to how the original decorations might have looked.

Farther into the room, you can't miss the display case of a statue's **torso** emblazoned with swastikas—a reminder that this symbol (carrying completely different meanings) predated Hitler by millennia.

In a glass case nearby, find the seated statue of **Zeus.** This painted clay Zeus dates from 520 B.C. The king of the gods was so lusty with his antics, he's still smirking.

• *Look out the museum's back window for a good, if distant...*

View of Paestum's Walls: The walls of ancient Paestum reach halfway to the mountain—a reminder that most of the site is still private property and yet to be excavated. The town up on the mountainside is Capaccio, established in the eighth century when inhabitants of the original city of Paestum were driven out by malaria and the city was abandoned.

• *Walk along the corridor at the back of the museum, which shows...*

Objects from Tombs: More than 1,000 tombs have been identified outside the ancient city's wall. About 100 were found decorated with frescoes or containing objects such as these.

• *At the far end of the corridor, turn left to see...*

The Tomb of the Diver: This is the museum's treasure and the most precious Paestum find. Dating from 480 B.C., it's not only the sole ancient Greek tomb fresco in the museum—it's the only

one ever found in southern Italy. Discovered in 1968, it has five frescoed slabs (four sides and a lid; the bottom wasn't decorated). The Greeks saw death as a passage: diving from mortality into immortality...into an unknown world. Archaeologists believe that the pillars shown on the fresco represent the Pillars of Hercules at Gibraltar, which in ancient times defined the known world. The ocean beyond the Mediterranean was the great unknown...like the afterlife. The Greek banquet makes it clear that this was an aristocratic man.

• *After the Tomb of the Diver, the next room displays...*

Lucanian Tomb Frescoes: The many other painted slabs in the museum date from a later time, around 350 B.C., when Paestum fell under Lucanian rule. These frescoes are cruder than their earlier Greek counterpart. The people who conquered the Greeks tried to appropriate their art and style, but they lacked the Greeks' distinctive light touch. Still, these offer fascinating glimpses into ancient life here at Paestum.

• *Beyond this room, you'll find yourself back at the entrance. Before you leave, go up the stairs by the bookshop for a glimpse at the mezzanine level, which focuses on prehistoric archaeology. The exhibit here has much better English translations than the ground floor. At the very least, near the end of the first hall, check out the...*

Film Footage from WWII: A 10-minute continuous film loop, subtitled in English, tells the story of Allied soldiers' encounters with the ruins in 1943. You'll see footage of soldiers hanging up their laundry and shaving in the temples, which they actually safeguarded well. Part of the film focuses on excavations directed by a British archaeologist who was attached to the invading forces.

• *The back wall of the mezzanine displays* **bronze vases,** *mostly from Gaudo, a half-mile from Paestum. If the vases downstairs are missing, here's your chance to see some rare surviving examples of this common Greek vessel.*

SLEEPING IN PAESTUM

Paestum at night, with views of the floodlit ruins, is magic. Accommodations here offer great value. You can sleep in a mansion for the same price you'd pay for a closet in Positano. All listings have free parking.

$ Il Granaio dei Casabella, a converted old granary with 14 attractive, reasonably priced rooms, is a 10-minute walk from the ruins. It has a beautiful garden and pretty common areas, and four rooms have temple views (RS%, family rooms, air-con, closed Dec-Feb, just west of the bus stop closest to Salerno at Via Tavernelle 84, tel. 0828-721-014, www.ilgranaiodeicasabella.com, info@ilgranaiodeicasabella.com, hospitable Celardo family).

$ Hotel Villa Rita is a tidy, quiet country hotel set on two acres within walking distance of the beach and the temples. It has 22 rooms, a kid-friendly swimming pool, and attractive grounds with grassy lawns and a little soccer field (RS%, extra bed possible, lunch or dinner-€22, air-con, closed Nov-mid-March, Via Nettuno 9, tel. 0828-811-081, www.hotelvillarita.it, info@hotelvillarita.it, Luigi). The hotel is a 10-minute walk west of the Hera entrance and public bus stop, and a 20-minute walk from the train station (they can usually pick you up, if you're arriving with luggage).

$ Hotel delle Rose, with 10 small, basic rooms with minuscule bathrooms, is near the Neptune entrance on the street bordering the ruins. It's an acceptable choice for those on a budget and is also the option closest to the ruins and the train station (RS%, family rooms, air-con, Via Magna Grecia 943, tel. 0828-199-0692, www.hotelristorantedellerose.com, info@hotelristorantedellerose. com, Luigi).

Outside of Town: $$ Agriturismo Seliano is a great option for drivers, with plush public spaces, a pool, and 14 grand, spacious rooms on a peaceful, once-elegant farm estate that's been in the same family for 300 years (air-con, closed Nov-March; one mile north of ruins on main road—Via Magna Grecia—a small *Azienda Agrituristica Seliano* sign directs you down long dirt driveway; Via Seliano, tel. 0828-723-634, www.agriturismoseliano.it, seliano@ agriturismoseliano.it). They serve a fine lunch or dinner for guests and nonguests—made with produce fresh from the garden—and can also organize cooking classes. The place is run by Cecilia—an English-speaking baroness—and her family, including about a dozen dogs.

PAESTUM CONNECTIONS

By Train: Ten slow, milk-run trains per day head to Salerno (30-40 minutes) and Naples (1.5 hours). In Salerno, you can change for the bus to Amalfi or walk down to the harbor to catch an Amalfi- or Positano-bound boat. You can buy train tickets at machines in the (unstaffed) Paestum station.

By Bus to Salerno: Buses depart from Paestum to Salerno roughly every hour (fewer on Sun; one-hour trip). Buy a ticket from one of the bars in Paestum, then go to either of the intersections that flank the ruins, flag down any northbound bus, and ask, "Salerno?" From Salerno, you can continue on to Amalfi or Positano by boat or walk up to the train station to catch an Amalfi-bound SITA bus or a train.

AMALFI COAST

PRACTICALITIES

This section covers just the basics on traveling in Italy (for much more information, see *Rick Steves Italy*). You'll find free advice on specific topics at www.ricksteves.com/tips.

Money

Italy uses the euro currency: 1 euro (€) = about $1.20. To convert prices in euros to dollars, add about 20 percent: €20 = about $24, €50 = about $60. (Check www.oanda.com for the latest exchange rates.)

The standard way for travelers to get euros is to withdraw money from an ATM (known as a *bancomat*) using a debit or credit card, ideally with a Visa or MasterCard logo. To keep your cash, cards, and valuables safe, wear a money belt.

Before departing, call your bank or credit-card company: Confirm that your card(s) will work overseas, ask about international transaction fees, and alert them that you'll be making withdrawals in Europe. Also ask for the PIN number for your credit card—you may need it for Europe's "chip-and-PIN" payment machines (see below; allow time for your bank to mail your PIN to you).

Dealing with "Chip and PIN": Most credit and debit cards now have chips that authenticate and secure transactions. European cardholders insert their chip card into the payment slot, then enter a PIN. (For most US cards, you provide a signature.) Any American card, whether with a chip or an old-fashioned magnetic stripe, will work at Europe's hotels, restaurants, and shops. But some self-service chip-and-PIN payment machines—such as those at train stations, toll roads, or unattended gas pumps—may not accept your card, even if you know the PIN. If your card won't work, look for a cashier who can process the transaction manually—or pay in cash.

Dynamic Currency Conversion: If merchants or hoteliers offer to convert your purchase price into dollars (called dynamic currency conversion, or DCC), refuse this "service." You'll pay extra in fees for the expensive convenience of seeing your charge in dollars. If an ATM offers to "lock in" or "guarantee" your conversion rate, choose "proceed without conversion." Other prompts might state, "You can be charged in dollars: Press YES for dollars, NO for euros." Always choose the local currency.

Staying Connected

The simplest solution is to bring your own device—mobile phone, tablet, or laptop—and use it just as you would at home (following the tips below, such as connecting to free Wi-Fi whenever possible).

To call Italy from a US or Canadian number: Whether you're phoning from a landline, your own mobile phone, or a Skype account, you're making an international call. Dial 011-39 and then the local number. (The 011 is our international access code, and 39 is Italy's country code.) If dialing from a mobile phone, you can enter + in place of the international access code—press and hold the 0 key.

To call Italy from a European country: Dial 00-39 followed by the local number. (The 00 is Europe's international access code.)

To call within Italy: Just dial the local number.

To call from Italy to another country: Dial 00 followed by the country code (for example, 1 for the US or Canada), then the area code and number. If you're calling European countries whose phone numbers begin with 0, you'll usually omit that 0 when you dial.

Tips: If you bring your own mobile phone, consider getting an international plan; most providers offer a global calling plan that cuts the per-minute cost of phone calls and texts, and a flat-fee data plan.

Use Wi-Fi whenever possible. Most hotels and many cafés offer free Wi-Fi, and you'll likely also find it at tourist information offices, major museums, and public-transit hubs. With Wi-Fi you can use your phone or tablet to make free or inexpensive domestic and international calls via a calling app such as Skype, FaceTime, or Google+ Hangouts. When you can't find Wi-Fi, you can use your cellular network to connect to the Internet, send texts, or make voice calls. When you're done, avoid further charges by manually switching off "data roaming" or "cellular data."

It's possible to stay connected without a mobile device. Most hotels have a computer in the lobby for guests to use. To make cheap international calls from any phone (even your hotel-room phone), you can buy a prepaid international phone card in Italy.

Sleep Code

Hotels are classified based on the average price of a standard double room with breakfast in high season.

$$$$	**Splurge:** Most rooms over €170
$$$	**Pricier:** €130-170
$$	**Moderate:** €90-130
$	**Budget:** €50-90
¢	**Backpacker:** Under €50
RS%	**Rick Steves discount**

Unless otherwise noted, credit cards are accepted, hotel staff speak basic English, and free Wi-Fi is available. Comparison-shop by checking prices at several hotels (on each hotel's own website, on a booking site, or by email). For the best deal, book directly with the hotel. Ask for a discount if paying in cash; if the listing includes **RS%,** request a Rick Steves discount.

Dial the toll-free access number, enter the card's PIN code, then dial the number. For more on phoning, see www.ricksteves.com/phoning. For a one-hour talk on "Traveling with a Mobile Device," see www.ricksteves.com/travel-talks.

Sleeping

I've categorized my recommended accommodations based on price, indicated with a dollar-sign rating (see sidebar). I recommend reserving rooms in advance, particularly during peak season. Once your dates are set, check the specific price for your preferred stay at several hotels. You can do this either by comparing prices on Hotels.com or Booking.com, or by checking the hotels' own websites. To get the best deal, contact my family-run hotels directly by phone or email. When you go direct, the owner avoids the online booking engine commission, giving them wiggle room to offer you a discount, a nicer room, or free breakfast. If you prefer to book online or are considering a hotel chain, it's to your advantage to use the hotel's website.

For complicated requests, send an email with the following information: number and type of rooms; number of nights; arrival date; departure date; and any special requests. Use the European style for writing dates: day/month/year. Hoteliers typically ask for your credit-card number as a deposit.

Some hotels are willing to make a deal to attract guests: Try emailing several to ask their best price. In general, hotel prices can soften if you do any of the following: offer to pay cash, stay at least three nights, or travel off-season.

While most taxes are included in the price, a variable city tax of €1.50-5/person per night is often added to hotel bills in Italy. Some hoteliers will ask to collect the city tax in cash to make their

---

Restaurant Price Code

I've assigned each eatery a price category, based on the average cost of a typical main course (pasta or *secondi*). Drinks, desserts, and splurge items (steak and seafood) can raise the price considerably.

$$$$	**Splurge:** Most main courses over €20
$$$	**Pricier:** €15-20
$$	**Moderate:** €10-15
$	**Budget:** Under €10

In Italy, pizza by the slice and other takeaway food is **$**; a basic trattoria or sit-down pizzeria is **$$**; a casual but more upscale restaurant is **$$$**; and a swanky splurge is **$$$$**.

---

bookkeeping and accounting simpler.

Eating

I've categorized my recommended eateries based on price, indicated with a dollar-sign rating (see sidebar). Italy offers a wide array of eateries. A *ristorante* is a formal restaurant, while a *trattoria* or *osteria* is usually more traditional and simpler (but can still be pricey). Italian "bars" are not taverns, but small cafés selling sandwiches, coffee, and other drinks. An *enoteca* is a wine bar with snacks and light meals. Take-away food from pizza shops and delis (*rosticcería*) makes an easy picnic.

Italians eat dinner a bit later than we do; better restaurants start serving around 19:00. A full meal consists of an appetizer (antipasto), a first course (*primo piatto*, pasta, rice, or soup), and a second course (*secondo piatto*, expensive meat and fish/seafood dishes). Vegetables *(verdure)* may come with the *secondo*, but more often must be ordered separately as a side dish (*contorno*). Desserts (*dolci*) can be very tempting. The euros can add up in a hurry, but you don't have to order each course. My approach is to mix antipasti and *primi piatti* family-style with my dinner partners (skipping *secondi*). Or, for a basic value, look for a *menù del giorno*, a three- or four-course, fixed-price meal deal (avoid the cheapest ones, often called a *menù turistico*).

At bars and cafés, getting a drink while standing at the bar (*banco*) is cheaper than drinking it at a table *(tavolo)* or sitting outside *(terrazza)*. This tiered pricing system is clearly posted on the wall. Sometimes you'll pay at a cash register, then take the receipt to another counter to claim your drink.

Good service is relaxed (slow to an American). You won't get the bill until you ask for it: *"Il conto?"* Many (but not all) restaurants in Italy add a cover charge *(coperto)* of €1-3.50 per person to your bill.

Tipping: Most restaurants include a service charge in their prices (check the menu for *servizio incluso*—generally around 10 percent). You can add on a tip, if you choose, by including a euro or two for each person in your party. If you order at a counter rather than from waitstaff, there's no need to tip.

Transportation

By Train: In Italy, most travelers find it's cheapest simply to buy train tickets as they go. To see if a rail pass could save you money, check www.ricksteves.com/rail. To research train schedules, visit Germany's excellent all-Europe website, www.bahn.com, or Italy's www.trenitalia.com. A private company called Italo also runs fast trains on major routes in Italy; see www.italotreno.it.

You can buy tickets at train stations (at the ticket window or at machines with English instructions) or from travel agencies. Before boarding the train, you must validate your train documents by stamping them in the machine near the platform (usually marked *convalida biglietti* or *vidimazione*). Strikes *(sciopero)* are common and generally announced in advance (but a few sporadic trains still run—ask around).

By Bus: Long-distance buses are catching on in Italy as an alternative to the train. They are usually cheaper, modern, and often (unlike trains) have free Wi-Fi. Some of the operators you'll see are Eurolines/Baltour (www.baltour.it), Flixbus (www.flixbus. com), and Marozzi (www.marozzivt.it).

By Car: It's cheaper to arrange most car rentals from the US. If you're planning a multicountry itinerary by car, be aware of often-astronomical international drop-off fees. For tips on your insurance options, see www.ricksteves.com/cdw, and for route planning, consult www.viamichelin.com. Theft insurance is mandatory in Italy ($15-20/day). In Italy, most car-rental companies' rates automatically include Collision Damage Waiver (CDW) coverage. Even if you try to decline CDW when you reserve your Italian car, you may find when you show up at the counter that you must buy it after all.

It's also required that you carry an International Driving Permit (IDP), available at your local AAA office ($20 plus two passport-type photos, www.aaa.com).

Italy's superhighway *(autostrada)* system is slick and speedy, but you'll pay a toll. Be warned that car traffic is restricted in many city centers—don't drive or park in any area that has a sign reading *Zona Traffico Limitato* (*ZTL,* often shown above a red circle)...or you might be mailed a ticket later.

Italians love to tailgate; otherwise, local road etiquette is similar to that in the US. Ask your car-rental company for details, or check the US State Department website (www.travel.state.gov, search for Italy in the "Learn about your destination" box, then click on "Travel and Transportation").

A car is a worthless headache in cities—park it safely (get tips from your hotelier). As break-ins are common, be sure your valuables are out of sight and locked in the trunk, or even better, with you or in your hotel room.

Helpful Hints

Emergency Help: For English-speaking **police** help, dial 113. To summon an **ambulance**, call 118. For passport problems, call the **US Embassy** (in Rome, 24-hour line—tel. 06-46741) or **US Consulates** (Milan—tel. 02-290-351, Florence—tel. 055-266-951, Naples—tel. 081-583-8111); or the **Canadian Embassy** (in Rome, tel. 06-854-442-911). If you have a minor illness, do as the locals do and go to a pharmacist for advice. Or ask at your hotel for help—they'll know of the nearest medical and emergency services. For other concerns, get advice from your hotelier.

Theft or Loss: Italy has particularly hardworking pickpockets—wear a money belt. Assume beggars are pickpockets and any scuffle is simply a distraction by a team of thieves. If you stop for any commotion or show, put your hands in your pockets before someone else does.

To replace a passport, you'll need to go in person to an embassy or consulate (see above). Cancel and replace your credit and debit cards by calling these 24-hour US numbers collect: Visa—tel. 303/967-1096, MasterCard—tel. 636/722-7111, American Express—tel. 336/393-1111. In Italy, to make a collect call to the US, dial 800-172-444; press zero or stay on the line for an operator. File a police report either on the spot or within a day or two; you'll need it to submit an insurance claim for lost or stolen rail passes or travel gear, and it can help with replacing your passport or credit and debit cards. For more information, see www.ricksteves.com/help.

Time: Italy uses the 24-hour clock. It's the same through 12:00 noon, then keep going: 13:00, 14:00, and so on. Italy, like most of continental Europe, is six/nine hours ahead of the East/West Coasts of the US.

Business Hours: Many businesses have now adopted the government's recommended 8:00 to 14:00 workday (although in tourist areas, shops are open longer). Still, expect small towns and villages to be more or less shut tight during lunch. Stores are also usually closed on Sunday, and often on Monday.

Sights: Opening and closing hours of sights can change unexpectedly; confirm the latest times with the local tourist information office or its website. Some major churches enforce a modest dress code (no bare shoulders or shorts) for everyone, even chil-

PRACTICALITIES

dren.

Holidays and Festivals: Italy celebrates many holidays, which can close sights and attract crowds (book hotel rooms ahead). For information on holidays and festivals, check Italy's website: www.italia.it. For a simple list showing major—though not all—events, see www.ricksteves.com/festivals.

Numbers and Stumblers: What Americans call the second floor of a building is the first floor in Europe. Europeans write dates as day/month/year, so Christmas 2019 is 25/12/19. Commas are decimal points and vice versa—a dollar and a half is 1,50, and there are 5.280 feet in a mile. Italy uses the metric system: A kilogram is 2.2 pounds; a liter is about a quart; and a kilometer is six-tenths of a mile.

Resources from Rick Steves

This Snapshot guide is excerpted from my latest edition of *Rick Steves Italy*, one of many titles in my ever-expanding series of guidebooks on European travel. I also produce a public television series, *Rick Steves' Europe*, and a public radio show, *Travel with Rick Steves*. My website, www.ricksteves.com, offers free travel information, a forum for travelers' comments, guidebook updates, my travel blog, an online travel store, and information on European rail passes and our tours of Europe. If you're bringing a mobile device, my free Rick Steves Audio Europe app features dozens of self-guided audio tours of the top sights in Europe—including sights in Rome, Florence, Venice, Milan, Naples, Pompeii, Siena, and Assisi—plus radio shows and travel interviews about Italy. You can get Rick Steves Audio Europe via Apple's App Store, Google Play, or the Amazon Appstore. For more information, see www.ricksteves.com/audioeurope.

Additional Resources

Tourist Information: www.italia.it
Passports and Red Tape: www.travel.state.gov
Packing List: www.ricksteves.com/packing
Travel Insurance: www.ricksteves.com/insurance
Cheap Flights: www.kayak.com or www.google.com/flights
Airplane Carry-on Restrictions: www.tsa.gov/travelers
Updates for This Book: www.ricksteves.com/update

How Was Your Trip?

To share your tips, concerns, and discoveries after using this book, please fill out the survey at www.ricksteves.com/feedback. Thanks in advance—it helps a lot.

Italian Survival Phrases

English	Italian	Pronunciation
Good day.	*Buon giorno.*	bwohn **jor**-noh
Do you speak English?	*Parla inglese?*	**par**-lah een-**gleh**-zay
Yes. / No.	*Sì. / No.*	see / noh
I (don't) understand.	*(Non) capisco.*	(nohn) kah-**pees**-koh
Please.	*Per favore.*	pehr fah-**voh**-ray
Thank you.	*Grazie.*	**graht**-see-ay
You're welcome.	*Prego.*	**preh**-go
I'm sorry.	*Mi dispiace.*	mee dee-spee-**ah**-chay
Excuse me.	*Mi scusi.*	mee **skoo**-zee
(No) problem.	*(Non) c'è problema.*	(nohn) cheh proh-**bleh**-mah
Good.	*Va bene.*	vah **beh**-nay
Goodbye.	*Arrivederci.*	ah-ree-veh-**dehr**-chee
one / two	*uno / due*	**oo**-noh / **doo**-ay
three / four	*tre / quattro*	tray / **kwah**-troh
five / six	*cinque / sei*	**cheeng**-kway / **seh**-ee
seven / eight	*sette / otto*	**seh**-tay / **oh**-toh
nine / ten	*nove / dieci*	**noh**-vay / dee-**ay**-chee
How much is it?	*Quanto costa?*	**kwahn**-toh **koh**-stah
Write it?	*Me lo scrive?*	may loh **skree**-vay
Is it free?	*È gratis?*	eh **grah**-tees
Is it included?	*È incluso?*	eh een-**kloo**-zoh
Where can I buy / find...?	*Dove posso comprare / trovare...?*	**doh**-vay **poh**-soh kohm-**prah**-ray / troh-**vah**-ray
I'd like / We'd like...	*Vorrei / Vorremmo...*	voh-**reh**-ee / voh-**reh**-moh
...a room.	*...una camera.*	**oo**-nah **kah**-meh-rah
...a ticket to ____.	*...un biglietto per ____.*	oon beel-**yeh**-toh pehr ____
Is it possible?	*È possibile?*	eh poh-**see**-bee-lay
Where is...?	*Dov'è...?*	doh-**veh**
...the train station	*...la stazione*	lah staht-see-**oh**-nay
...the bus station	*...la stazione degli autobus*	lah staht-see-**oh**-nay **dehl**-yee **ow**-toh-boos
...tourist information	*...informazioni per turisti*	een-for-maht-see-**oh**-nee pehr too-**ree**-stee
...the toilet	*...la toilette*	lah twah-**leh**-tay
men	*uomini / signori*	**woh**-mee-nee / seen-**yoh**-ree
women	*donne / signore*	**doh**-nay / seen-**yoh**-ray
left / right	*sinistra / destra*	see-**nee**-strah / **deh**-strah
straight	*sempre dritto*	**sehm**-pray **dree**-toh
What time does this open / close?	*A che ora apre / chiude?*	ah kay **oh**-rah **ah**-pray / kee-**oo**-day
At what time?	*A che ora?*	ah kay **oh**-rah
Just a moment.	*Un momento.*	oon moh-**mehn**-toh
now / soon / later	*adesso / presto / tardi*	ah-**deh**-soh / **preh**-stoh / **tar**-dee
today / tomorrow	*oggi / domani*	**oh**-jee / doh-**mah**-nee

In an Italian Restaurant

English	Italian	Pronunciation
I'd like...	Vorrei...	voh-**reh**-ee
We'd like...	Vorremmo...	vor-**reh**-moh
...to reserve...	...prenotare...	preh-noh-**tah**-ray
...a table for one / two.	...un tavolo per uno / due.	oon **tah**-voh-loh pehr **oo**-noh / **doo**-ay
Is this seat free?	È libero questo posto?	eh **lee**-beh-roh **kweh**-stoh **poh**-stoh
The menu (in English), please.	Il menù (in inglese), per favore.	eel meh-**noo** (een een-**gleh**-zay) pehr fah-**voh**-ray
service (not) included	servizio (non) incluso	sehr-**veet**-see-oh (nohn) een-**kloo**-zoh
cover charge	pane e coperto	**pah**-nay ay koh-**pehr**-toh
to go	da portar via	dah **por**-tar **vee**-ah
with / without	con / senza	kohn / **sehnt**-sah
and / or	e / o	ay / oh
menu (of the day)	menù (del giorno)	meh-**noo** (dehl **jor**-noh)
specialty of the house	specialità della casa	speh-chah-lee-**tah** deh-lah **kah**-zah
first course (pasta, soup)	primo piatto	**pree**-moh pee-**ah**-toh
main course (meat, fish)	secondo piatto	seh-**kohn**-doh pee-**ah**-toh
side dishes	contorni	kohn-**tor**-nee
bread	pane	**pah**-nay
cheese	formaggio	for-**mah**-joh
sandwich	panino	pah-**nee**-noh
soup	zuppa	**tsoo**-pah
salad	insalata	een-sah-**lah**-tah
meat	carne	**kar**-nay
chicken	pollo	**poh**-loh
fish	pesce	**peh**-shay
seafood	frutti di mare	**froo**-tee dee **mah**-ray
fruit / vegetables	frutta / legumi	**froo**-tah / lay-**goo**-mee
dessert	dolce	**dohl**-chay
tap water	acqua del rubinetto	**ah**-kwah dehl roo-bee-**neh**-toh
mineral water	acqua minerale	**ah**-kwah mee-neh-**rah**-lay
milk	latte	**lah**-tay
(orange) juice	succo (d'arancia)	**soo**-koh (dah-**rahn**-chah)
coffee / tea	caffè / tè	kah-**feh** / teh
wine	vino	**vee**-noh
red / white	rosso / bianco	**roh**-soh / bee-**ahn**-koh
glass / bottle	bicchiere / bottiglia	bee-kee-**eh**-ray / boh-**teel**-yah
beer	birra	**bee**-rah
Cheers!	Cin cin!	cheen cheen
More. / Another.	Di più. / Un altro.	dee pew / oon **ahl**-troh
The same.	Lo stesso.	loh **steh**-soh
The bill, please.	Il conto, per favore.	eel **kohn**-toh pehr fah-**voh**-ray
Do you accept credit cards?	Accettate carte di credito?	ah-cheh-**tah**-tay **kar**-tay dee **kreh**-dee-toh
tip	mancia	**mahn**-chah
Delicious!	Delizioso!	day-leet-see-**oh**-zoh

For more user-friendly Italian phrases, check out *Rick Steves' Italian Phrase Book & Dictionary* or *Rick Steves' French, Italian, & German Phrase Book*.

INDEX

INDEX

Our website enhances this book and turns

Explore Europe

At ricksteves.com you can browse through thousands of articles, videos, photos and radio interviews, plus find a wealth of money-saving travel tips for planning your dream trip. And with our mobile-friendly website, you can easily access all this great travel information anywhere you go.

TV Shows

Preview the places you'll visit by watching entire half-hour episodes of Rick Steves' Europe (choose from all 100 shows) on-demand, for free.

your travel dreams into affordable reality

Radio Interviews

Enjoy ready access to Rick's vast library of radio interviews covering travel

tips and cultural insights that relate specifically to your Europe travel plans.

Travel Forums

Learn, ask, share! Our online community of savvy travelers is a great resource

for first-time travelers to Europe, as well as seasoned pros. You'll find forums on each country, plus travel tips and restaurant/hotel reviews. You can even ask one of our well-traveled staff to chime in with an opinion.

Travel News

Subscribe to our free Travel News e-newsletter, and get monthly updates from Rick on what's happening in Europe.

Experience maximum Europe

Save time and energy

This guidebook is your independent-travel toolkit. But for all it delivers, it's still up to you to devote the time and energy it takes to manage the preparation and logistics that are essential for a happy trip. If that's a hassle, there's a solution.

Rick Steves Tours

A Rick Steves tour takes you to Europe's most interesting places with great

guides and small groups of 28 or less. We follow Rick's favorite itineraries, ride in comfy buses, stay in family-run hotels, and bring you intimately close to the Europe you've traveled so far to see. Most importantly, we take away the logistical headaches so you can focus on the fun.

Join the fun

This year we'll take thousands of free-spirited travelers—nearly half of them repeat customers—along with us on four dozen different itineraries, from Ireland to Italy to Athens. Is a Rick Steves tour the right fit for your travel dreams? Find out at ricksteves.com, where you can also request Rick's latest tour catalog. Europe is best experienced with happy travel partners. We hope you can join us.

A Guide for Every Trip

BEST OF GUIDES

Full color easy-to-scan format, focusing on Europe's most popular destinations and sights.

Best of France
Best of Germany
Best of England
Best of Europe
Best of Ireland
Best of Italy
Best of Spain

COMPREHENSIVE GUIDES

City, country, and regional guides with detailed coverage for a multi-week trip exploring the most iconic sights and venturing off the beaten track.

Amsterdam & the Netherlands
Barcelona
Belgium: Bruges, Brussels,
  Antwerp & Ghent
Berlin
Budapest
Croatia & Slovenia
Eastern Europe
England
Florence & Tuscany
France
Germany
Great Britain
Greece: Athens & the Peloponnese
Iceland
Ireland
Istanbul
Italy
London
Paris
Portugal
Prague & the Czech Republic
Provence & the French Riviera
Rome
Scandinavia
Scotland
Spain
Switzerland
Venice
Vienna, Salzburg & Tirol

E BEST OF ROME

Italy's capital, is studded with
remnants and floodlit-fountain
s. From the Vatican to the Colos-
s, with crazy traffic in between, Rome
erful, huge, and exhausting. The
the heat, and the weighty history

of the Eternal City where Caesars walked
can make tourists wilt. Recharge by taking siestas, gelato breaks, and after-dark
walks, strolling from one atmospheric
square to another in the refreshing evening air.

*Pantheon—which
dome until the
,000 years old
ver 1,500).*

*thens in the Vat-
the humanistic*

*iators fought
her, entertaining*

*ome ristorante,
t St. Peter's
iously.*

Rick Steves guidebooks are published by Avalon Travel,
an imprint of Perseus Books, a Hachette Book Group compa

OCKET GUIDES

ompact, full color city guides with e essentials for shorter trips.

msterdam	Paris
thens	Prague
arcelona	Rome
orence	Venice
aly's Cinque Terre	Vienna
ondon	
unich & Salzburg	

NAPSHOT GUIDES

ocused single-destination coverage.

asque Country: Spain & France
openhagen & the Best of Denmark
ublin
ubrovnik
dinburgh
ill Towns of Central Italy
rakow, Warsaw & Gdansk
sbon
oire Valley
adrid & Toledo
ilan & the Italian Lakes District
aples & the Amalfi Coast
orthern Ireland
ormandy
orway
eykjavik
evilla, Granada & Southern Spain
t. Petersburg, Helsinki & Tallinn
ockholm

CRUISE PORTS GUIDES

Reference for cruise ports of call.

Mediterranean Cruise Ports
Northern European Cruise Ports

Complete your library with...

TRAVEL SKILLS & CULTURE

Study up on travel skills and gain insight on history and culture.

Europe 101
European Christmas
European Easter
European Festivals
Europe Through the Back Door
Postcards from Europe
Travel as a Political Act

PHRASE BOOKS & DICTIONARIES

French
French, Italian & German
German
Italian
Portuguese
Spanish

PLANNING MAPS

Britain, Ireland & London
Europe
France & Paris
Germany, Austria & Switzerland
Ireland
Italy
Spain & Portugal

Avalon Travel
Hachette Book Group
1700 Fourth Street
Berkeley, CA 94710

Text © 2018 by Rick Steves' Europe, Inc. All rights reserved.
Maps © 2018 by Rick Steves' Europe, Inc. All rights reserved.
Printed in Canada by Friesens
Second printing June 2018

Fifth Edition
ISBN 978-1-63121-675-6

For the latest on Rick's lectures, guidebooks, tours, public radio show, and public television series, contact Rick Steves' Europe, Inc., 130 Fourth Avenue North, Edmonds, WA 98020, tel. 425/771-8303, www.ricksteves.com, rick@ricksteves.com.

Rick Steves' Europe

Managing Editor: Jennifer Madison Davis
Special Publications Manager: Risa Laib
Assistant Managing Editor: Cathy Lu
Editors: Glenn Eriksen, Tom Griffin, Katherine Gustafson, Mary Keils, Suzanne Kotz, Rosie Leutzinger, Carrie Shepherd
Editorial & Production Assistant: Jessica Shaw
Editorial Intern: Claire Connor
Researchers: Virginia Agostinelli, Ben Cameron, Sarah Murdoch
Contributor: Gene Openshaw
Graphic Content Director: Sandra Hundacker
Maps & Graphics: David C. Hoerlein, Lauren Mills, Mary Rostad

Avalon Travel

Senior Editor and Series Manager: Madhu Prasher
Editor: Jamie Andrade
Associate Editor: Sierra Machado
Copy Editor: Maggie Ryan
Proofreaders: Patrick Collins, Suzie Nasol, Patty Mon
Indexer: Stephen Callahan
Production and Typesetting: Krista Anderson, Rue Flaherty, Jane Musser
Cover Design: Kimberly Glyder Design
Maps & Graphics: Kat Bennett

Photo Credits

Front Cover: © Buena Vista Images/Getty
Title Page: Piazza dei Signori, Padu © Dominic Arizona Bonuccelli
Additional Photography: Sistine Chapel, p. 887 © Erich Lessing/Art Resources, NY; Dominic Arizona Bonuccelli, Ben Cameron, Trish Feaster, Simon Griffith, Jennifer Hauseman, Cameron Hewitt, David C. Hoerlein, Suzanne Kotz, Gene Openshaw, Michael Potter, Robyn Stencil, Rick Steves, Bruce VanDeventer, Laura VanDeventer, Ian Watson, Wikimedia Commons (PD-Art/PD-US). (Photos are used by permission and are the property of the original copyright owners.)

ABOUT THE AUTHOR

RICK STEVES

 Since 1973, Rick has spent about four months a year exploring Europe. His mission: to empower Americans to have European trips that are fun, affordable, and culturally broadening. Rick produces a best-selling guidebook series, a public television series, and a public radio show, and organizes small-group tours that take over 20,000 travelers to Europe annually. He does all of this with the help of a hardworking, well-traveled staff of 100 at Rick Steves' Europe in Edmonds, Washington, near Seattle. When not on the road, Rick is active in his church and with advocacy groups focused on economic justice, drug policy reform, and ending hunger. To recharge, Rick plays piano, relaxes at his family cabin in the Cascade Mountains, and spends time with his partner Trish, son Andy, and daughter Jackie. Find out more about Rick at www.ricksteves.com and on Facebook.

Want More Italy?
Maximize the experience with Rick Steves as your guide

Guidebooks
Venice, Florence, and Rome guides make side-trips smooth and afford[ab]

Phrase Books
Rely on Rick's Italian Phrase Book and Dictionary

Rick's DVDs
Preview where you're going with 15 shows on Italy

Free! Rick's Audio Europe™ App
Get free audio tours for Italy's top sights

Small-Group Tours
Rick offers a dozen great itineraries through Italy

For all the details, visit ricksteves.com